A Treasury of
CROCHETED
SWEATERS

A Treasury of
CROCHETED SWEATERS

Sedgewood® Press

Published by Sedgewood Press

For Sedgewood ® *Press*
Editorial Director   Elizabeth P. Rice
Associate Editor   Leslie Gilbert
Production Manager   Bill Rose

Produced for Sedgewood ® Press by
Marshall Cavendish Books Limited
58 Old Compton Street
London W1V 5PA

For Marshall Cavendish
House Editor   Elizabeth Longley
Editor   Eleanor Van Zandt
Designer   Brenda Morrison

First Printing 1985

ISBN   0-02-496730-0

Library of Congress Catalog Card
Number 84-52752

Printed in the United States of America

INTRODUCTION

If you're a crochet fan you'll find this book a great source of inspiration. In these pages are 44 beautiful, stylish crocheted garments for women, men and children, chosen to appeal to all tastes and ages. There are warm cardigans and jackets for out-of-doors, glamorous evening sweaters, cool cotton tops for summer, charming little sweaters for babies and warm, handsome pullovers for men – to name but a few. The wonderful range of crochet textures is well represented: bobbles, filet work, lace patterns, woven crochet, as well as the basic fabric stitches, are all here. And if you've ever wanted to learn Tunisian (afghan) crochet or hairpin lace, here is your chance, for we've included several garments using these techniques, along with photographs and step-by-step instructions to make it easy.

Most of the other projects, too, include illustrated instructions for a special technique used in that project – for example, how to work a shell lace edging, how to work surface slip stitch and how to make a toggle loop.

Yarns needed for the projects are specified by generic type (e.g. knitting worsted weight, fingering, medium-weight mohair), rather than by brand name. We strongly recommend that you buy good-quality yarn for any crochet project – those made of natural fibers, such as wool and cotton, or natural-synthetic blends. There are some good all-synthetic yarns available, but many are of poor quality. The colors are less attractive and they are unpleasant to the touch. Often they do not wear well, losing their resilience after a few washings. Today even some pure wool yarns are machine washable; and hand-washing is not really such a chore when the sweater is a treasured part of your wardrobe. So, avoid cheap yarns – they're a false economy.

When buying any yarn, check the wrapper or ask the salesperson to make sure that it is appropriate for the garment. The right choice of yarn will help to ensure that the garment is fun to make and to wear.

Before you begin work on a project, remember to check your gauge. This step is *absolutely essential* if you are to obtain a garment of the correct size. Even professional crocheters make a gauge swatch to make sure that they get the same number of stitches (and sometimes rows) to the inch as did the designer of the pattern. The sample should be at least four inches square. If you get more or fewer stitches per inch than the stated gauge, try a larger or smaller hook, respectively, until you get the right gauge. The short time you spend at the outset getting the gauge correct may save you hours of wasted time making something the wrong size.

CONTENTS

LACY BLOUSE

Made in white or a pastel color, this blouse is perfect for a summer day. Made in black, with ribbon threaded through the rows, it becomes an elegant evening top.

Sizes
Misses' sizes 12-16
Length from shoulder 19 in

Materials
11 oz (or 1350 yd) of a size 5 pearl cotton
Size 0 steel crochet hook

Gauge
20 dc and first 17 rows of pat should measure 4 in worked on size 0 steel hook

To save time, take time to check gauge.

Back and front (worked in one piece)
Beg at center back: make 95 ch.
1st row 1 dc into 3rd ch from hook, 1 dc into each ch to end, turn. 93 tr.
2nd row Ch 3, 1 dc into each st to end, turn.
3rd row Ch 1, 1 sc into each st to end, turn.
4th row Working into front loops only, work a row of crab st (sc worked from left to right) back along the row, do not turn.
5th row Ch 1, working into back loops of row 3, work 1 sc into each st to end, do not turn.
6th row As row 4.
7th row As 5th row working into back loops of row 5, do not turn.
8th row As row 4.
9th row As row 5, working into back loops of row 7, turn.
10th row Ch 3, 1 dc into each st to end, turn.
11th row Ch 4, * skip next dc, 1 dc into next dc, ch 1. rep from * to end of row, ending with 1 dc into last st, turn.
12 row Ch 3, * 1 dc into next 1 ch sp, 1 dc into next dc, rep from * to end of row, turn.
13th row Ch 3, 1 dc into each of next 4 dc, * skip 1 dc, ch 1, 1 dc into each of next 7 dc, rep from * to end of row, ending with 1 dc into each of last 6 dc, turn.
14th row Ch 3, 1 dc into each of next 4 dc, * ch 1, skip next dc, (yo, insert hook into 1 ch sp, draw through a loop) 5 times, yo, draw through 10 loops, yo, draw through rem 2 loops on hook (1 puff st), ch 1, skip next dc, 1 dc into each of next 5 dc, rep from * to end ending with 1 dc into each of last 4 dc, turn.
15th row Ch 3, 1 dc into each of first 3 dc, * 1 dc into next 1 ch sp, ch 1, 1 dc into next 1 ch sp, 1 dc into each of next 5 dc, rep from * to end of row, ending with 1 dc into each of last 4 dc, turn.
16th row As 10th.
17th row As 11th.
18th row As 12th.
Work rows 3-12 twice.
39th row Ch 4, * skip next dc, 1 puff st into next dc, ch 1, rep from * to end of row ending with 1 dc into last st, turn. 45 puff sts.
40th row Ch 3, * 1 puff st into next 1 ch sp, ch 1, rep from * to end ending with 1 puff st into last 1 ch sp, 1 dc into 3rd of 4 ch, turn.
41st row Ch 3, * 1 dc into top of puff st, 1 dc into next 1 ch sp, rep from * to end of row, ending with 1 dc into top of turning ch, turn.
42nd row As 11th.
43rd row As 12th.
44th row As 11th.
45th row As 12th.
Divide for armhole
46th row Ch 3, 1 dc into each of next 42 dc, leave rem of dc unworked.
47th row Make 52 ch. 1 dc into 4th ch from hook, 1 dc into each ch, then 1 dc into each dc to end of row, turn. 93 dc.
Work rows 11 and 12 twice.
52nd row As 39th.
53rd row As 40th.
54th row As 41st.
55th row As 11th.
56th row As 12th.
Work rows 3-9.
64th row Ch 3, 1 dc into each of next 50 sts, turn.
65th row Sl st over next 2 sts, ch 4, skip next dc, 1 dc into next dc, *ch 1, skip next dc, 1 dc into next dc, rep from * to end of row, turn.
66th row Ch 3, * 1 dc into next 1 ch sp, 1 dc into next dc, rep from * 22 times, turn. 47 dc.
Decreasing 1 st at neck edge on every row until there are 41 sts, work rows 3-9, turn.
74th row Ch 3, 1 dc into each dc to end of row, turn. 41 sts.

SPECIAL TECHNIQUE
Corded ribbing

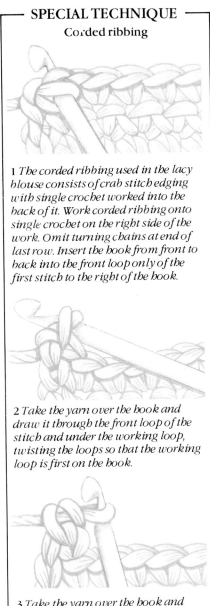

1 *The corded ribbing used in the lacy blouse consists of crab stitch edging with single crochet worked into the back of it. Work corded ribbing onto single crochet on the right side of the work. Omit turning chains at end of last row. Insert the hook from front to back into the front loop only of the first stitch to the right of the hook.*

2 *Take the yarn over the hook and draw it through the front loop of the stitch and under the working loop, twisting the loops so that the working loop is first on the hook.*

3 *Take the yarn over the hook and draw through two loops on the hook to complete the first crab stitch single crochet.*

4 *Insert the hook from front to back into the front loop only of the next stitch to the right of the hook, and work another crab stitch as before.*

75th row As 11th.
76th row As 12th.
77th row Ch 3, 1dc into each of next 3dc, * skip 1dc, ch 1, 1dc into each of next 7dc, rep from * to end of row, ending with 1dc into each of last 4dc, turn.
78th row Ch 3, 1dc into each of next 2dc, * ch 1, skip next dc, 1 puff st into next 1 ch sp, ch 1, skip next dc, 1dc into each of next 5dc, rep from * to end, ending with 1dc into each of last 3dc, turn.
79th row Ch 3, 1dc into each of next 2dc, * 1dc into next 1ch sp, ch 1, 1dc into next 1ch sp, 1dc into each of next 5dc, rep from * to end of row, ending with 1dc into each of last 3dc, turn.
80th row As 10th. 41dc.
81st row As 11th.
82nd row As 12th.
Work rows 3-12 twice.
103rd row As 75th.
104th row As 76th.
105th row As 77th.
106th row As 10th.
107th row As 11th.
108th row As 12th.
109th row Ch 1, 2sc into next dc, 1sc into each dc to end. 42 sts.
110th row Work crab st into front loops only.
111th row Ch 1, working into back loops, work 2sc into next st, 1sc into each st to end. 43 sts.
112th row Work crab st into front loops only.
113th row Ch 1, working into back loops, work 2sc into next st, 1sc into each st to end. 44 sts.
114th row Work crab st into front loops only.
115th row Ch 1, working into back

5 *Continue to work into the front loop of each stitch in the same way. Make sure you twist the loops each time to achieve a corded effect.*

loops, work 2sc into next st, 1sc into each st to end, turn. 45 sts.
116th row Ch 3, work 1dc into each st to last 2 sts, 2dc into each of next 2 sts, turn. 47dc.
117th row Ch 4, 1dc into next dc, * ch 1, skip next dc, 1dc into next dc, rep from * to end of row, turn.
118th row Ch 3, * 1dc into 1ch sp, 1dc into next dc, rep from * to last sp, 2dc into last sp, 1dc into 3rd of turning ch, turn. 50dc.
119th row Make 44ch. 1sc into 2nd ch from hook, 1sc into each ch, then 1sc into each dc to end of row. 93sc. Work rows 4-12.
Now work rows 39-63.
Next row As 10th.
Next row As 11th.
Next row As 12th.
Now work rows 3-18, then rows 3-10.
Next row Ch 3, 1dc into each dc to end, fasten off.

Yoke
Make 52ch.
1st row 1dc into 3rd ch from hook, 1dc into each of next 22ch, ch 1, skip 1ch, 1 puff st into next ch, skip 1ch, 1dc into each of next 24dc, turn.
2nd row Ch 3, 1dc into dc at base of 3ch, 1 puff st into 1ch sp, ch 1, 1 puff st into next 1ch sp, 1dc into each of next 21dc, 2dc into each of next 2dc, turn.
3rd row Ch 3, 1dc into dc at base of 3ch, 1dc into each of next 5dc, ch 1, skip 1dc, 1dc into each of next 10dc, ch 1, skip 1dc, 1dc into each of next 7dc, ch 1, 1 puff st into next 1ch sp, ch 1, skip next puff st, 1dc into each of next 7dc, ch 1, skip 1dc, 1dc into each of next 10dc, ch 1, skip 1dc, 1dc into each of next 5dc, 2dc into last dc, turn.

6 *To complete the first corded ribbing row, make one chain, then work a single crochet into the back loop of each stitch worked in the previous row, working behind the crab stitch row.*

4th row Ch 3, 1dc into dc at base of 3ch, 2dc into next dc, 1dc into each of next 5dc, ch 1, 1dc into each of next 10dc, ch 1, 1dc into each of next 7dc, 1dc into next 1ch sp, ch 1, skip next puff st, 1dc into next 1ch sp, 1dc into each of next 7dc, ch 1, 1dc into each of next 10dc, ch 1, 1dc into each of next 5dc, 2dc into each of last 2dc, turn.

5th row Ch 3, 1dc into each of next 8dc, ch 1, 1 puff st into next 1ch sp, ch 1, 1dc into each of next 9dc, ch 1, skip 1dc, 1 puff st into next sp, ch 1, skip next dc, 1dc into each of next 7dc, ch 1, 1dc into each of next 7dc, skip next dc, 1 puff st into next sp, skip 1dc, ch 1, 1dc into each of next 9dc, ch 1, 1 puff st into next 1ch sp, ch 1, 1dc into each of last 9dc, turn.

6th row Ch 3, 1dc into each of next 7dc, ch 1, skip 1dc, 1 puff st into next sp, ch 1, 1 puff st into next sp, ch 1, skip 1dc, 1dc into next 7dc, ch 1, skip 1dc, 1 puff st into next 1ch sp, ch 1, 1 puff st into next sp, ch 1, skip 1dc, 1dc into each of next 6dc, ch 1, 1dc into next 6dc, ch 1, skip 1dc, 1 puff st into next sp, ch 1, 1 puff st into next sp, ch 1, skip next dc, 1 puff st into next sp, ch 1, 1 puff st into next sp, ch 1, skip 1dc, 1dc into each of last 8dc, turn.

7th row Ch 3, 1dc into each of next 7dc, 1dc into 1ch sp, ch 1, 1 puff st into next sp, ch 1, 1dc into next sp, 1dc into each of next 7dc, 1dc into next sp, ch 1, 1 puff st into next sp, ch 1, 1dc into next sp, 1dc into each of next 6dc, ch 1, 1dc into each of next 6dc, 1dc into next sp, ch 1, 1 puff st into next sp, ch 1, 1dc into next sp, 1dc into each of next 7dc, 1dc into next sp, ch 1, 1 puff st into next sp, ch 1, 1dc into next sp, 1dc into each of last 8dc, turn.

8th row Ch 3, 1dc into each of next 8dc, 1dc into next sp, ch 1, 1dc into next sp, 1dc into each of next 9dc, 1dc into next sp, ch 1, 1dc into next sp, 1dc into each of next 7dc, ch 1, 1dc into each of next 7dc, 1dc into next sp, ch 1, 1dc into next sp, 1dc into each of next 9dc, 1dc into next sp, ch 1, 1dc into next sp, 1dc into each of last 9dc, turn.

9th row Ch 3, 1dc into each of next 9dc, ch 1, 1dc into each of next 11dc, ch 1, 1dc into each of next 8dc, ch 1, 1dc into each of next 8dc, ch 1, 1dc into each of next 11dc, ch 1, 1dc into

each of next 10dc, turn.

10th row Ch 3, 1dc into each of next 8dc, ch 1, skip next dc, 1 puff st into next sp, ch 1, skip next dc, 1dc into each of next 9dc, ch 1, skip 1dc, 1 puff st into next sp, ch 1, skip next dc, 1dc into each of next 7dc, ch 1, 1dc into each of next 7dc, ch 1, skip next dc, 1 puff st into next sp, ch 1, skip next dc, 1dc into each of next 9dc, ch 1, skip next dc, 1 puff st into next sp, ch 1, skip 1dc, 1dc into each of last 9dc, turn.

11th row Ch 3, 1dc into each of next 7dc, 1dc, skip 1dc, 1 puff st into next sp, ch 1, 1 puff st into next sp, ch 1, skip 1dc, 1dc into next 7dc, ch 1, skip 1dc, 1 puff st into next 1ch sp, ch 1, 1 puff st into next sp, ch 1, skip 1dc, 1dc into each of next 5dc, 1 puff st into top of next dc, ch 1, 1 puff st into top of next dc, 1dc into each of next 5dc, ch 1, skip 1dc, 1 puff st into next sp, ch 1, 1 puff st into next sp, ch 1, skip next dc, 1dc into each of next 7dc, ch 1, skip next dc, 1 puff st into next sp, ch 1, 1 puff st into next sp, ch 1, skip 1dc, 1dc into each of last 8dc, turn.

12th row Ch 3, 1dc into each of next 7dc, 1dc into sp, ch 1, 1 puff st into next sp, ch 1, 1dc into next sp, 1dc into next 7dc, 1dc into next sp, ch 1, 1 puff st into next sp, ch 1, 1dc into next sp, (ch 1, skip next st, 1dc into next st) 3 times, 1 puff st into next sp, 1dc into next st, (ch 1, skip next st, 1dc into next st) 3 times, ch 1, 1 puff st into next sp, ch 1, 1dc into next sp, 1dc into next 7dc, 1dc into next sp, ch 1, 1 puff st into next sp, ch 1, 1dc into next sp, 1dc into each of last 8dc, turn.

13th row Ch 3, 1dc into each of next 8dc, 1dc into next sp, 1dc into next st, 1dc into next sp, 1dc into each of next 7dc, ch 1, skip next dc, 1dc into next dc, (ch 1, 1dc into next st) 5 times, ch 1, skip puff st, 1dc into next st, (ch 1, 1dc into next st) 5 times, ch 1, skip next dc, 1dc into each of next 7dc, 1dc into next sp, 1dc into next st, 1dc, into next sp, 1dc into each of last 9dc, turn.

14th row Ch 3, 1dc into each of next 16dc, ch 1, skip 1dc, 1dc into next dc, (ch 1, 1dc into next dc) 13 times, ch 1, skip next dc, 1dc into each of last 17dc, turn.

15th row Ch 3, 1dc into each of next 14dc, ch 1, skip 1dc, 1dc into next dc, (ch 1, 1dc into next dc) 15 times, ch 1, skip next dc, 1dc into each of last 15dc, turn.

16th row Ch 3, 1dc into each of next 12dc, ch 1, skip 1dc, 1dc into next dc, (ch 1, 1dc into next dc) 17 times, ch 1, skip next dc, 1dc into each of last 13dc, turn.

Divide for neck

Next row Ch 3, 1dc into each of next 12dc, turn.

Work another 12 rows of dc on these 13 sts. Fasten off.

Rejoin yarn to other side of neck and work 13 rows of dc over the 13dc. Fasten off.

To finish

Join center back and shoulder seams. Work a row of crab st around front neck edge of main bodice piece. Sew yoke in place using slipstitch.

Waistband

Join yarn to the lower edge at one side and work approx 155dc around lower edge. Work 2 more rows in dc.

Next row Ch 4, skip 1dc, * 1dc into each of next 10dc, ch 1, skip next dc, rep from * ending with a sl st into 3rd

of 4ch.

Next row Ch 3, 1 puff st into next sp, ch 1, skip next dc, * 1dc into each of next 8dc, ch 1, 1 puff st into next sp, ch 1, skip next dc, rep from * to end ending with a sl st into top of 3ch.

Next row Ch 4, * 1dc into next sp, 1dc into each of next 8dc, 1dc into next sp, ch 1, rep from * to end ending with a sl st into 3rd of 4ch.

Now work another 3 rows of dc working into every st.

Next row Ch 4, 5tr into same place as 4ch, * skip 2dc, 6tr into next dc, rep from * to end, ending with a sl st into top of 4ch. Fasten off.

Armhole edging

Join yarn at underarm; ch 4, 5tr into same place as 4ch, skip 4dc along armhole edge, * work 4tr into sp between next 2dc, skip next 4dc, rep from * ending with a sl st into top of 4ch. Fasten off.

Neck edging

Work a row of sc evenly around neck edge. Work shell edge as for armhole, skipping 3sc between each shell. Fasten off.

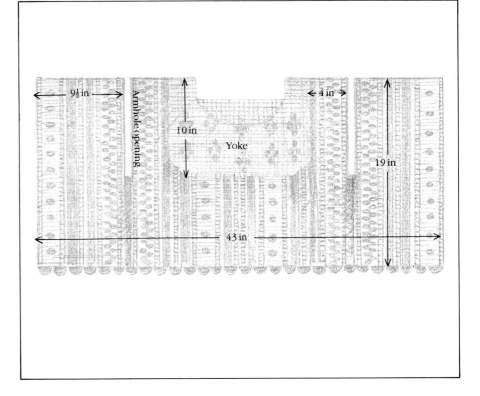

SOFT
SUMMER BLOUSE

A double row of shell edging finishes the neckline of this flattering blouse.

Sizes

Misses' sizes 10-12
Length from shoulder *19½in*
Sleeve seam *6in*

Materials

11oz (or 1320 yd) of size 5 pearl cotton
9 buttons in ⅜ in diameter
Size B crochet hook
Pair of size 3 knitting needles

Gauge

22dc and 11 rows to 4in worked on size B hook

To save time, take time to check gauge.

Front

Make 92ch. 1dc into 4th ch from hook, 1dc into each ch to end, turn.

Next row Ch 3, 1dc into each dc to end, turn. 90dc.

Rep this row 29 more times.

Shape armholes

Sl st across first 5dc, 1hdc into next dc, 1dc into each of next 78dc, 1hdc into next dc, turn.

Next row Skip first hdc, sl st into each of first 2dc, 1hdc into next dc, 1dc into each of next 72dc, 1hdc into next dc, turn.

Next row Skip first hdc, sl st into next dc, 1hdc into next dc, 1dc into each of next 68dc, 1hdc into next dc, turn.

Next row Ch 3, 1dc into each dc to end, turn. 68dc.

Rep this row 13 more times.

Shape neck

Next row Ch 3, 1dc into each of next 22dc, 1hdc into next dc, turn.

Next row Sl st into first hdc and next dc, 1hdc into next dc, 1dc into each dc to end, turn.

Next row Ch 3, 1dc into each of next 18dc, turn.

Work 3 more rows of dc on these 19 sts. Fasten off.
Skip center 20dc; rejoin yarn to work 2nd side of neck, matching first side and reversing all shapings.

Back (worked in two pieces)
Make 45ch. 1dc into 4th ch from hook, 1dc into each ch to end, turn.
Next row Ch 3, 1dc into each dc to end, turn. 43dc.
Rep this last row 29 more times.
Shape armholes
Sl st across first 3dc, 1hdc into next dc, 1dc into each dc to end, turn.
Next row Ch 3, 1dc into each of next 35dc, 1hdc into next dc, turn.
Next row Skip 1hdc, sl st into next dc, 1hdc into next dc, 1dc into each dc to end, turn.
Next row Ch 3, 1dc into each dc to end, turn. 34dc.
Rep this last row 19 more times.
Shape shoulders
Next row Ch 3, 1dc into each of next 18dc. Fasten off.
Work other back piece to match, reversing all shapings.

Sleeves
Make 61ch. 1dc into 4th ch from hook, 1dc into each ch to end, turn.
Next row Ch 3, 1dc into each dc to end, turn. 59dc.
Work 9 more rows in dc.
Next row (inc row) Ch 3, 1dc into each of next 2dc, * 2dc into next dc, 1dc into each of next 3dc, rep from * to end, turn. 73dc.
Work 4 rows in dc.
Rep inc row working only 1dc after last inc. 91dc.
Work 3 rows in dc.

Shape sleeve cap
Next row Sl st over first 4dc, 1hdc into next dc, 1dc into each of next 81dc, 1hdc into next dc, turn.
Next row Sl st into hdc, 1hdc into next dc, 1dc into each of next 79dc, 1hdc into next dc, turn.
Next row Sl st into hdc, 1hdc into next dc, 1dc into each of next 77dc, 1hdc into next dc, turn.
Cont dec as on last row working 2dc less on each row until 37dc rem.
Fasten off.

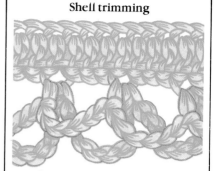

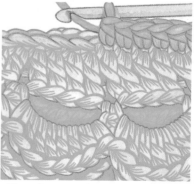
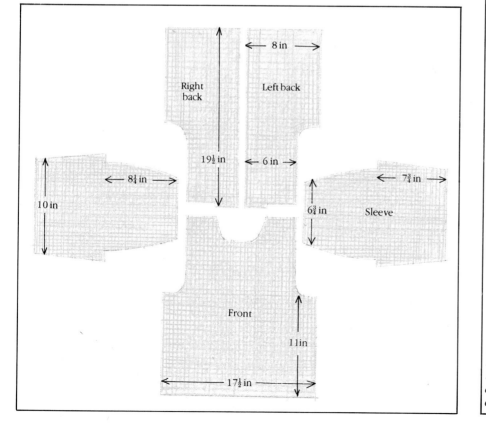

Right back

Left back

8 in

19½ in

6 in

8¼ in

10 in

7¾ in

6¾ in

Sleeve

Front

11 in

17½ in

Working buttonholes

Where small buttons are used on a crocheted garment, they are often fastened simply by inserting them between the fabric stitches. However, buttonholes can easily be worked in crochet – either horizontally or vertically, into the main fabric or into a separate band. If you are making separate button and buttonhole bands, make the button band first and mark the button positions with pins. Use these marks as guides when placing the buttonholes.

Horizontal buttonholes

1 Work in single crochet to position for first buttonhole. Make 2 chains to form top of medium-sized hole. The number of chains depends on size of hole required

2 Skip next 2 single crochets and work into the following stitch. The number of stitches skipped is always the same as the number of chains.

3 On the next row, work in single crochet into the chains made in the previous row to complete the top of the buttonhole.

To finish

Join side seams. Using knitting needles pick up and K133 sts along lower edge.
1st row K1, * P1, K1, rep from * to end.
2nd row P1, * K1, P1, rep from * to end.
Work 7 more rows in ribbing. Bind off loosely in ribbing.

Buttonhole

Using crochet hook work approx 112dc along center back edge.
Rep for buttonhole band (the sps between dc serve as buttonholes).
Sew on buttons, spacing them evenly.

Sleeve edging

Join yarn at side edge; using crochet hook work 1sc into sp between first 2dc, * 1hdc between next 2dc, (1dc between next 2dc) 3 times, 1hdc between next 2dc, 1sc between next 2dc, rep from * to end. Fasten off. Join sleeve seam, join shoulder seams. Set in sleeves gathering excess at cap of sleeve.

Collar

Make 93ch. 1dc into 4th ch from hook, 1dc into each ch to end. 91dc.
Next row * Ch 7, skip the next 5dc, sl st into next dc, rep from * to end, turn.
Next row Into each 7ch loop work 13dc.
Next row *Ch 10, sl st into the same place as sl st of 7ch loop, rep from * to end, turn.
Next row Into each 10ch loop work 14dc. Fasten off.
Hold collar in place along neck edge, placing WS of collar to RS of neck, and work a row of hdc through both thicknesses.
Fasten off.

Vertical buttonholes

1 Work across row to position for first buttonhole. Here the band is 6 stitches wide, with 3 stitches on each side of buttonhole. Turn and work 2 rows (or more, for a longer buttonhole) on these stitches, ending at inner edge.

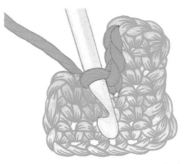

2 Slip stitch down side of buttonhole and into single crochet immediately below.
Chain 1 to count as first single crochet, work to end of row, so that there are 3 stitches on second side.

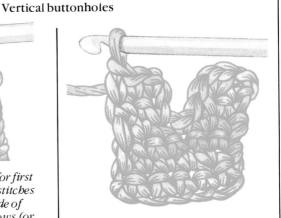

3 Work 2 rows on these stitches, ending at side edge so that second side of buttonhole is same height as first.

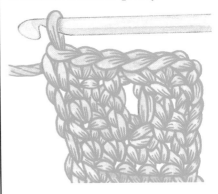

4 Work in single crochet across both sides of buttonhole, joining the two sides in this way.

LATTICEWORK TOP

Mouthwatering ice cream colors are used for this cool cotton sweater decorated with horizontal and vertical stripes.

Sizes

Misses' sizes 10 [12:14]
Length from shoulder $22\frac{1}{2}$ in
Sleeve seam 5 in
Note *Instructions for larger sizes are in brackets [ ]; where there is one set of figures it applies to all sizes.*

Materials

6oz of a sport-weight smooth cotton yarn in each of two colors: A and B
1oz in contrasting color C
Size H crochet hook
Pair of size 5 knitting needles

Gauge

11 tr and 5 rows to $4\frac{1}{4}$ in worked on size H hook

To save time, take time to check gauge.

Note *When shaping, work edge sts at a slightly looser tension to keep work flat.*

Back

* * Using crochet hook and A, make 47 [49:51] ch *loosely.*
Base row 1 tr into 5th ch from hook, 1 tr into each ch to end.
Turn. 44 [46:48] sts.
Pat row Ch 4, skip first tr, 1 tr into each tr, 1 tr into top of turning ch. Turn.
Work 12 more rows in pat.
Shape armholes
1st row Sl st into each of first 4 tr, ch 4, 1 tr into each tr to last 3 sts, turn. 38 [40:42] sts. * *
2nd row Ch 4, skip first tr, leaving last loop of each st on hook, work 1 tr into each of next 3 sts, yo and draw through all 4 loops – 2 tr dec –, 1 tr into each tr to last 4 sts, dec 2 tr over next 3 sts, 1 tr into top of turning ch. Turn. 34 [36:38] sts. Pat 8 rows.
Fasten off.

Front

Work as back from * * to * *.
Shape left neck
1st row Ch 4, skip first tr, dec 2 tr over next 3 sts, 1 tr into each of next 7 [8:9] tr, dec 2 tr over next 3 sts, 1 tr into next tr, turn. Cont on these 11 [12:13] sts for first side of neck.
2nd row Ch 4, skip first tr, dec 2 tr over next 3 sts, 1 tr into each of next 6 [7:8] sts, 1 tr into top of turning ch. Turn.
3rd row Ch 4, skip first tr, 1 tr into each of next 4 [5:6] tr, dec 2 tr over next 3 sts, 1 tr into top of turning ch. Turn. 7 [8:9] sts.
Work in pat for 7 rows.
Fasten off.
Note *There is 1 more row on front than on back, making the shoulder seams fall slightly toward the back.*
Shape right neck
1st row Skip center 8 tr after right neck and join A to next tr, ch 4, dec 2 tr over next 3 sts, 1 tr into each of next 7 [8:9] tr, dec 2 tr over next 3 sts, 1 tr into top of turning ch.
Turn.
2nd row Ch 4, skip first tr, 1 tr into each of next 6 [7:8] sts, dec 2 tr over next 3 sts, 1 tr into top of turning ch. Turn.
3rd row Ch 4, skip first tr, dec 2 tr over next 3 sts, 1 tr into each of next 4 [5:6] tr, 1 tr into top of turning ch. Turn.
Work in pat for 7 rows.
Fasten off.

Sleeves (alike)

Using crochet hook and A, make 39 ch.
Work base row as for back. 36 sts.
Work in pat for 4 rows.
Shape top
1st row As first row of armhole shaping of back. 30 sts.
2nd row As 2nd row of armhole shaping of back.
3rd row Ch 4, skip first tr, leaving last loop of each st on hook, work 1 tr into each of next 2 sts, yo and draw through all 3 loops – 1 tr dec –, 1 tr into each tr to last 3 sts, dec 1 tr over next 2 sts, 1 tr into top of turning ch. Turn.
Rep 2nd and 3rd rows twice. 12 sts.
Fasten off.

Waistbands

With RS facing and using knitting needles, join A to first ch of base row of back. Pick up and K60 [62:64] sts evenly along base edge. Work $1\frac{1}{2}$ in in K1, P1 ribbing. Bind off *very loosely* in ribbing.
Work other waistband to match.

Horizontal stripes

With RS of back facing and using crochet hook, join B to the top of first st of base row.
Stripe row Ch 4, 1 tr into top of each st of base row. Fasten off.
Skip the next 2 rows. Rep stripe row into the top of next row.
Cont in this way to shoulders.
Work front and sleeves to match.

Vertical stripes

Note *When working vertical stripes, work through the corresponding sps of horizontal stripe and background tog where appropriate. Work the vertical stripes at a slightly tighter tension than the background to draw the work up and reduce the length slightly.*
1st stripe With RS of back facing and using crochet hook, join C to the sp between the center 2 sts of base row. Keep yarn at back of work. Fold each horizontal stripe downward toward the waistband. Yo, (insert hook into same sp as joining, yo and draw through loop on hook) twice, *insert hook into corresponding sp of next row, yo and draw through loop on

hook, insert hook into same sp, yo and draw through loop on hook, rep from * to top.
Fasten off.

2nd stripe Skip the next 3 sps to the right and join C to the next sp between sts. Fold each horizontal stripe upward toward the top of the work. Work as for first stripe.

Cont in this way over all the back, skipping 3 sps between each stripe and folding horizontal stripes alternately downward and upward as shown in the photograph.

Work front and sleeves to match.

To finish
Join shoulders. Join side and sleeve seams. Set in sleeves.
Neck edging
1st round With RS facing and using crochet hook, join A to neck edge at shoulder. Work sc evenly around neck, working a multiple of 5sc plus 1 extra, sl st into first sc.
2nd round 1sc into first sc, *1hdc into each sc, 1dc into each of next 2sc, 1hdc into next sc, 1sc into next sc, rep from * to end, sl st into first sc. Fasten off.
Sleeve edging
Work as for neck edging.

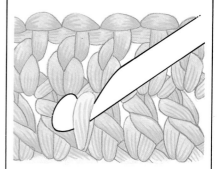
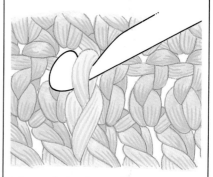

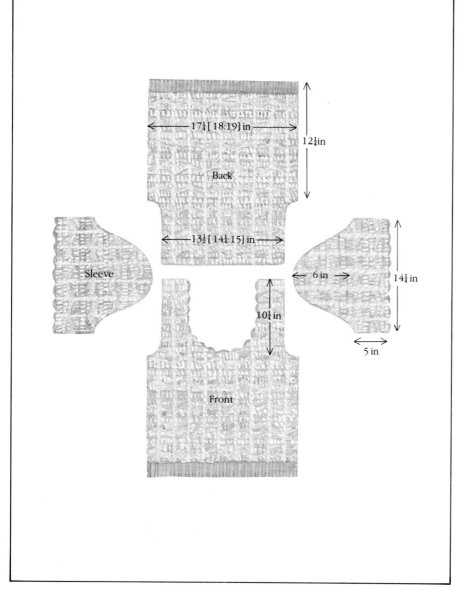

17¼[18:19] in

12¼in

Back

13½[14½:15] in

6 in

14¼ in

Sleeve

10½ in

5 in

Front

19

FILET CROCHET BLOUSE

This simple blouse can be worn for daytime or evening, depending on how you accessorize it, and requires the minimum of shaping.

Main piece

(worked in one piece to armholes)
Make 349 [365:389:409] ch.
Foundation row (RS) 1dc into 7th ch from hook, *ch 1, skip 1ch, 1dc into next ch; rep from * to end.
172 [180:192:202] sps.
Next row Ch 4, (to count as first 1dc, ch 1), 1dc into next dc, *ch 1, 1dc into next dc; rep from * to end of row. Rep this row once more. Work from filet pat chart 1, starting at first [26th:20th:15th] sp/block, rep the first pat row 5 [6:6:6] times complete, then rep it once more, ending on the 27th [2nd:8th:13th] sp/block.
Beg the next row on the 27th [2nd:8th:13th] square of chart. Work even in filet pat until work measures 12in.

Divide for armholes

Pat across 44 [46:49:52] sps, turn and cont on these sts for right front. Work 3 [3:5:5] more rows.

Shape sleeve

Inc 1sp at armhole edge at end of next row by working (ch 1, 1dc) into same place as the last dc. Inc 1sp at armhole edge on every following 6th row until there are 50 [52:55:57] sps, working extra sts into the filet pat.

4th size only

Work even for 7 rows, then inc 1sp at armhole edge on next row. 58sps.

All sizes

Work 1 more row, finishing at neck edge. Front now measures 19 [19¼:19¾:20] in.

Shape shoulder

Keeping filet pat correct, shape shoulder as follows:
1st row Work across 49 [51:54:57] sps, turn.
2nd row Sl st over 2sps, pat to end.
3rd row Pat to last 1 [2:2:2] sps, turn.
4th row Sl st over 2 [1:2:2] sps, pat to end.
5th row As 3rd.
6th row Sl st over 2 [2:1:2] sps, pat to end.

1st and 2nd sizes only

Next row Work across 40 [41] sps, turn.
Next row Sl st over 2sps, pat to end.

All sizes

Shape neck

Still dec at shoulders, shape neck.

Next row (RS) Sl st over 5sps, pat across 32 [32:38:41] sps, turn.
Next row Sl st over 2 [1:2:2] sps, pat to last 4sps, turn.
Next row Sl st over 2sps, pat to last 1 [2:2:2] sps, turn.
Next row Sl st over 2sps, pat to last sp, turn leaving last sp unworked.
Next row Sl st over sp, pat to last 1 [1:1:2] sps, turn.
Next row Sl st over 2sps, work across 15 [15:20:22] sps, turn.
Next row Sl st over 1sp, pat to last 1 [2:2:1] sp, turn.
Next row Sl st over 2 [1:2:2] sps, pat to last sp, turn, leaving last sp unworked. Neck shaping is now finished for first, 2nd and 3rd sizes.
Next row Sl st over 0 [0:0:1] sp, pat to last 1 [2:2:2] sps, turn.
Next row Sl st over 2 [2:1:2] sps, pat to last 0 [0:0:1] sp, turn. Neck shaping is now finished for 4th size.
Next row Pat to last 1 [1:2:2] sps, turn.
Next row Sl st over 2sps, pat to end.
Next row Pat over 2 [2:5:6] sps, turn.

3rd and 4th sizes only

Next row Sl st over 2sps, pat to end.
Next row Pat over 2sps.

All sizes

Fasten off.
With RS facing, rejoin yarn to last st of right front at underarm, ch 3, work across 84 [88:94:98] sps/blocks, and continue in filet pat across these sts for back. Work even for 3 [3:5:5] more rows. Inc 1sp each end of next and every following 6th row until there are 96 [100:106:109] sps/blocks, working inc sts into filet pat.

4th size only

Work even for 7 rows, then inc 1sp at each end of next row. 110sps. Work 1 more row so that back measures same as front to start of shoulder shaping. Keeping filet pat correct, shape shoulders as follows:
1st row (RS) Sl st over 1sp, work across 94 [98:104:108] sps, turn.
2nd row Sl st over 2sps, pat to last 2sps, turn.
3rd row Dec 1 [2:2:2] sps at each end.
4th row Dec 2 [1:2:2] sps at each end.
5th row As 3rd.
6th row Dec 2 [2:1:2] sps at each end.
7th row Dec 1 [1:2:1] sps at each end.
8th row As 2nd.

Sizes

Misses' sizes 10 [12:14:16]
Length from shoulder 19 [19¼:19¾:20] in
Note *Instructions for larger sizes are in brackets []; where there is only one set of figures it applies to all sizes.*

Materials

10 [12:13:15] oz, or 1230 [1400:1600:1760] yd of a size 5 pearl cotton
Size 7 steel crochet hook
8 buttons

Gauge

18 sps and 19 rows to 4in over filet pat

To save time, take time to check gauge.

9th row As 3rd.
10th row As 4th.
11th row Dec 1 [2:1:2] sps at each end.
12th row As 2nd.
13th row As 7th.
14th row As 2nd.
15th row As 3rd.
16th row Dec 2 [1:1:2] sps at each end.
17th row As 3rd.
18th row As 2nd.
19th row As 7th. 40 [38:38:42] sps.
Shape neck
Next row (WS) Sl st over 2sps, work across 10 [9:9:11] sps, turn.
Next row Sl st over 6 [6:6:7] sps, work over 2sps. Fasten off. Skip center 16 sts, (WS facing) rejoin yarn to next st, ch 4, pat to last 2sps, turn.
Next row Sl st over 2 [1:1:2] sps, pat over 2sps, turn. Fasten off.
Shape front
With RS of work facing, rejoin yarn to last st of back at underarm, ch 3, work in filet pat to end. 44 [46:49:52] sps. Cont on these sts as for left front and finish to correspond with right front, reversing all shapings.

Collar

Make 141 [141:141:153] ch; work foundation row as for main part. 68 [68:68:74] sps. Work 10 rows of filet from chart 2, working the pat rep

11 [11:11:12] times and finishing with 2sps at end of row. Fasten off.

To finish

Press very lightly on WS.
Button border
With RS facing, start at beg of neck shaping and work 1 row of sc down left front to lower edge.
2nd-4th rows Ch 1, 1sc in each st to end. Fasten off.
Buttonhole border
Work as for button border, starting at lower edge and working 8 buttonholes on the 3rd row, the first $\frac{1}{2}$ in above lower edge, the last at top of border and the rest spaced evenly between.
To work buttonhole Ch 3, skip 3sc, 1sc into next sc. Work 3sc into each 3ch sp on following row.
Sleeve borders
With RS facing, work 1 row of sc along edge of each sleeve. Fasten off.
Lower border
Work as for sleeve borders, starting and ending at center front. Place a marker on neck shaping $\frac{3}{4}$ in from front edge of front borders. Sew last row of collar between markers.
Collar and neck border
Work as for sleeve borders, beg and ending at center front. Join seams and sew on buttons.

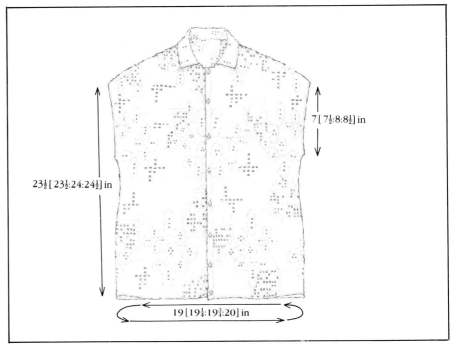

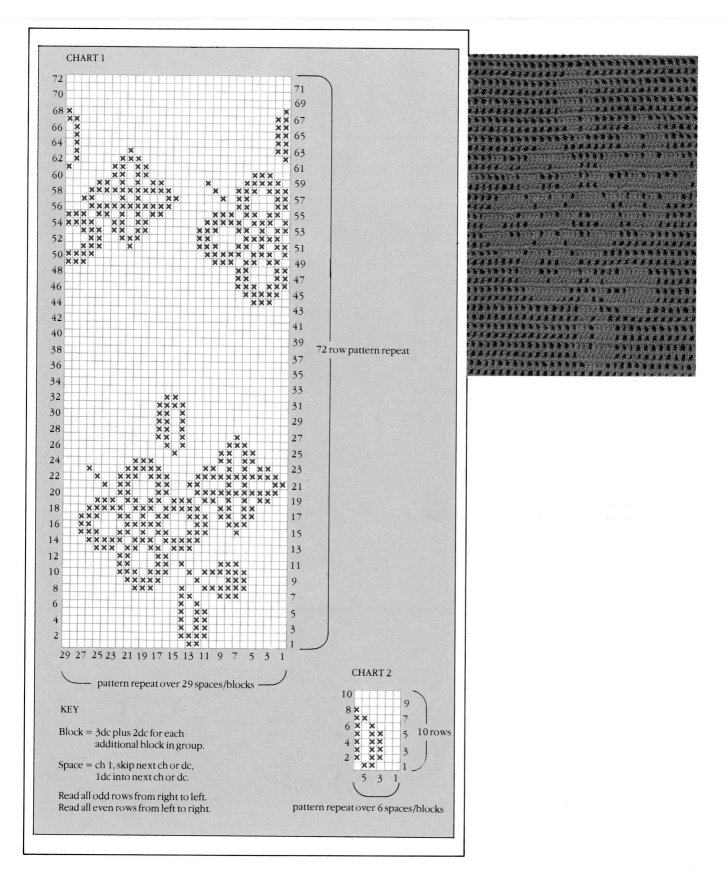

CHART 1

72 row pattern repeat

pattern repeat over 29 spaces/blocks

KEY

Block = 3dc plus 2dc for each
          additional block in group.

Space = ch 1, skip next ch or dc,
          1dc into next ch or dc.

Read all odd rows from right to left.
Read all even rows from left to right.

CHART 2

10 rows

pattern repeat over 6 spaces/blocks

FLOWER-TRIMMED TOP

Crocheted flowers make a pretty trim for lingerie or a simple blouse like this one.

Back

Using knitting needles cast on 108 sts.
Ribbing row * K1, P1, rep from * to end.
Rep ribbing row until work measures 2in, ending with WS facing. Bind off loosely in ribbing until one loop rem. Transfer loop to larger crochet hook.
Next row (RS) Ch 3 to count as first dc, 1dc into each bound-off st to end. 108dc.
Next row Ch 3, 1dc into each dc to end. Rep this last row until work measures 13in.
Next row Ch 4, 1dc into 4th ch from hook (2dc inc), 1dc into each dc to end, turn.
Rep this row once more. 112dc.
Work even until back measures 18in.
Shape shoulders
Sl st across 7dc, ch 3, work to last 7dc, turn. Rep this row once more. 84dc.
Shape neck
Sl st across 7dc, ch 3 to count as first dc, 1dc into each of next 20dc, turn.
Next row Sl st across 7dc, ch 3, 1dc into each of next 6dc.
Fasten off.

With RS facing, skip center 28dc, rejoin yarn and work across 21dc, turn leaving 7dc unworked.
Next row Sl st across 7dc, ch 3, 1dc into each of next 6dc. Fasten off.

Front

Work as for back until work measures 15½ in.
Shape neck
Work across 45dc, turn. Dec 1dc at neck edge on next and every following row until 35dc rem. Work even until front measures same as back to start of shoulder shaping, ending at armhole edge.
Shape shoulders
Sl st across 7dc, work in dc to end of row, turn.
Next row Ch 3 to count as first dc, 1dc into each of next 20dc, turn.
Next row Sl st over 7dc, work in dc to end of row, turn.
Next row Ch 3, 1dc into each of next 6dc. Fasten off.
Skip center 20dc, rejoin yarn for 2nd side of neck and work across 45dc.
Work as for first side of neck, reversing all shaping.

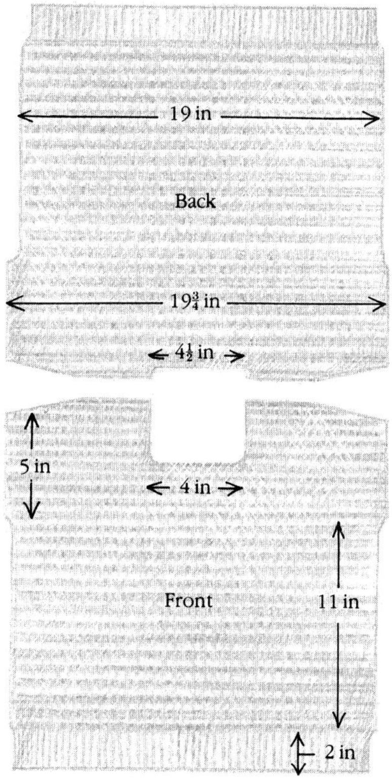

Sizes

Misses' sizes 12-16
Length from shoulder *18in*

Materials

9oz, or 1220 yd, of a pearl cotton in main color
1oz, or 230 yd, of size 20 crochet cotton in each of five contrasting colors
Size C crochet hook
Size 7 steel crochet hook
Pair of sizes 00 knitting needles

Gauge

22dc and 14 rows to 4in worked on size C hook

To save time, take time to check gauge.

19 in

Back

19¾ in

4½ in

5 in

4 in

Front

11 in

2 in

Working a flower motif

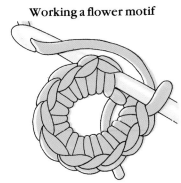

1 Begin by working the number of chains specified in the pattern and joining them with a slip stitch to form a ring. Work 12 single crochets into the ring. The first and last stitches of each round are joined with a slip stitch.

To finish

Join shoulder and side seams.

Armhole edging

With RS facing join yarn to underarm seam, 1sc into same place, skip first row end, * 5dc into next row end, skip next row end, 1sc into next row end, skip next row end, rep from * around armhole, sl st to first sc. Fasten off. Rep around 2nd armhole.

Neck edging

Join yarn to left shoulder seam and work shell edging around neck as for armhole, but skipping 2dc between sts, instead of 1 row end, when working across top edge of dc.

Flowers

Using size 7 steel hook, make 9ch, sl st to form a ring.

Ch 1, 18sc into ring, sl st to first sc.

2nd round 1sc into same place as sl st, * ch 3, skip 2sc, 1sc into next sc, rep from * ending with ch 3, skip 2sc, 1sl st into first sc.

3rd round Into each 3ch loop work 1sc, 1hdc, 3dc, 1hdc, 1sc.

4th round * Ch 5, 1sc around first sc of 2nd round inserting hook from back of work, * ch 5, 1sc around next sc of 2nd round, rep from * to end of round.

5th round Into each 5ch loop work (1sc, 1hdc, 5dc, 1hdc, 1sc), sl st to first sc. Fasten off.

Make 26 flowers using different colors as desired. Sew them to blouse as shown.

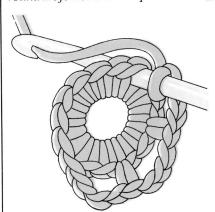

2 Work one single crochet into the same place as the slip stitch, work three chains, skip one single crochet, work one single crochet into the next stitch. Repeat all the way around.

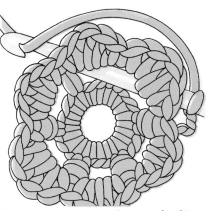

4 Work one single crochet into the slip stitch of previous round, work five chains, then work one single crochet around the back of the stitch which separated the previous round of loops.

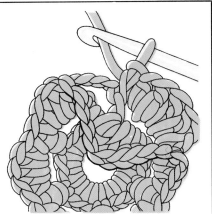

6 Into the first five-chain loop work one single crochet, one half double, three doubles, one half double and one single crochet.

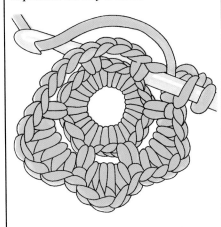

3 Into every three-chain loop work one single crochet, one half double, one double, one half double and one single.

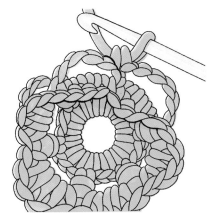

5 Make a five-chain loop in the same way behind each petal on the previous round.

7 Work a petal in the same way into each five-chain loop all around.

TWO EASY PIECES

. . . make up this checked cotton top. The front fastens with a button; the back forms a low V.

Size

Misses' sizes 12 [14]
Length from shoulder *17¾* [*19½*] *in*
Note *Instructions for the larger size are in brackets* [ ]; *where there is one set of figures it applies to both sizes.*

Materials

9 [*13*] *oz of a sport-weight cotton yarn in main color A*
2 [*4*] *oz in each of four contrasting colors: B, C, D and E*
Size E [*F*] *crochet hook*
Pair of size 3 knitting needles
1 button

Gauge

16 [*14*] *dc and 9* [*7¾*] *rows over check pat worked on size E* [*F*] *hook; each square measures 1⅛ × 1⅛* [*1½ × 1½*] *in.*

To save time, take time to check gauge.

Right half

Using size E [F] hook and A, make 38ch *loosely.*
1st row (RS) Using A, 1dc into 4th ch from hook, 1dc into each of next 4dc, changing to B on last st. With B, 1dc into each of next 6ch, weaving A across back of work and changing to A on last dc. With A, 1dc into each of next 6ch, changing to C on last st. With C, 1dc into each of next 6ch, weaving A across back of work and changing to A on last st. With A, 1dc into each of next 6ch, changing to D on last dc. With D, 1dc into each of next 6ch, turn. 6 squares, each consisting of 6dc. 36 sts.
2nd row (WS) Ch 3 to count as first dc, 1dc into each st to end, following chart for colors and working last dc into top of turning ch. Turn.
3rd row As 2nd.
Keeping edges of work as neat as possible cont in dc, working check pat from chart until 66 rows in all have been worked. 22 vertical squares in all. Fasten off.

Left half

Work as for right half, reversing check pat so that first row of chart is WS.

Waistbands

With RS of two halves facing, pin two pieces tog as shown in diagram so that lower edge of right half overlaps lower edge of left half by two squares for front. Pin two pieces in same way in back so that lower edge of left half overlaps lower edge of right half by two squares. With RS of front facing, using knitting needles and A, pick up and K60 [70] sts along lower edge, taking care to pick up sts through both layers at center front overlap.
Work firmly in K2, P2 ribbing until work measures 2¼in.
Bind off loosely in ribbing. Pick up and K60 [70] sts on back and work in K2, P2 ribbing as for front.

To finish

Steam-press lightly on WS, avoiding ribbing. Count up 5 squares from ribbing at each side and pin side seams, taking care to match squares. Using finer cotton thread in a matching color, join side seams on WS, taking extra care with ribbing. Count up 6 squares at center front and sew button to left front on 2nd dc from edge; use turning ch on right front as button loop.

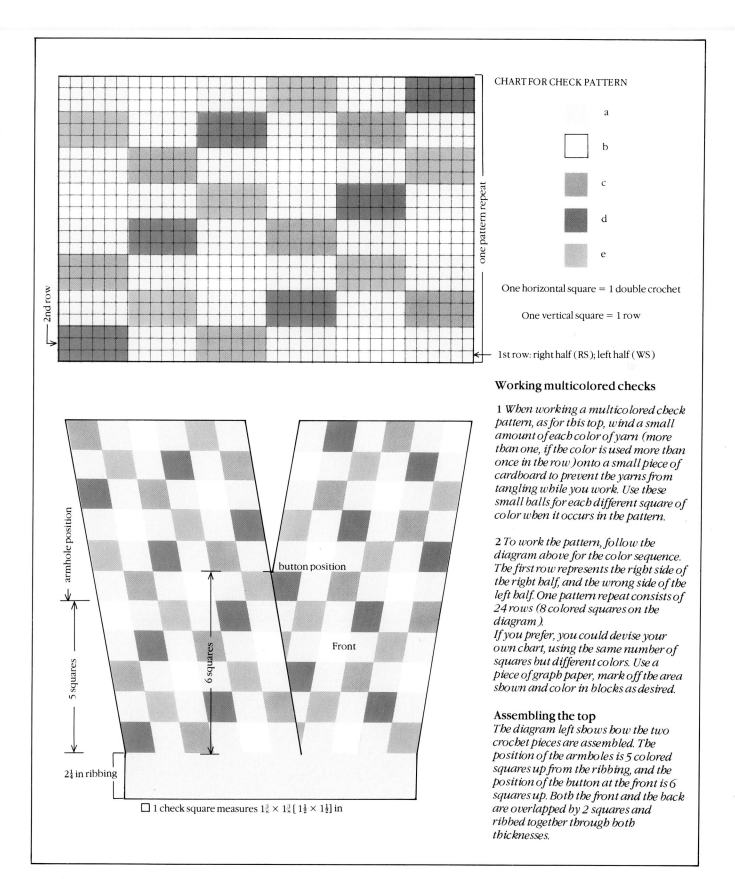

CHART FOR CHECK PATTERN

a

b

c

d

e

One horizontal square = 1 double crochet

One vertical square = 1 row

1st row: right half (RS); left half (WS)

one pattern repeat

2nd row

Working multicolored checks

1 *When working a multicolored check pattern, as for this top, wind a small amount of each color of yarn (more than one, if the color is used more than once in the row) onto a small piece of cardboard to prevent the yarns from tangling while you work. Use these small balls for each different square of color when it occurs in the pattern.*

2 *To work the pattern, follow the diagram above for the color sequence. The first row represents the right side of the right half, and the wrong side of the left half. One pattern repeat consists of 24 rows (8 colored squares on the diagram).*
If you prefer, you could devise your own chart, using the same number of squares but different colors. Use a piece of graph paper, mark off the area shown and color in blocks as desired.

Assembling the top

The diagram left shows how the two crochet pieces are assembled. The position of the armholes is 5 colored squares up from the ribbing, and the position of the button at the front is 6 squares up. Both the front and the back are overlapped by 2 squares and ribbed together through both thicknesses.

armhole position

button position

Front

6 squares

5 squares

2¼ in ribbing

☐ 1 check square measures 1¾ × 1¾ [1½ × 1½] in

SKY-BLUE JACKET

Soft chenille yarn is used for this comfortable jacket, which is trimmed with knitting worsted in a harmonizing or contrasting shade.

Back

Using larger hook and A, make 51 [54:57:60] ch.

Base row (RS) 1dc into 4th ch from hook, 1dc into each ch to end. Turn. 49 [52:55:58] sts.

1st row Ch 3 to count as first dc, 1dc between first and 2nd dc, 1dc between 2nd and 3rd dc, cont to work 1dc between each 2dc to end, 1dc into turning ch. Turn. First row forms pat and is rep throughout. Cont in pat until work measures 16in, ending with a WS row.

Shape armholes

Next row Sl st across first 5 sts, sl st into next sp between dc, ch 3, pat to last 6 sts, turn, leaving rem sts unworked.

39 [42:45:48] sts. Work even until work measures 23½ [23½:24:24] in, ending with a WS row.

Shape shoulders

1st row Sl st across first 4 sts, 1sc into next sp between dc, pat to last 6 sts, skip next dc, 1sc into next dc, turn. Rep last row once.

3rd row Sl st across first 3 [4:5:6] sts, 1sc into next sp between dc, pat to last 5 [6:7:8] sts, skip next dc, 1sc into next dc. 17 [18:19:20] sts. Fasten off.

Pocket linings (make 2)

Using larger hook and A, make 17 ch. Work base row as for back. 15 dc. Work 9 rows in pat as for back on these 15 sts. Fasten off.

Right front

Using larger hook and A, make 30 [32:33:35] ch and work base row as for back. 28 [30:31:33] sts.

Cont in pat as for back, work 10 rows.

Make buttonhole and pocket linings

Next row Ch 3, pat 2dc, ch 2, skip next 2 sts (buttonhole formed), pat 6 [7:8:9] dc, pat across 15 pocket lining sts, skip next 15 sts, pat to end.

Cont in pat until work measures 16in.

Shape armhole

Dec 5 sts at side edge on next row. Cont on rem 23 [25:26:28] sts until work measures 5 rows less than back to beg of shoulder shaping, ending at front edge.

Shape neck

Dec 7 [8:8:9] sts on next row, 2 sts at front edge on next row and 1 st at front edge on following 3 rows, ending at armhole edge and working 1sc at front edge to achieve a good curve.

Shape shoulder

Work to match back shoulder shaping, dec 4 sts at armhole edge on following 2 rows. Fasten off, leaving rem 3 [4:5:6] sts as part of shoulder edge.

Left front

Work as for right front, omitting buttonhole, reversing shaping and position of pocket on the front.

Sleeves

Using larger hook and A, work 30 [30:32:32] ch. Work base row as for back. 28 [28:30:30] sts. Cont in pat as for back, inc one st at each end of 4th and every following 4th row 5 times in all, then every following 3rd row twice. 44 [44:46:46] sts. Work even until work measures 17¼in. Place a contrasting marker at each end of last row. Work even for 3 more rows to fit armhole. Fasten off.

Collar

Using larger hook and A, make 54 [56:58:60] ch. Work base row as for back. 52 [54:56:58] sts. Work 5 rows in pat as for back.

Next row Sl st across first 16 [17:17:18] sts, 1sc into next st, pat 18 [18:20:20] dc, 1sc into next st. Fasten off, leaving rem 16 [17:17:18] sts unworked.

To finish

Join shoulder seams. Sew top edges of sleeves to sides of armholes and last rows above markers to armhole shaping. Join side and sleeve seams. Sew shaped edge of collar to neck edges, leaving 5 sts free on each front neck edge.

Borders

Using smaller hook and B, work 5 rows sc across lower edge, taking care not to work too tightly as this will pucker main fabric. Work 5 rounds of sc around lower edge of each sleeve border. Join each round with sl st and turn work each time to achieve same effect as lower border.

Sizes

Misses' sizes 10 [12:14:16]

Length from shoulder *23½ [23½:24:24] in, excluding border*

Sleeve seam *17¼in, excluding border*

Note: *Instructions for larger sizes are in brackets [ ]; where there is only one set of figures it applies to all sizes.*

Materials

24 [25:26:26] oz of a medium-weight chenille yarn (A)

4oz of a knitting worsted (B)

Size E crochet hook

Size H crochet hook

1 button

Gauge

11½ sts and 8 rows to 4in over pat worked on size H hook

To save time, take time to check gauge.

Edging the fabric with crochet

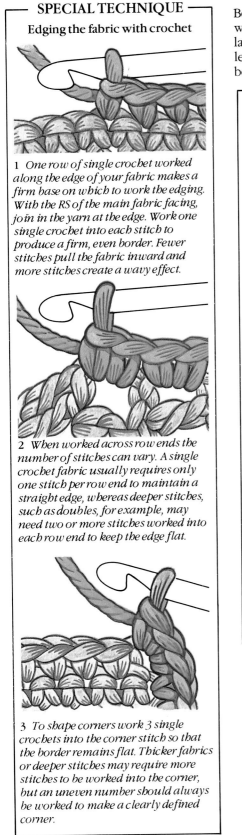

1 *One row of single crochet worked along the edge of your fabric makes a firm base on which to work the edging. With the RS of the main fabric facing, join in the yarn at the edge. Work one single crochet into each stitch to produce a firm, even border. Fewer stitches pull the fabric inward and more stitches create a wavy effect.*

2 *When worked across row ends the number of stitches can vary. A single crochet fabric usually requires only one stitch per row end to maintain a straight edge, whereas deeper stitches, such as doubles, for example, may need two or more stitches worked into each row end to keep the edge flat.*

3 *To shape corners work 3 single crochets into the corner stitch so that the border remains flat. Thicker fabrics or deeper stitches may require more stitches to be worked into the corner, but an uneven number should always be worked to make a clearly defined corner.*

Beg at lower edge of lower border, work in sc up right front, across top of lapels, all around edge of collar, down left side and across end of lower border. Work 4 more rows in same way, inc at outer edge of lapels and collar corners and dec at inner corners to keep work flat. Work 5 rows sc in same way across pocket opening. Sew pocket linings to WS. Sew on button.

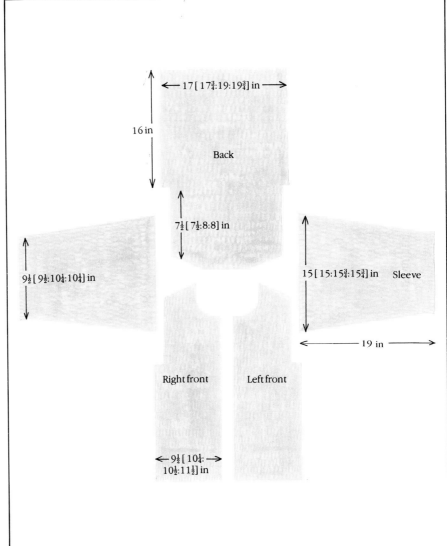

MOSAIC PATTERN SWEATER

This pretty sweater is designed on classic lines with raglan sleeves and a V-neckline. Make it in soft pastel shades, using one of them for the knitted waistband and borders.

Sizes

Misses' sizes 10 [12:14:16]
Length from back neck 24 [24½:24¾:25] in
Sleeve seam 17¼in
Note *Instructions for the larger sizes are in brackets []; where there is only one set of figures it applies to all sizes.*

Materials

13[13:15:15] oz of a knitting worsted in main color A
9[9:11:11] oz in each of contrasting colors B and C
Size F crochet hook
Pair of size 2 knitting needles

Gauge

20 sts and 19½ rows to 4in worked on size F hook (1sc, 1ch = 2 sts)

To save time, take time to check gauge.

Note *Carry yarns not in use loosely up side of work. Join in new color by drawing it through last two loops on hook in old color.*

Back

Using A, make 93[99:105:111] ch.
Base row (RS) Using A, 1sc into 3rd ch from hook, * ch 1, skip next ch, 1sc into next ch, rep from * to end. Turn. 92[98:104:110] sts. Working in color sequence of 1 row B, 1 row C, 1 row A, cont in pat thus:
Pat row Ch 1 to count as first sc, skip first st, * 1sc into next 1ch sp, ch 1, skip next sc, rep from * ending last rep with 1sc into last st. Turn.
Cont in pat until work measures 12in, ending with a row in A.
Shape raglan armholes
Keeping pat and color sequence correct:
1st row Sl st across first 3 sts, pat to last 2 sts, turn. 88[94:100:106] sts.
2nd row Work in pat.
3rd row Dec 1 st at each end of the row. Rep last 2 rows 16 more times. 54[60:66:72] sts.
Rep 3rd row only 11[13:15:17] more times. 32[34:36:38] sts. Fasten off.

Front

Work as for back until 2[4:4:4] rows less have been worked to beg of raglan, thus ending with a row in B[C:C:C].
Divide for neck
Keeping pat and color sequence correct:
Next row Pat first 43[46:49:52] sts, turn and cont on these sts for first side of neck.
Next row Work in pat.
2nd, 3rd and 4th sizes only
Next row Dec 1 st at neck edge. Work 1 row in pat.
All sizes
Shape raglan armhole
Next row Sl st over first 3 sts, pat to end.
Dec 1 st at armhole edge on next 17 alternate rows and then on the following 8[8:12:16] rows *and at the same time* shape neck edge by dec 1 st at neck edge on 2nd row and every following 4th row until 11[12:13:14] sts in all have been dec at neck edge. 5[7:5:3] sts. Dec 1 st at armhole edge on the next 3[5:3:1] rows.
Fasten off rem 2 sts.
Return to sts left at beg of neck shaping. With RS facing, skip next 6 sts and rejoin appropriate color to next st, pat to end. 43[46:49:52] sts. Complete to match first side of neck, reversing all shaping.

Sleeves

Using A, make 59[61:63:65]ch.
Base row Using A, work as for back. 58[60:62:64] sts.
Work 8[8:7:7] rows in pat as for back.
Next row Inc 1 st at each end of row.
Inc 1 st at each end of every following 9th [9th:8th:8th] row 6[6:7:7] more times. 72[74:78:80] sts.
Work even in pat until work measures 15in, ending with a row in A.
Shape raglan top
Keeping pat and color sequence correct:
1st row Sl st over first 3 sts, pat to last 2 sts, turn.
68[70:74:76] sts.
2nd row Work in pat.
3rd row Dec 1 st at each end of row.
Rep 2nd and 3rd rows 13[14:14:15] more times, ending with a 3rd row. 40[40:44:44] sts.
Rep 3rd row only 17[17:19:19]more times. 6 sts. Fasten off.

Waistbands

With RS facing, using knitting needles and A, pick up and K 79[83:89:93] sts along lower edge of front and back.
Work 3¼in in K1, P1 ribbing. Bind off in ribbing.

Cuffs

With RS facing, using knitting needles and A, pick up and K 49[51:53:55] sts along lower edge of sleeve.
Work 2½in in K1, P1 ribbing.
Bind off in ribbing.

Raglan borders (make 4)

Using knitting needles and A, cast on 9 sts.
1st row (RS) K2, * P1, K1, rep from * to last st, K1.
2nd row P2, * K1, P1, rep from * to last st, P1.
Rep these 2 rows until strip, when slightly stretched, fits raglan from beg of dec at underarm to neck edge. Bind off in ribbing.
Sew borders to raglans on front and back. Sew raglan edges of sleeves to borders.

Neck border

Using knitting needles and A, cast on 7 sts and work in ribbing as for raglan borders until border, when slightly stretched, fits around neck opening, beg and ending at center front. Bind off in ribbing.
Sew border to neck edge, lapping the right end over the left at the center front.

To finish

Press or block, as appropriate. Join side and sleeve seams, joining ends of raglan borders at underarm. Press seams very lightly.

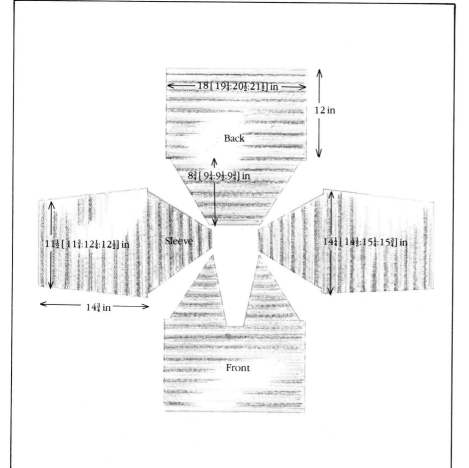

18[19¼:20½:21½] in

12 in

Back

8¾[9¼:9½:9¾] in

11½[11¾:12¼:12½] in

Sleeve

14¼[14½:15¼:15¾] in

14¾ in

Front

SPECIAL TECHNIQUE
Three-color mosaic

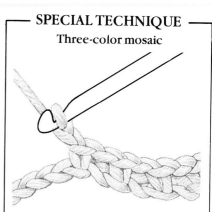

1 *The sweater is worked in a three-color single crochet and chain mosaic. Work the base row in the main color as instructed, so forming a row of alternating chain spaces and single crochet.*

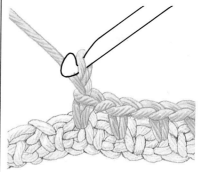

2 *Join in the second color on the last stitch of the base row. On the following row work a single crochet into each chain space and a chain above each single crochet.*

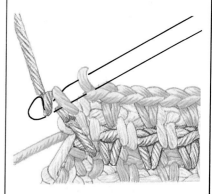

3 *Introduce the third color for the next row and work as in step 2. Continue in this way using the three different colors in sequence. Do not cut the end of old yarn when changing color, but leave it at the edge of the work ready for the next row in that color.*

RIBBON-THREADED TOPS

Satin ribbon provides the finishing touch on these pretty tops worked in filet crochet.

Woman's mesh top

Back

Using crochet hook, make 140 [149:158] ch.
Base row 1dc into 8th ch from hook, (ch 2, skip next 2ch, 1dc into next ch) 44 [47:50] times. Turn. 45 [48:51] sps.
Pat row Ch 5, skip first dc, 1dc into next dc, *ch 2, 1dc into next dc, rep from * to turning ch, ch 2, 1dc into sp formed by turning ch. Turn.
Rep pat row 44 more times.
Shape sleeves
Next row Make 73ch, 1dc into 8th ch from hook, (ch 2, skip next 2ch, 1dc into next ch) 21 times, (ch 2, 1dc into next dc) 45 [48:51] times, ch 2, 1dc into sp formed by turning ch, ch 2, 1dtr into same sp, (ch 2, 1dtr into sp formed by previous dtr) 22 times.
Turn. 91 [94:97] sps.
Rep pat row 24 more times.
Fasten off.

Front

Work as for back for 60 rows.

Shape neck

1st row Ch 5, skip first dc, 1dc into next dc, (ch 2, 1dc into next dc) 39 [40:42] times, 1tr into next dc, turn.
2nd row Ch 3, skip first tr and dc, 1dc into next dc, *ch 2, 1dc into next dc, rep from * to end, ending with 1dc into sp formed by turning ch. Turn.
3rd row Ch 5, skip first dc, 1dc into next dc, (ch 2, 1dc into next dc) 37 [38:40] times, 1tr into next dc. Turn.
4th row As 2nd row.
5th row Ch 5, skip first dc, 1dc into next dc, (ch 2, 1dc into next dc) 35 [36:38] times, 1tr into next dc. Turn.
6th row As 2nd row.
7th row Ch 5, skip first dc, 1dc into next dc, (ch 2, 1dc into next dc) 33 [34:36] times, 1tr into next dc. Turn.
8th row As 2nd row.
Work even in pat for 3 more rows.
Fasten off.
Join yarn to first st on other sleeve and work other side of neck to match.

To finish

If necessary, block or press lightly, as appropriate for yarn used.

Woman's mesh top

Sizes
Misses' sizes 10 [12:14]
Length from shoulder *23½ in.*
Sleeve seam *10½ in.*

Note *Instructions for larger sizes are in brackets [ ]; where there is only one set of figures it applies to all sizes.*

Materials
8 [9:10] oz of a firmly-spun fingering yarn
Approx 4½ yd of ¼ in-wide single-faced satin ribbon in each of three colors: A, B and C
Size E crochet hook
Pair of size 2 knitting needles

Gauge
10 sps and 13 rows to 4in over filet mesh pat worked on size E hook

To save time, take time to check gauge.

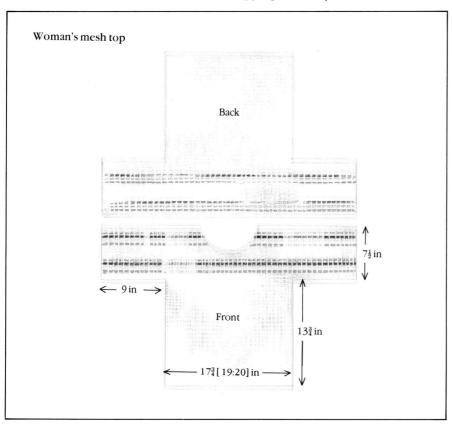

Woman's mesh top

Back

Front

7½ in

9 in

13¾ in

17¾ [19:20] in

SPECIAL TECHNIQUE
Ribbon weaving

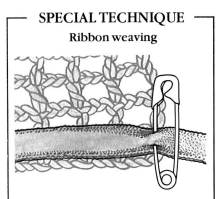

1 To prevent fraying, cut the ribbon diagonally, cutting it 5 in longer than needed. Estimating the length may be difficult, so make a trial weave across the mesh and note the amount required. Using a safety pin, anchor the ribbon to the right-hand edge of mesh, leaving about 3 in of ribbon extending over the edge.

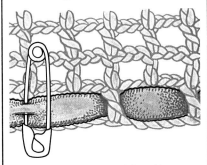

2 Trim the other end of the ribbon diagonally. When using fine ribbon, thread this other end into a large tapestry needle. Thicker ribbon must be drawn through the mesh with a safety pin inserted about 1 in from the end.

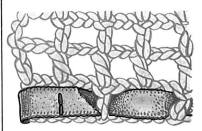

3 Weave the ribbon through the mesh in your chosen pattern, guiding the ribbon through your fingers to prevent it from twisting. When one row of weaving is complete, remove the safety pin or needle. Fold the ends of ribbon to the wrong side at the side edges and secure with small backstitches, or enclose the ends later when seaming.

Join shoulder seams.

Cuffs (alike)
Using knitting needles and with RS facing, pick up and K 82 sts from cuff edge. Work in K1, P1 ribbing for 1½ in. Bind off in ribbing.

Waistbands
Using knitting needles and with RS facing, pick up and K 110 sts from lower edge of front. Work in K1, P1 ribbing for 2¼ in.
Bind off in ribbing.
Work back waistband in the same way.

Neck edging
Using crochet hook and with RS facing, join yarn to center-back neck.

1st round Ch 1, 2sc into each sp all around neck, sl st to first ch.
2nd round Ch 1, skip first sc, 1sc into each sc to end, sl st to first ch.
3rd round Sl st into each sc to end.
Fasten off.

Ribbon weaving
Back Beg at RH edge, weave A through each sp on 6th row above sleeve shaping. Using B and C, weave next 2 rows in the same way. Skip next 10 rows and weave next 3 rows as before.
Front Weave A, B and C into same rows as on back, omitting neck opening.
Join side and sleeve seams, enclosing ends of ribbon with side seams.

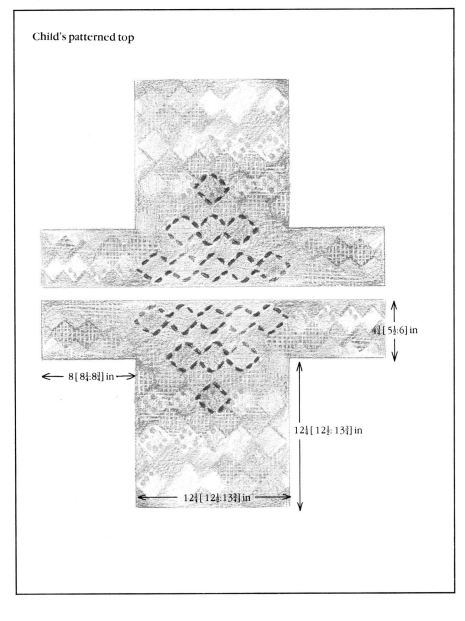

Child's patterned top

4¾[5½:6] in

8[8¼:8¾] in

12¼[12½:13¾] in

12¼[12½:13¾] in

Child's patterned top

Back and front (alike)

Make 98 [104:110] ch.
Base row 1dc into 8th ch from hook,
(ch 2, skip next 2ch, 1dc into next ch)
30 [32:34] times. Turn. 31 [33:35] sps.
Next row Ch 5, skip first dc, * 1dc into
next dc, ch 2, rep from * to end, 1dc
into sp formed by turning ch. Turn.
Last row forms mesh pat row.
Rep mesh pat row 2 [1:1] more times.
Next row Ch 5, skip first dc, 1dc into
next dc, (ch 2, 1dc into next dc) 2 [3:4]
times, 2dc into next 2ch sp, 1dc into
next dc – block formed –, * (ch 2, 1dc
into next dc) 5 times, 2dc into next
2ch sp, 1dc into next dc, rep from * 3
more times, (ch 2, 1dc into next dc) 3
[4:5] times, working last dc into sp
formed by turning ch. Turn.
* * Beg with 2nd row, work rem 6
rows of filet diamond pat from chart A.
Work mesh pat row 4 [5:6] times.
Work first row of chart A. * *
Rep from * * to * * twice more.
Work 2nd and 3rd rows of chart A, so
that 40 [42:45] rows have been
worked from beg.

Shape sleeves

Next row Make 65 [62:68] ch, 1dc into
4th ch from hook, 1dc into next ch –
first block formed –, cont working 4th
row of chart B to other side edge,
remove hook from loop, join a
separate length of yarn to base of last
dc worked, make 62 [59:65] ch and
fasten off, return to main yarn and cont
working 4th row of chart B across
foundation ch just made.
Turn.
Work 5th-7th rows of chart B.
Work mesh pat row 4 [5:6] times.
Work first-7th rows of chart B.
Work mesh pat row 2 [3:3] times.
Fasten off.

To finish

Join shoulder seams, leaving center 23
[23:27] sps for neck open.
Ribbon weaving
Beg at RH edge, weave ribbon through
sps above and below block diamond
pat on front and backs as shown in the
measurement diagram, twisting
ribbon at corners as necessary.
Join side and sleeve seams; for 3¼ in
above cuff edge place WS tog, so
reversing seam.
Lower edge
With RS facing and using crochet hook,
join yarn to lower edge at a side seam.
1st round Ch 1, 2sc into each sp to end,
sl st to first ch.
2nd round Ch 1, skip first sc, work in
crab st (sc worked from left to right) to
end, sl st to first ch. Fasten off.
Turn back cuffs twice (1½ in, then 1¾
in) and catch to sleeve seam if
necessary.

Child's patterned top
Sizes
C-3 [C-5:C-7]
Length from shoulder *17 [18:19¾] in*
Sleeve seam *(with cuff turned back)*
4¾ [5:5½] in

Note *Instructions for larger sizes are in
brackets []; where there is only one set of
figures it applies to all sizes.*

Materials
*6 [7:8] oz of a firmly-spun fingering yarn
Approx 2¼ yd of ¾-in-wide double-faced
satin ribbon
Size E crochet hook*

Gauge
*10 sps and 13 rows to 4in in filet mesh pat
worked on size E hook.*

To save time, take time to check gauge.

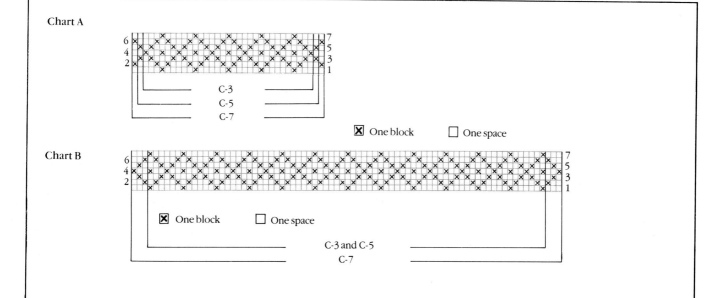

HAIRPIN CROCHET BEDJACKET

This pretty bedjacket is worked in three contrasting colors in a soft mohair blend yarn.

Note: *Instructions for working hairpin crochet are on pages 164-166. The crochet is worked with yarn double throughout.*

Back and fronts

Using yarn double, make 9 strips in color A, 6 in B and 6 in C, all 20in long (60 loops along each edge). Then make 1 strip each in A and C to measure 17in (51 loops on each edge)

and 2 strips each in A and C to measure 12¼in (36 loops along each edge). Arrange the strips as shown in the diagram on page 42. Start at the right front edge and join the left side of one 17in-long strip in C to the other side of a 20in strip in B, starting at the lower edge and leaving 9 loops free on the longer strip at the top (see page 166). Join the remaining strips in the same way, using the shorter strips for the underarm sections (leaving 24 loops free at the top of the longer strips).

Sleeves

For each sleeve work 12 strips 16½in long (49 loops on each edge), 4 in each of the colors (24 strips in all for both sleeves). Join the strips for each sleeve, alternating colors as on the main body of the jacket.

Join the sleeve seam by looping the first and last strips together, leaving 7 loops open at the top. Bind of these 7 loops by inserting the crochet hook through the first loop and drawing the next loop through it, then continuing to draw successive loops through the preceding loop on the hook. Sew the last loop to finish the bound-off edge.

Edging strips

To make the sleeve edgings take one strand each from two of the colors and make 2 two-tone strips 10½in long (32 loops along each edge); then work 2 more two-tone strips to the same length but using a different color combination. Loop one strip of each color together and join them to form a ring. Gather the wrist edge of each sleeve and sew the edgings neatly in place.

For the waist, work 2 two-tone strips 24in long (72 loops along each edge) or to the desired length, but do not join them to the garment yet. Make two more two-tone strips to measure 17¼in (52 loops along each edge) to go from the lower edge up to the neck edge on the right front, and 2 strips 15¾in long (48 loops) to go around the neck edge.

To finish

Do not press. Join the shoulder seams,

Size
Misses' sizes 10-12
Length from shoulder approx 23in
Sleeve seam approx 14½in

Note: *The size can easily be adjusted by adding or subtracting strips, by lengthening or shortening the waistband or by lengthening or shortening the vertical strips.*

Materials
6oz of a medium-weight mohair blend in each of three colors: A, B and C
3½yd of narrow ribbon in each of two colors to match yarn
4 snaps
1½in hairpin loom (or adjustable loom fixed at this width)
Size F crochet hook

Gauge
Two strips of hairpin crochet, worked with yarn double and joined with sc should measure approx 20in long (60 loops on each side) and 3in wide.

To save time, take time to check gauge.

then set in the sleeves, placing the bound-off edges at the underarm edges of the armholes and keeping the free loops along the armholes on the main body to the right side of the work to make a fluffy edge.

Bind off the loops along the neck edge (the 9 loops at each side) and along each front.

Gather the lower edge of the jacket to fit the waist measurement and sew the edging neatly in place. Sew the right front edging in place, fitting it from the neck edge to the lower edge, stitching along the center of the edging and making sure that it laps over the bound-off edge.

Thread two rows of ribbon through the wrist, neck edge and waist and tie them in bows.

Sew four snaps at equally-spaced intervals down the front edges.

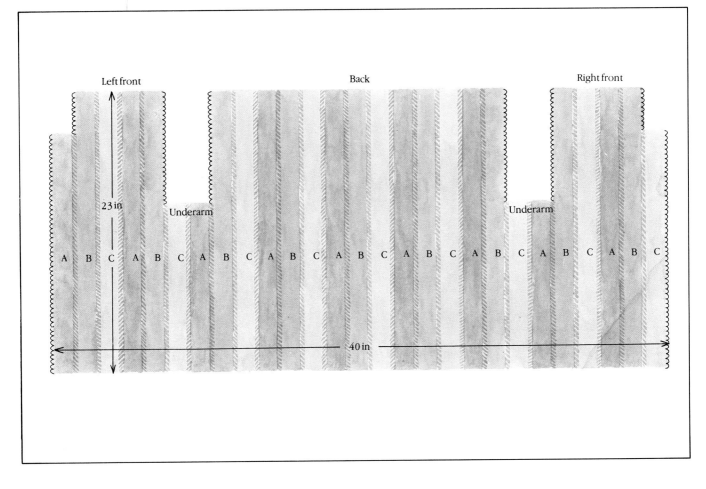

BOBBLES 'N' STRIPES

Subtle pastel colors worked in stripes and bobbles make an attractive pullover – and a sensational addition to your wardrobe!

Sizes
Misses' sizes 12 [14:16]
Length from shoulder $24\frac{1}{4}$ [$24\frac{3}{4}$: $25\frac{1}{2}$] in
Sleeve seam *19 in*

Note *Instructions for larger sizes are in brackets [ ]; where there is only one set of figures it applies to all sizes.*

Materials
11 [12:14] oz of a sport-weight yarn in main color A
9 [11:11] oz in each of two contrasting colors, B and C
Size C crochet hook
Pair of size 1 knitting needles

Gauge
22 dc and $12\frac{1}{2}$ rows to 4 in worked on size C hook

To save time, take time to check gauge.

Back
Using knitting needles and A, cast on 126 [132:138] sts.
1st row (RS) (K1, P1) to end.
2nd row (P1, K1) to end.
Rep first and 2nd rows until work measures $2\frac{3}{4}$ in, ending with a RS row. Bind off in ribbing, transferring last st to crochet hook.
Next row With RS facing and using A, ch 1 to count as first sc, skip first st at base of first ch, work 105 [109:113] sc evenly into last row of waistband. Turn. 106 [110:114] sts.
Beg pat
1st row (WS) Using B, ch 3, skip first st, 1 dc into each st to end. Turn.
2nd row Using A, as first row.
3rd row Using C, as first row.
4th row Using A, as first row.
5th row Using B, as first row.
6th, 8th, 10th, 12th, 14th, 16th, 18th, 20th and 22nd rows Using A, ch 1 to count as first sc, skip first st, 1 sc into each st to end. Turn.
7th row Using C, ch 1 to count as first sc, skip first st, 1 sc into each of next 3 sts, *leaving last loop of each st on hook work 3 tr into next st, yo and draw through all 4 loops on hook – bobble formed –, 1 sc into each of next 3 sts, rep from * to last 2 sts, bobble into next st, 1 sc into last st. Turn.
9th row Using B, ch 1 to count as first sc, skip first st, 1 sc into next st, *bobble into next st, 1 sc into each of next 3 sts, rep from * to end. Turn.
11th-22nd rows Rep 7th-10th rows 3 more times.
23rd row Using C, as first row.
24th row Using A, as first row.
25th row Using B, as first row.
26th row Using A, as first row.
27th row Using C, as first row.
28th-44th rows As 6th-22nd rows, reading B for C and C for B.
First-44th rows form pat.
Cont in pat until work measures 16 [$16\frac{1}{2}$: $16\frac{1}{2}$] in, ending with a WS row.
Shape armholes
Next row Keeping pat correct, sl st across first 5 [6:7] sts, pat to last 4 [5:6] sts, turn. 98 [100:102] sts.
Next row Sl st across first 3 sts, pat to last 2 sts, turn. 94 [96:98] sts.
Next 2 rows Work first 2 sts tog, pat to last 2 sts, work last 2 sts tog.

Turn. 90 [92:94] sts.
Work even in pat until armhole measures $8\frac{1}{4}$ [$8\frac{1}{2}$:9] in, ending with a WS row.
Shape shoulders and neck
Next row Sl st across first 9 sts, pat next 16 sts, turn.
Next row Pat 8 sts.
Fasten off.
With RS facing, return to sts skipped at beg of neck shaping, skip next 42 [44:46] sts, and keeping pat correct, join yarn to next st.
Next row Pat 16 sts, turn.
Next row Sl st across first 9 sts, pat to end. Fasten off.

Front
Work as for back until work measures $23\frac{3}{4}$ [$24\frac{1}{2}$:25] in.
Shape neck
Next row Pat 37 [38:39] sts, turn.
Next row Sl st across first 4 sts, pat to end. Turn. 34 [35:36] sts.
Next row Pat to last 3 sts, turn. 31 [32:33] sts.
Rep last 2 rows once more. 25 [26:27] sts.
Next row Sl st across first 2 [3:4] sts, pat to end. Turn. 24 sts.
Work even in pat until armhole matches back armhole to beg of shoulder shaping, ending at armhole edge.
Shape shoulder
Next row Sl st across first 9 sts, pat to end. Turn. 16 sts.
Next row Pat first 8 sts.
Fasten off.
With RS facing, return to sts skipped at beg of neck shaping, skip next 16 sts and keeping pat correct, join yarn to next st.
Next row Pat to end. Turn. 37 [38:39] sts.
Complete to match first side of neck, reversing all shaping.

Sleeves (alike)
Using knitting needles and A, cast on 50 [52:54] sts.
Work in K1, P1 ribbing as for back for $2\frac{1}{4}$ in, ending with a RS row.
Bind off in ribbing, transferring last st to size C hook.
Next row With RS facing and using A, ch 1 to count as first sc, skip first st at

base of first ch, 1sc into each bound-off st to end. Turn. 50 [52:54] sts.

1st-5th rows As 23rd-27th rows of back pat.

Shape sleeve

6th row As 28th row of back pat, inc one st at each end of row. 52 [54:56] sts.

7th-22nd rows As 29th-44th rows of back pat, inc one st at each end of every following 4th row. 60 [62:64] sts. Cont in pat as for back, at the same time inc one st at each end of every following 4th row until there are 64 [66:68] sts. Work even in pat as for back until work measures approx 19 in, ending with same row as back at beg of armhole shaping.

Shape top

Next row Sl st across first 5 sts, pat to last 4 sts, turn. 56 [58:60] sts.

Next 3 rows Work first 2 sts tog, pat to last 2 sts, work last 2 sts tog. Turn. 50 [52:54] sts.

Work even in pat for 2 [2¼:2¾] in.

Next row Work first 2 sts tog, pat to last 2 sts, work last 2 sts tog. Turn. 48 [50:52] sts.

Next row Pat to end. Turn.

Rep last 2 rows until 32 sts rem.

Work even in pat until work measures 26¾ [27:27½] in.

Fasten off.

Neckband

Join left shoulder seam.

With RS facing, using knitting needles and A, pick up and K 65 sts across back neck and 75 sts across front neck. 140 sts. Work 7 rows of K1, P1 ribbing. Bind off in ribbing.

To finish

Do not press.

Join right shoulder seam.

Set in sleeves, matching stripes.

Join side and sleeve seams, matching stripes.

Note *Use backstitch for shoulder seams and a flat seam for the remaining seams, so as to prevent excess bulk.*

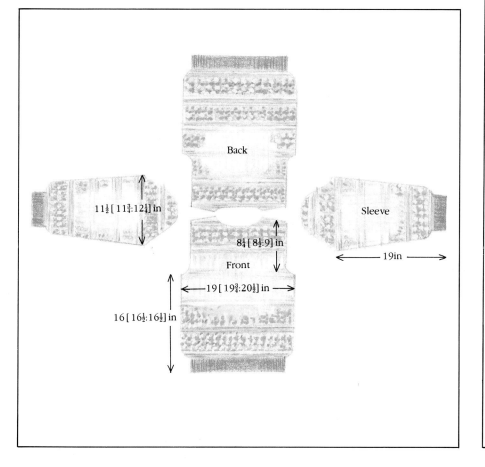

SPECIAL TECHNIQUE

Triple bobbles

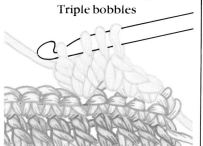

1 *The bobbles on the sweater are formed on the wrong side of the work by bending triple clusters. With the right side facing, work a row of single crochet and turn. Change to the first contrasting color and work in single crochet to the position of the first bobble.*

Leaving the last loop of each stitch on the hook, work three triples into the next stitch.

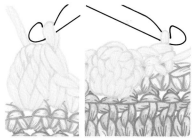

2 *Wind the yarn around the hook and draw it through all four loops on the hook to form the first triple cluster (above left). Work one single crochet into each of the next three stitches to bend the cluster, so forming the first bobble on the right side of the work (above right). If necessary, push the bobble to the right side with the blunt end of the crochet hook.*

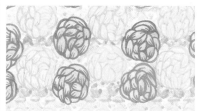

3 *Continue in this way to the end of the row. Change back to the first color and work a row of single crochet. Work another row of bobbles using the second contrasting color and slightly altering the positions of the bobbles as instructed in the pattern. Continue alternating bobble and single crochet rows for the required length.*

Figure labels (on diagram): Back, Sleeve, Front, 11½ [11¾:12¼] in, 8¼ [8½:9] in, 19in, 19 [19¾:20½] in, 16 [16½:16½] in

45

TUNISIAN PULLOVER

Warm colors in Tunisian crochet stripes make this attractive pullover with a slash neck.

Note: *Instructions for working Basic Tunisian stitch (Tst), Tunisian double stitch (Tdst), Tunisian triple (Ttr) and Tunisian purl (Tp) are on pages 161-162.*

Back and front (alike)
Using afghan hook and A, make 58 [62:64:68] ch.
1st row Work 1 Ttr into 4th ch from hook. Work in Ttr to end.
2nd row With B, work as for 2nd row of Tst – called "return row."
3rd row Tdst in B.
4th row Return row in C.
5th row Work Tp in C.
6th row Return row in A.
7th row Ttr in A.
8th row Return row in C.
9th row Tdst in C.
10th row Return row in B.
11th row Tp in B.
12th row Return row in A.
13th row Ttr in A.
Rows 2-13 form the striped pattern used for the main part of the sweater.
Cont in pat until work measures $17\frac{3}{4}$ [$17\frac{3}{4}$:$19\frac{3}{4}$:$19\frac{3}{4}$] in, finishing with a Ttr row in A.
To finish the top, work a return row, then 1 row Tp and another return row, all in A. Make 1 row sl st from right to left.

Sleeves
Work 50 [52:54:56] ch in A.
1st row Ttr to end of row in A.
Change to B and work in pat as for front until work measures 16 [16:$17\frac{3}{4}$:$17\frac{3}{4}$] in, ending with 1 row Ttr in A.
Finish the top of the sleeve in A with 1 row Tdst, a return row and then 1 row sl st from right to left.

Waistband
Using ordinary crochet hook and A, make 11ch.
1st row 1sc into 2nd ch from hook, sc to end of row. Turn. 10sc.
2nd row Work sc into the back loops of the sc of the previous row. Turn.
Rep 2nd row to form a crochet rib, which is worked sideways and can be sewn or crocheted onto the garment.
Cont working in ribbing until strip measures $28\frac{1}{4}$ [30:$32\frac{1}{4}$:$34\frac{1}{4}$] in.

Bring the two ends tog and join the last row to the first 10ch with sc.

Cuffs
Make 15ch in A. Work in sc as for waistband until work measures $6\frac{1}{4}$ in. Join last row to first 14ch.

To finish
Darn in all ends and block or press the pieces lightly on WS as appropriate for yarn used.
Place front and back tog with RS facing and sew tog at shoulders for $3\frac{1}{4}$ in on each side.
Place center of sleeve top at shoulder seam. RS facing, and join seams. Join side and sleeve seams.
Sew the waistband and cuffs in position.

Size
Misses' sizes 8 [10:12:14]
Length from shoulder *$21\frac{1}{4}$ [$21\frac{1}{4}$:$23\frac{1}{4}$:$23\frac{1}{4}$] in*
Sleeve seam *20 [20:$21\frac{1}{4}$:$21\frac{1}{4}$] in*

Note *Instructions for larger sizes are in brackets [ ]; where there is only one set of figures it applies to all sizes.*

Materials
*10 [10:12:12] oz of a knitting worsted-weight yarn in main color A
3 [4:4:4] oz in contrasting color B
3 [5:5:5] oz in contrasting color C
Size K afghan hook
Size I ordinary crochet hook*

Gauge
14 sts and 10 rows to 4in worked on size K afghan hook.

To save time, take time to check gauge.

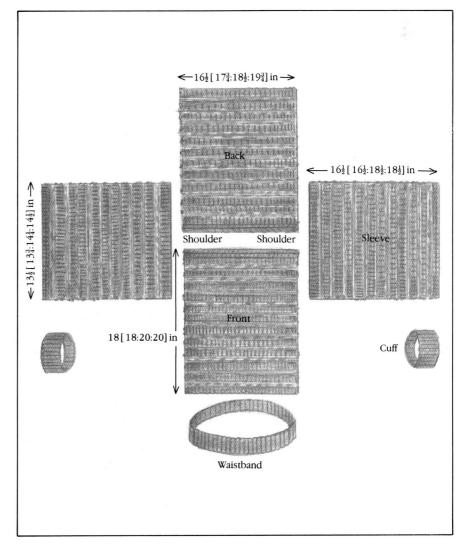

HOT PINK DIAMONDS

Open-work diamond motifs embellished with puff stitches make this pretty pullover.

Size

Misses' sizes 10-14
Length from shoulder $22\frac{1}{2}$ in
Sleeve seam $17\frac{3}{4}$ in

Materials

21oz of a sport-weight glossy yarn
Size E crochet hook
Pair of size 2 knitting needles

Gauge

1 pat rep (16 sts) to $3\frac{1}{4}$ in and 1 pat rep (10 rows) to $4\frac{1}{4}$ in, worked on size E hook

To save time, take time to check gauge.

Back

Using knitting needles, cast on 99 sts.
1st row (K1, P1) to last st, K1.
2nd row (P1, K1) to last st, P1.
Rep first and 2nd rows until work measures $2\frac{1}{4}$ in, ending with a 2nd row. Bind off loosely in ribbing, leaving last st on needle.
Transfer last st to crochet hook.
Next row (RS) Ch 1 to count as first sc, skip first st at base of first ch, 1sc into each bound-off st to end. Turn. 99 sts.
Next row Ch 3, skip first st, 1dc into next st, *ch 3, skip next 3 sts, (yo, insert hook into st and draw through a loop) 4 times into next st, yo and draw through first 8 loops on hook, yo and draw through rem 2 loops on hook – puff st formed –, (ch 1, skip next st, puff st into next st) 4 times, ch 3, skip next 3 sts, 1dc into next st, rep from * to last st, 1dc into last st.
Turn.

Beg pat

1st row (RS) Ch 3, skip first st, 1dc into next dc, *1dc into next ch, ch 3, skip next 2ch, (puff st into next ch, ch 1) 3 times, puff st into next ch, ch 3, skip next 2ch, 1dc into next ch, 1dc into next dc, rep from * to last st, 1dc into last st. Turn.
2nd row Ch 3, skip first st, 1dc into next dc, *1dc into next dc, 1dc into next ch, ch 3, skip next 2ch, (puff st into next ch, ch 1) twice, puff st into next ch, ch 3, skip next 2ch, 1dc into next ch, 1dc into each of next 2dc, rep from * to last st, 1dc into last st. Turn.
3rd row Ch 3, skip first st, 1dc into next st, *1dc into each of next 2dc, 1dc into next ch, ch 3, skip next 2ch, puff st into next ch, ch 1, puff st into next ch, ch 3, skip next 2ch, 1dc into next ch, 1dc into each of next 3dc, rep from * to

last st, 1dc into last st. Turn.
4th row Ch 3, skip first st, 1dc into next st, *1dc into each of next 3dc, 1dc into next ch, ch 3, skip next 2ch, puff st into next ch, ch 3, skip next 2ch, 1dc into next ch, 1dc into each of next 4dc, rep from * to last st, 1dc into last st. Turn.
5th row Ch 3, skip first st, puff st into next dc, * (ch 1, skip next dc, puff st into next dc) twice, ch 3, 1dc into next puff st, ch 3, puff st into next dc, (ch 1, skip next dc, puff st into next dc) twice, rep from * to last st, 1dc into last st. Turn.
6th row Ch 4, skip first 2 sts, * puff st into next ch, ch 1, puff st into next ch, ch 3, skip first 2ch, 1dc into next ch, 1dc into next dc, 1dc into next ch, ch 3, skip next 2ch, (puff st into next ch, ch 1) twice, rep from * to last st, 1dc into last st. Turn.
7th row Ch 3, skip first st, puff st into first ch, *ch 1, puff st into next ch, ch 3, skip next 2ch, 1dc into next ch, 1dc into each of next 3dc, 1dc into next ch, ch 3, skip next 2ch, puff st into next ch, ch 1, puff st into next ch, rep from * to last st, ending last rep with puff st into 4th turning ch, 1dc into 3rd turning ch. Turn.
8th row Ch 4, skip first 2 sts, *puff st into next ch, ch 3, skip next 2ch, 1dc into next ch, 1dc into each of next 5dc, 1dc into next ch, ch 3, skip next 2ch, puff st into next ch, ch 1, rep from * to last st, 1dc into last st. Turn.
9th row Ch 3, skip first st, puff st into first ch, *ch 3, skip next 2ch, 1dc into next ch, 1dc into each of next 7dc, 1dc into next ch, ch 3, skip next 2ch, puff st into next ch, rep from * to last st, ending last rep with puff st into 4th turning ch, 1dc into 3rd turning ch. Turn.
10th row Ch 3, skip first st, 1dc into

next puff st, *ch 3, (puff st into next dc, ch 1, skip next dc) 4 times, puff st into next dc, ch 3, 1dc into next puff st, rep from * to last st, 1dc into last st. Turn. First-10th rows form pat. Cont in pat until work measures approx 22½ in from cast-on edge, ending with a 6th row. Fasten off.

Front

Work as for back until work measures approx 15½ in from cast-on edge, ending with an 8th row.

Divide for neck

Next row Ch 3, skip first st, *puff st into next ch, ch 3, skip next 2ch, 1dc into next ch, 1dc into each of next 8dc, 1dc into next ch, ch 3, rep from * twice more, ending last rep with ch 2, 1dc into next puff st. Turn.

Shape left neck

1st row Ch 3, puff st into first dc, pat to end. Turn.

2nd row Work 2 pat reps, 1dc into next ch, ch 3, skip next 2ch, (puff st into next ch, ch 1, skip next ch) 3 times, puff st into next ch, 1dc into top of turning ch. Turn.

3rd row Ch 3, puff st into next ch, pat to end. Turn.

4th row Ch 3, work 2 pat reps, 1dc into each of next 2dc, 1dc into next ch, ch 3, skip next 2ch, puff st into next ch, ch 1, puff st into next ch, 1dc into top of turning ch. Turn.

5th row As 3rd row.

6th row Ch 3, work 2 pat reps, (ch 1, skip next dc, puff st into next dc) twice, 1dc into top of turning ch. Turn.

7th row As 3rd row.

8th row Ch 3, work 2 pat reps, ch 1, puff st into next ch, 1dc into top of turning ch. Turn.

9th row As 3rd row.

10th row Ch 3, work 2 pat reps, puff st into next st, 1dc into top of turning ch. Turn.

11th row Ch 3, skip first st, 1dc into first puff st, pat to end. Turn.

12th row Ch 3, work 2 pat reps, 1dc into 3rd turning ch. Turn.

13th row Ch 3, skip first st, 1dc into next st, pat to end. Turn.

14th row Work 2 pat reps, omitting 1dc from end of last rep. Turn.

15th row As 13th row.

Keeping pat correct, work even in pat until work matches back to shoulder, ending with a 6th row. Fasten off.

With RS facing and using crochet hook, return to sts left at beg of neck shaping and rejoin yarn to next puff st.

Next row Ch 5, skip first 2ch, 1dc into next ch, pat to end. Turn.

Shape right neck

1st row Work 3 pat reps, ending last rep with puff st into last dc, 1dc into 3rd turning ch. Turn.

2nd row Ch 3, skip first st, puff st into first ch, pat to end. Turn.

Complete to match left side of neck, reversing shaping as shown.

Sleeves (alike)

Using knitting needles, cast on 45 sts. Rep first and 2nd ribbing rows as for back for 2in, ending with a 2nd row. Bind off loosely in ribbing, leaving last st on needle. Transfer last st onto crochet hook.

Next row (RS) Ch 1 to count as first sc, skip first st at base of first ch, work 82sc into bound-off edge. 83 sts. Cont as for back until work measures approx 17¾ in from cast-on edge, ending with a 9th row. Fasten off.

To finish

Do not press. Join right shoulder seam, matching pats.

Neckband

With RS facing, using knitting needles and beg at top of left neck, pick up and K 60 sts down left neck, one st from ch lying between 2 puff sts at beg of V, (mark this st with contrasting yarn) 60 sts up right neck and 46 sts across back neck. 157 sts.

Next row (WS) (K1, P1) to within 2 sts of marked st, K2 tog, P1, K2 tog, (P1, K1) to end.

Next row (P1, K1) to within 2 sts of marked st, P2 tog, K1, P2 tog, (K1, P1) to end.

Rep last 2 rows for 1¼in.

Bind off loosely in ribbing, dec one st at each side of marked st as before.

Place contrasting markers 8in from shoulders on both side edges of back and front, i.e. on a 5th pat row.

Set in sleeves between markers, easing top edges to fit.

Join side and sleeve seams.

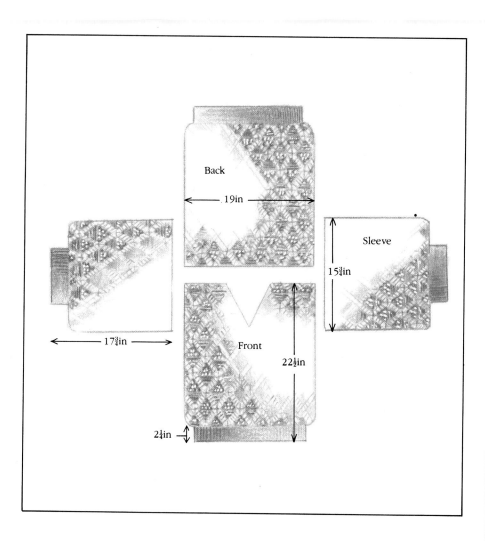

Back

19in

Sleeve

15¾in

17¾in

Front

22½in

2¼in

SPECIAL TECHNIQUE

Working an approximate foundation

1 *It can be difficult, especially when using fine yarn, to count accurately the number of chains required for the base row. This problem can be avoided by working an approximate foundation chain. Work roughly the required number of chains plus about 25 more. Work the base row as instructed, leaving a length of unworked chain.*

2 *Using sharp scissors, cut across the first chain worked, so removing the beginning slip knot. Discard the short piece of yarn now caught in the second foundation chain. Insert the point of the crochet hook into the loop at the end of the chain and draw through the loose length of yarn.*

3 *Continue drawing through yarn and undoing chains in this way until one loop remains. Do not draw through the yarn, but instead pull it firmly to tighten the last chain. The remaining end of yarn can now be used for seaming or can be darned into the edge of the work as usual.*

CROSS-STITCH SWEATER

Contrasting patterns of crossed stitches give an interesting texture to this two-tone pullover.

Back (See chart, page 54.)
Using A, make 90 [94:98] ch.
Base row 1sc into 2nd ch from hook, 1sc into each ch to end. Turn. 89 [93:97] sc.
1st row (WS) Ch 3, skip first sc, (skip next sc, 1dc into next sc, working behind last dc work 1dc into skipped sc – 1 pair of crossed dc or Xdc worked) 7 [8:9] times, 1dc into each of next 22sc, skip next 3sc, 1tr into each of next 3sc, working behind tr work 1tr into each of 3 skipped sc – back cable worked – 1dc into each of next 3sc, skip next 3sc, 1tr into each of next 3sc, working in front of tr work 1tr into each of 3 skipped sc – front cable worked – 1dc into each of next 22 sc, (1 pair Xdc into next 2sc) 7 [8:9] times, 1dc into last sc. Turn.
2nd row Ch 3, skip first st, (1 pair Xdc into next 2 sts) 7 [8:9] times, 1dc into next st, inserting hook from front of work, from right to left, work 1dc around stem of next st – 1dc front worked – * (skip next 2 sts, inserting hook from front of work, from right to left, work 1tr around stem of next dc – 1tr front worked – working behind tr work 1dc into each of 2 skipped sts, skip next st, 1dc into each of next 2 sts, 1tr front around stem of skipped dc) 3 times – tr V pat worked * – 1dc front around stem of next dc, (1dc into next st, 1sc into each of next 6 sts, 1dc into next st, 1dc front around stem of next st) twice, rep from * to * once, 1dc front around stem of next dc, 1dc into next st, (1 pair Xdc into next 2 sts) 7 [8:9] times, 1dc into top of turning ch. Turn.
3rd row Ch 3, skip first dc, (1 pair Xdc into next 2 sts) 7 [8:9] times, 1dc into next st, inserting hook from back of work, from right to left, work 1dc around stem of next st – 1dc back worked – 1dc into each of next 18 sts, 1dc back around stem of next st, 1dc into next st, work front cable over next 6 sts, 1dc into next st, 1dc back around stem of next st, 1dc into next st, work back cable over next 6 sts, 1dc into next st, 1dc back around stem of next st, 1dc into each of next 18 sts, 1dc back around stem of next st, 1dc into next st, (1 pair Xdc into next 2 sts) 7 [8:9] times, 1dc into turning ch. Turn.

4th row As 2nd row.
5th row As 3rd row working back cable in place of front cable and front cable in place of back cable.
Rep 2nd – 5th rows for pat.
Cont in pat until a total of 62 [63:64] rows have been worked.
Shape neck
1st row Pat across 27 [29:31] sts, turn.
2nd row Keeping pat correct, pat to end. Fasten off.
2nd side, 1st row Skip center 35 sts, rejoin yarn to next st and pat to end. Pat 1 row. Fasten off.

Front
Work as for back until a total of 44 rows of pat have been worked.
Shape neck
1st row Pat across 44 [46:48] sts, turn. Keeping pat correct cont on these sts only for first side.
2nd row Ch 3, skip first dc, 1sc into each of next 6 sts, 1dc into next st, 1dc front around stem of next st, skip next 2 sts, 1tr around stem of next st, working behind tr and leaving last loop of each st on hook, work 1dc into each of 2 skipped sts – 1dc dec worked –, pat to end. Turn.
3rd row Work in pat to last 2 sts of tr V pat, dec 1dc over next 2 sts, pat to end. Turn.
4th row Work in pat to first 2 sts of tr V pat, dec 1dc over next 2 sts, pat to end. Turn. Cont to dec 1dc in this way on every row until 27 [29:31] sts rem. Pat 2 [3:4] rows straight. Fasten off.
2nd side, 1st row Skip center st, rejoin yarn to next st and complete to match first side, reversing shaping.

Sleeves (alike)
Using A, make 52 [56:60] ch.
Base row Work as for back. 51 [55:59] sc.
1st row (WS) Ch 3, skip first sc, (1 pair Xdc into next 2 sts) 7 [8:9] times, 1dc into each of next 3 sts, work back cable over next 6 sts, 1dc into each of next 3 sts, work front cable over next 6 sts, 1dc into each of next 3 sts, (1 pair Xdc into next 2 sts) 7 [8:9] times, 1dc into last sc. Turn.
2nd row Ch 3, skip first st, (1 pair Xdc into next 2 sts) 7 [8:9] times, 1dc into next st, 1dc front around stem of next

Sizes
Misses' sizes 12 [14:16]
Length from shoulder $24\frac{3}{4}$ [$25\frac{1}{4}$:$25\frac{1}{2}$] in
Sleeve seam $16\frac{1}{2}$ [$17\frac{1}{4}$:18] in

Note *Instructions for larger sizes are in brackets [ ]; where there is only one set of figures it applies to all sizes.*

Materials
26 [28:30] oz of a knitting worsted-weight yarn in main color A
8oz in contrasting color B
Size F crochet hook

Gauge
20 sts and 11 rows to 4in over Xdc (crossed dc) pat worked on size F hook.

To save time, take time to check gauge.

st, (1dc into next st, 1sc into each of next 6 sts, 1dc into next st, 1dc front around stem of next dc) twice, 1dc into next dc, (1 pair Xdc into next 2 sts) 7 [8:9] times, 1dc into top of turning ch. Turn.

With sts as set, inc 1 st at end of every row until there are 63 [67:71] sts, working inc sts into pat. Work even until a total of 42 [44:46] rows has been worked in pat.
Fasten off.

To finish

Join shoulder seams. With center of sleeve to shoulder seam, sew sleeves to front/back section. Join side and sleeve seams.

Cuffs

With RS facing join B to lower edge of sleeve at seam and work into other side of foundation ch thus:
1st round Ch 3, 1dc into each ch, sl st to top of 3ch. Turn. 52 [56:60] sts.
2nd round Ch 3, skip turning ch, 1dc back around stem of first dc, *1dc front around stem of next dc, 1dc back around stem of next dc, rep from * to end, sl st to top of 3ch. Turn.
3rd round Ch 3, skip turning ch, 1dc front around stem of first dc, *1dc back around stem of next dc, 1dc front around stem of next dc, rep from * to end, sl st to top of 3ch. Turn.
Rep 2nd and 3rd rounds twice.
Fasten off.

Waistband

Work around lower edge of back and front as for cuffs on 180 [188:196] sts; rep 2nd and 3rd rounds 3 times.

Pockets

Using B, make 27ch.
Base row Work as for back. 26 sc.
1st row Ch 3, skip first sc, *1 pair Xdc into next 2 sts, rep from * to last st, 1dc into last st. Turn.
Rep last row 13 times but do not turn at end of last row.
Edging
1st round Ch 1, *work sc evenly along row ends to corner, ch 1*, 1sc into each ch along other side of foundation ch, ch 1, rep from * to *once, 1sc into each st along top edge, sl st to first ch. Turn.
2nd round 1sc into each st to end, sl st to first sc.
Fasten off.
Press or block and sew to front as shown.

Collar

With RS facing, join C to center front st of V neck.
1st row Ch 1, work in sc evenly around neck edge working an odd number of sts, sl st to first ch. Turn.
2nd row Ch 3, skip first 2sc, skipping 1sc at each shoulder seam, work 1dc into each sc to last 2sc, skip next sc, 1dc into last sc. Turn.
3rd row Ch 3, skip first 2dc, *1dc front

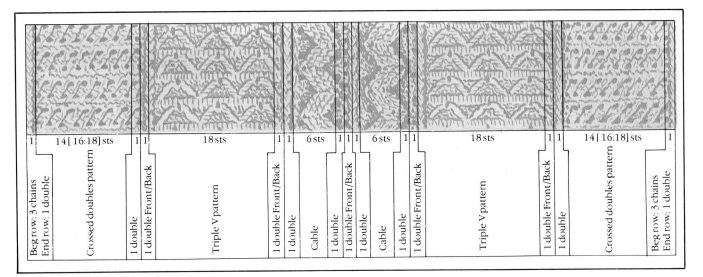

around stem of next dc, 1dc back around stem of next dc, skipping 1dc at each shoulder seam, rep from * to last 3 sts, 1dc front around stem of next dc, skip next dc, 1dc into top of turning ch. Turn.

4th row Ch 3, skip first 2dc, rib as set to last 2 sts, skip next dc, 1dc into top of turning ch. Turn.

Rep 4th row 3 times.

Next row Ch 3, skip first st, rib as set to last st, 1dc into top of turning ch. Turn. Rep last row once.

Next row Ch 3, 1dc into first dc, rib as set to last st, 2dc into top of turning ch. Turn.

Working extra sts into ribbing, rep last row 9 times but do not turn at end of last rep.

Edging

Next row Ch 1, work 1 row of sc evenly down shaped edge of collar to center, skip 1 st at center, work sc evenly up other edge of collar to corner. Fasten off.

Press seams lightly.

Cross-stitch cable

1 *"Cable" panels are formed by slanting blocks of stitches to the right or left. After a base row of single crochet, the cables begin on the next (wrong side) row. To cable to the right, skip the next three stitches and work one triple into each of the next three stitches.*

2 *Then, working behind the three triples, work one triple into each of the three stitches just skipped. You will find these stitches easier to work if you fold the first three triples toward you.*

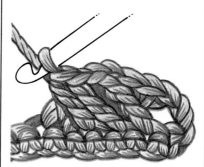

3 *Cable to the left by skipping three stitches and working three triples as in step 1. Then, from the front of the work, work one triples into each of the three skipped stitches. This will be easier if you fold the first three triples away from you.*

Garment schematic:

Back — 17¾ [18½ : 19¼] in

12½ [13½ : 15] in

Sleeve 10¼ [11 : 11¾] in

15 [15¾ : 16½] in

Front — 22¾ [23¼ : 23½] in

15¾ in

SKI SWEATER AND CAP

The Yugoslavian province of Bosnia is the home of firmly-textured, multicolored crochet. Use the simple technique shown here to make this striking pullover and matching hat.

Sizes

Sweater
Misses' sizes 10-12 [14-16]
Length from shoulder 25[26]in
Sleeve seam 16½[17¾]in
Hat *To fit average head*

Note *Instructions for larger size are in brackets [ ]; where there is only one set of figues it applies to both sizes.*

Materials

Sweater
21[22]oz of a knitting worsted-weight yarn in main color A
2oz in each of two contrasting colors, B and C
Size E crochet hook
Set of four size 3 double-pointed knitting needles
Hat
2oz of a sport-weight yarn in main color A
1oz in each of two contrasting colors, B and C
Size B crochet hook
Set of four size 1 double-pointed knitting needles

Gauge

Sweater *20 sts and 20 rows to 4in over tubular sc pat worked on size E hook*
Hat *24 sts and 32 rows to 3¼in over tubular sl st pat worked on size B hook*

To save time, take time to check gauge.

Sweater

Note *Sweater is worked in three tubes —one for body and one each for sleeves —joined at the yoke. Work into back loop only of each stitch and with RS facing throughout the work. (See page 59.)*

Body

Using larger hook and A, make 180 [204] ch; join with a sl st to first ch to form a ring.
1st round Ch 1, 1sc into each ch to end, sl st into first ch, making sure that ch is not twisted. 180 [204] sts.
Mark end of round with a contrasting thread.
Pat round Ch 1, working into back loop only of each st work 1sc into each sc to end, sl st to first ch.
Pat 2 more rounds in A.
Cont in pat, work 12 rounds of Chart A (page 58).
Break off B and C and, using A, cont in pat until work measures 13½in.
Fasten off.
Shape back armholes
Skip first 4 [5] sts of round and rejoin A to next st.
* * **Next row** Ch 1 to count as first sc, skip st at base of first ch, 1sc into back loop of each of next 81 [91]sc. Fasten off and do not turn. 82 [92] sts.
Next row Return to beg of row and rejoin A to 2nd st, ch 1 to count as first sc, skip st at base of first ch, 1sc into back loop of each st to within last st. Fasten off. 80 [90] sts.
Rep last row 3 [5]more times. 74 [80] sts.
Fasten off. * *
Shape front armholes
Return to end of first row of back armholes, skip next 8 [10] sts and rejoin A to next st.

Work from * * to * * once more.

Sleeves (alike)

Using larger hook and A, make 58 [70]ch.
Work base row and pat row as for body until 3 rounds have been worked.
Inc round Ch 1, working into back loop of each st, work 1sc into first st, 2sc into next st, 1sc into each st to last 2 sts, 2sc into next st, 1sc into last st, sl st to first ch. 60 [72] sts. Cont in pat, working 12 rounds of Chart A (page 58).
Break off B and C and cont with A only.
Next round Work as for inc round.
Work even in pat for 6 rounds.
Rep last 7 rounds until there are 72 [80] sts. Work even in pat until work measures 14¼ [15¼]in. Fasten off.
Shape armhole
Skip first 4 [5] sts and rejoin A to next st.
Next row Ch 1 to count as first sc, skip st at base of first ch, 1sc into back loop of each of next 63 [71] sts. Fasten off. 64 [72] sts.
Next row Return to beg of row and rejoin yarn to 2nd st, ch 1 to count as first sc, skip st at base of first ch, pat to within last st. Fasten off. 62 [70] sts.
Rep last row 3 [5] more times. 56 [60] sts. Fasten off.

Yoke

With RS facing, rejoin A to first st on last row of back.
Next round Ch 1, pat 74 [80] sts of back, pat 56 [60] sts of first sleeve, pat 74 [80] sts of front, pat 56 [60] sts of 2nd sleeve. 260 [280] sts. Pat 2 more rounds.
Next round Ch 1, pat first 11 [12] sts, work next 2sc tog, * pat next 11 [12] sts, work next 2sc tog, rep from * to

end, sl st to first ch. 240 [260] sts.

2nd size only

Work even in pat for 3 more rounds.

Next round Ch 1, pat first 11 sts, work next 2sc tog, * pat next 11 sts, work next 2sc tog, rep from * to end, sl st to first ch. 240 sts.

Both sizes

Cont in pat, working 12 rounds of Chart B (below), working decs on 4th and 8th rounds as shown. 200 sts.

Break off B and C and cont in A only.

Next round Ch 1, pat first 8 sts, work next 2sc tog, * pat next 8 sts, work next 2sc tog, rep from * to end, sl st to first ch. 180 sts.

Work even for 4 rounds.

Next round Ch 1, pat first 7 sts, work next 2sc tog, * pat next 7 sts, work next 2sc tog, rep from * to end, sl st to first sc. 160 sts.

Work even in pat for 4 rounds.

Next round Ch 1, pat first 6 sts, work next 2sc tog, * pat next 6 sts, work next 2sc tog, rep from * to end, sl st to first ch. 140 sts.

Cont in pat, working 12 rounds of

Chart C (below), working decs on 4th and 8th rounds as shown. 100 sts.

Break off B and C and, using A only, work even in pat for one round.

Fasten off.

To finish

Do not press.

Join underarm seams.

Waistband

With RS facing and using size 3 double-pointed needles and A, pick up and K 180 [204] sts from lower edge of body.

Work in rounds of K2, P2 ribbing for 2½in.

Bind off loosely.

Cuffs (alike)

With RS facing, using size 3 double-pointed needles and A, pick up and K 40 [48] sts evenly from lower edge of sleeve.

Complete cuffs as instructed for waistband.

Turtleneck collar

With RS facing, using size 3 double-pointed needles and A, pick up

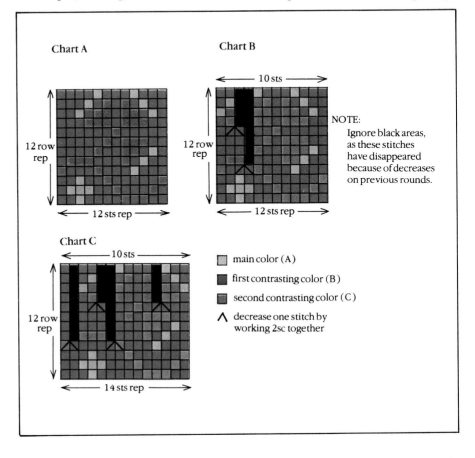

Chart A

12 row rep

12 sts rep

Chart B

10 sts

12 row rep

12 sts rep

NOTE:
Ignore black areas, as these stitches have disappeared because of decreases on previous rounds.

Chart C

10 sts

12 row rep

14 sts rep

☐ main color (A)

◼ first contrasting color (B)

◼ second contrasting color (C)

∧ decrease one stitch by working 2sc together

and K 100 sts evenly around neck edge. Work in rounds of K2, P2 ribbing for 7in.

Hat

Note *Hat is worked in continuous rounds. Work into back loop only of each stitch and with RS facing as shown in the Special Technique at right.*

To make

Using smaller hook and A, make 132ch; sl st to first ch to form a ring.
1st round Sl st into each ch to end, making sure that ch is not twisted. Mark end of round with a contrasting thread.
Pat round Working into back loop of each st, work 1 sl st into each sl st to end. Pat 8 more rounds in A.
Cont in pat, work 12 rounds of Chart A (see page 58).
Break off B and C and, using A, cont in pat for 4 more rounds.
Cont in pat, work 12 rounds of Chart A.

Break off B and C and, using A, cont in pat.
Shape crown
Next round * Sl st into each of next 10 sts, skip next st, rep from * to end. Pat one round without shaping.
Next round * Sl st into each of next 9 sts, skip next st, rep from * to end.
Work even in pat for one round.
Cont in this way, dec 12 sts on every alternate round until 12 sts rem.
Next round * Sl st into next st, skip next st, rep from * to end, sl st into first st. Fasten off, leaving a long end of yarn.

To finish

Run end of yarn through last round and draw up tightly to close hole. Secure yarn firmly on WS of work.
Brim
With RS facing, using size 1 double-pointed needles and A, pick up and K 132 sts from lower edge of hat.
Work in K2, P2 ribbing for 4in.
Bind off loosely.
Turn up brim as desired.

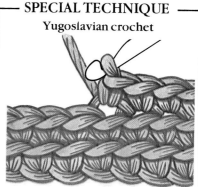

1 *The ridges of Yugoslavian crochet are formed by working into the back loop of each stitch. When working in rounds of single crochet as on the sweater, begin each round with one chain. Work one single crochet into the back loop of the first and every following stitch. Slip stitch the last stitch to the first chain.*

2 *When working in slip stitch, as on the basic hat, work in continuous rounds. Work one slip stitch into the back loop of each stitch as instructed. To make it easier to work the hat, mark the beginning of each round with a contrasting thread.*

3 *Traditional Yugoslavian crochet is always worked with the right side facing. This is easy in tubes or continuous rounds, but more difficult in rows, as for the armhole shaping on this sweater. Work the first row and fasten off. Do not turn, but with the right side facing, rejoin the yarn to the beginning of the row and pattern to the end. Repeat as required.*

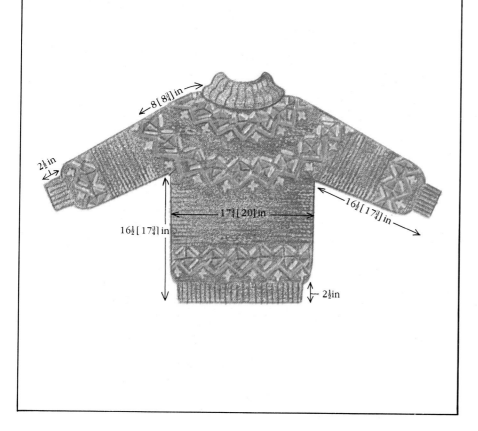

8 [8¾] in

2½ in

17¾ [20] in

16½ [17¾] in

16½ [17¾] in

2½ in

2½in

STRIPED EVENING SWEATER

This glamorous striped sweater is very simple to make and the glitter yarn gives it extra sparkle.

Sizes

Misses' sizes 12-14
Length from shoulder *20in, excluding waistband*
Sleeve seam *16½in, excluding cuff*

Materials

8oz of a fine glitter yarn in main color A
1oz in contrasting color B
Size C crochet hook
Pair of size 2 knitting needles
Set of 4 double-pointed size 2 knitting needles

Gauge

9dc and 7 rows to 2in worked on size C hook

To save time, take time to check gauge.

Back

Using knitting needles, and A, cast on 108 sts.
Work ribbing as follows: * K1, P1, rep from * to end. Rep ribbing row 17 times.
Bind off *loosely* until 1 loop rem. Place loop on crochet hook.
1st row Ch 3, 1dc into each st to end, turn. Rep this row 4 times, join in B at end of last row.
6th row Ch 1, 1sc into each st to end, join in A, turn.
7th row Ch 3, 1dc into each st to end, turn. Rep 7th row 8 times, join in B at end of last row. Rep rows 6-15 three times, then rep rows 6 and 7 once more.

Shape armholes

48th row Sl st into first 9 sts, ch 3, dec 1 st as follows: yo, insert hook into next st and draw loop through, yo and draw through 2 loops on hook, yo, insert hook into next st and draw loop through, yo and draw through 2 loops, yo and draw through all 3 loops; work in pat to last 11 sts, dec 1 dc into next st, turn.
49th row Ch 3, dec 1, dc into each st to last 3 sts, dec 1, dc into last st, turn. Rep last row 4 times for 50th-53rd rows. 80 sts.

Shape neck

54th row Ch 3, dc into next 19 sts, dec 1, dc into next st, turn.
55th row Ch 3, dec 1, dc into each st to end, join in B, turn.
56th row Ch 1, sc into each st to end, join in A, turn.
57th row as 55th.
58th row Ch 3, dc into each st to last 3 sts, dec 1, dc into last st, turn.
59th row as 55th. 18 sts. Work even in dc for 6 more rows, then work 1 row sc in B, and then 3 rows dc in A. Fasten off. Return to 53rd row, skip 34 sts at center, rejoin A with a sl st to next st.
54th row Ch 3, dec 1, dc into each st to end, turn.
Cont to match other side, reversing shaping

Front

Work as for back to 53rd row, then work even in pat for 6 more rows. Shape neck as for back on next (60th) row, i.e. work rows 60-64 as for rows 54, 55, 56, 57 and 58 of back. Work even until 69 rows are complete. Complete other side to match.

Sleeves (alike)

Using A and pair of knitting needles, cast on 60 sts. Work 18 rows of K1, P1 ribbing as for back; bind off *loosely,* insert crochet hook in rem loop. Work 4 rows as for back.
5th row Ch 3, 2dc into next st, dc into each st to last 2sts, 2dc into next st, dc into last st, change to B, turn.
6th-14th rows Work as for rows 6-14 of back.
15th row Work as for 5th row of sleeve.
Rep rows 6-15 three more times. 70 sts.
Work even for 10 more rows, keeping color sequence correct.
Work 1 row sc in B, then work 1 more row dc in A.

Shape top

58th row Sl st into first 9 sts, ch 3, dec 1, dc into each st to last 11 sts, dec 1, dc into next st, turn.
59th row Ch 3, dec 1, dc into each st to last 3 sts, dec 1, dc into last st, turn. Rep last row 6 times, then work 1 row sc in B, then work 59th row twice more.
69th row Sl st into 2nd st, ch 3, dec 1, dc into each st to last 4 sts, dec 1, dc into next st, turn. Rep last row twice. 22 sts.

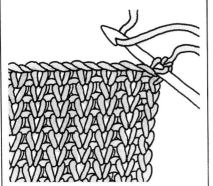

1 The evening sweater has knitted ribbing waistband and cuffs, which give a closer fit than crocheted ribbing. The crochet is then worked directly onto the ribbing. Complete the knitting and bind off. Break the yarn, leaving a long end. Insert the hook into the knitted edge, one row below bound-off edge.

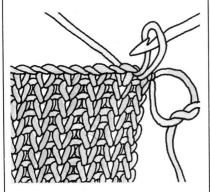

2 Draw the yarn through and knot the loose end of crochet yarn to the knitting yarn to secure it.

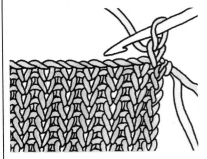

3 Holding the knitting in the left hand, take the yarn around the hook and draw through a loop to form one chain to count as the first single crochet (chain two if working double crochet).

72nd row Sl st into first 5 sts, ch 1, sc into next 3 sts, dc into next 6 sts, sc into next 4 sts. Fasten off.

To finish
Join shoulder, side and sleeve seams; set in sleeves. Using set of 4 double-pointed needles, pick up and K 210 sts evenly around neck. Work 20 rows in K1, P1 ribbing as for back, bind off *loosely* and turn under and sew bound-off edge to base of ribbing.

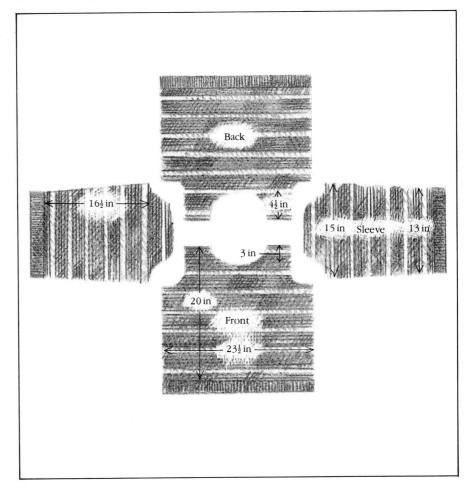

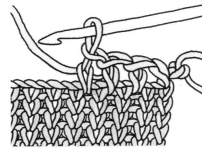

4 Insert the hook into the next appropriate stitch, draw a loop through, take the yarn around the hook and draw through the two loops on hook. Repeat to the end for the required number of stitches. In some cases — depending on the relative gauges of the knitted and the crocheted stitches — the pattern may instruct you to work fewer crochet stitches (which tend to be larger) into the knitted ribbing. For example, you might need to skip one knitted stitch every inch or so.

CHEVRON CARDIGAN AND SCARF

For those very special evenings – an elegant cardigan and scarf in a glittery yarn.

Sizes
Cardigan: Misses' sizes 12 [14:16]
Length from shoulder *25in approx*
Sleeve seam *19in*
Scarf *measures 60in approx by 8in*

Note *Instructions for larger sizes are in brackets [ ]; where there is only one set of figures it applies to all sizes.*

Materials
Cardigan *11 [13:15] oz of a fingering-weight glitter yarn in main color A*
10 [12:14] oz in contrasting color B
Scarf *4oz of a fingering-weight glitter yarn in main color A*
4oz in contrasting color B
Size C crochet hook
6 buttons

Gauge
26dc and 13 rows to 4in in pat worked on size C hook

To save time, take time to check gauge.

Note *To keep the edges of the work straight, one stitch has been increased at the end of a row where the zigzag points downward at the edge, and one stitch has been decreased where the zigzag points upward. When shaping the fronts or sleeves, count the stitches carefully, so that the correct number is increased or decreased. Count the 3 double crochets worked into one stitch as 3, and the 3 double crochets worked together as 1.*

Note *When measuring the work, measure between its farthest points — that is, between a downward-pointing zigzag on the lower edge and an upward-pointing zigzag on the top edge.*

Scarf
Using A, make 55ch.
Base row 1dc into 4th ch from hook, 1dc into each of next 3ch, * 3dc into next ch, 1dc into each of next 5ch, (yo, insert hook into next ch, yo, draw through a loop, yo, draw through 2 loops on hook) 3 times, yo, draw through all 4 loops on hook – called work 3dc tog –, 1dc into each of next 5ch*, rep from * to * twice more, 3dc into next ch, 1dc into each of last 5ch. Turn. 55 sts.
Pat row Ch 3, skip first 2dc, 1dc into each of next 4dc, **3dc into center dc of 3dc group, 1dc into each of next 5dc, work 3dc tog, 1dc into each of next 5dc**, rep from ** to ** twice more, 3dc into next dc, 1dc into each of next 4dc, skip next dc, 1dc into top of turning ch. Turn.
Rep pat row throughout, working 1 more row in A and cont in stripe sequence as follows: 2 rows B, 2 rows A, 1 row B, 1 row A, 3 rows B, 2 rows A, 2 rows B, 1 row A, 1 row B, 3 rows A. Cont in pat, working stripe sequence, until work measures approx 60in, ending with 3 rows in A.
Fasten off.

Cardigan
Back
Using A, make 123 [127:137] ch.
Base row 1dc into 4th ch from hook, 1dc into each of next 2 [4:2]ch, work from * to * as for base row of Scarf 8 [8:9] times, 3dc into next ch, 1dc into each of last 4 [6:4]ch. Turn. 123 [127:137] sts.

Pat row Ch 3, skip first 2dc, 1dc into each of next 3 [5:3]dc, **3dc into center dc of 3dc group, 1dc into each of next 5dc, work 3dc tog, 1dc into each of next 5dc**, rep from ** to ** 7 [7:8] more times, 3dc into next dc, 1dc into each of next 3 [5:3] dc, skip next dc, 1dc into top of turning ch. Turn.
Rep pat row throughout, working 1 more row in A, and working stripe sequence as set for Scarf until work measures 17in. Mark both ends of the last row with contrasting threads.
Cont in pat in stripe sequence until work measures 25in, ending with a row in A.
Straighten top edge
Using A, ch 3, 1dc into each of next 1 [3:1] dc, 1hdc into each of next 2dc, *1sc into next dc, dc, sl st into center dc of 3dc group, 1sc into next dc, 1hdc into each of next 2dc, 1dc into each of next 2dc, 1tr into each of next 3dc, 1dc into each of next 2dc, 1hdc into each of next 2dc, rep from *7 [7:8] more times, 1sc into next dc, sl st into center dc of 3dc group, 1sc into next dc, 1hdc into each of next 2dc, 1dc into each of next 1 [3:1] dc, 1dc into top of turning ch. Fasten off.

Left front
Using A, make 67 [70:73] ch.
Base row 1dc into 4th ch from hook, 1dc into each of next 2 [4:4] ch, work from * to * as for base row of Scarf 4 times, 3dc into next ch, 1dc into each of last 4 [5:8] dc. Turn. 67 [70:73] sts.
Working in pat and stripe sequence as for back, cont until work measures 17in.
Mark beg of last row for armhole.
Shape neck edge
Keeping armhole edge straight, dec 1 st at neck edge on every row until 40 [42:44] dc rem.
Work even in pat until work measures same as back, ending with a row in A.
Straighten top edge
Using A, straighten edge as for back, working sl st into center of 3dc group and working 3tr over 3dc worked tog. Fasten off.

Right front
Work as for left front, reversing shaping.

Sleeves (alike)

Using A, make 55ch.
Work base row and pat row as for Scarf. 55sts.
Cont in pat and stripe sequence as for Scarf, inc 1dc at each end of every alternate row until there are 111sts.
Work even until work measures 19in, ending with a row in A.
Straighten top edge as for back.
Fasten off.

Front band

Join shoulder seams.
With RS facing, join A to right front at the inner corner of the lower edge.
Work 2sc into each row end up right front, across back neck and down left front. Work 5 more rows of sc, ending at lower right front. Turn.
Buttonhole row Ch 1, skip first sc, 1sc into each of next 3sc, * ch 3, skip next 3sc, 1sc into each of next 16sc, rep from * 4 more times, ch 3, skip next 3sc, 1sc into each sc to end. Turn.
Next row Ch 1, skip first sc, 1sc into each st to end, working 3sc into 3ch sp of previous row.
Work 5 more rows in sc.
Fasten off.

To finish

Set in sleeves. Sew side and sleeve seams. Sew on buttons.

Working chevrons

1 *The zigzag effect of chevrons is produced by alternately increasing and decreasing stitches at intervals along row. The zigzags point upward where stitches have been increased and downward where stitches have been decreased.*

2 *When working some chevron patterns it can be difficult to keep the edges straight. Patterns will therefore suggest that you increase one stitch where the zigzag points downward at the end of a row and decrease one stitch at the side edge where the zigzag points upward.*

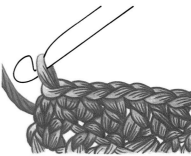

3 *To straighten top edges, work gradually longer stitches to the lowest point of the zigzag, working the longest stitch into the center stitch of the decreasing, and then work shorter stitches to the highest point, working the shortest stitch into the center stitch of the increasing.*

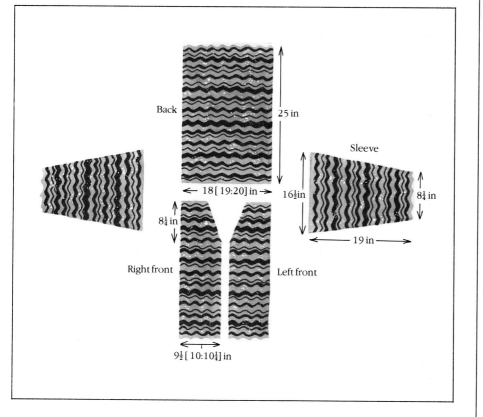

Back

25 in

← 18 [19:20] in →

16½ in

Sleeve

8¼ in

19 in

8¼ in

Right front

Left front

9½ [10:10¼] in

PINEAPPLE LACE BLOUSE

Made as two semicircles joined at the shoulders, this glamorous top can be enlarged to fit any size by continuing to work more of the pattern. The knitted ribbing can be adjusted as required.

Size
Total width from cuff to cuff, 48in.

Materials
18oz of a fine, silky fingering yarn
Size B crochet hook
Pair of size 1 knitting needles
Matching sewing thread

Gauge
One pineapple measures $2\frac{3}{4} \times 2\frac{3}{8}$ in.

To save time, take time to check gauge.

Back
Make 84ch.
1st row 1sc into 2nd ch from hook, 1sc into each ch to end, turn.
2nd row Ch 3, skip first sc, (2dc, ch 2, 2dc) into next sc, * ch 6, skip 3sc, (2dc, ch 2, 2dc) into next sc, rep from * to last sc, 1dc into last sc, turn. 21 groups.
3rd row Ch 3, (2dc, ch 2, 2dc) into next 2ch sp, * ch 3, 13tr into next 2ch sp, ch 3, (2dc, ch 2, 2dc) into next 2ch sp, rep from * ending with 1dc into top of turning ch, turn.
4th row Ch 3, (2dc, ch 2, 2dc) into next 2ch sp, * ch 3, (1tr into next tr, ch 1), 12 times, 1tr into next tr, ch 3, (2dc, ch 2, 2dc) into next 2ch sp, rep from * ending with 1dc into top of turning ch, turn.
5th row Ch 3, (2dc, ch 2, 2dc) into next 2ch sp, * (ch 3, 1sc into next 1ch sp) 12 times, ch 3, (2dc, ch 2, 2dc) into next 2ch sp, rep from * ending with 1dc into top of turning ch, turn.
6th row Ch 3, (2dc, ch 2, 2dc) into next 2ch sp, * skip next 3ch sp, (ch 3, 1sc into next 3ch sp) 11 times, ch 3, (2dc, ch 2, 2dc) into next 2ch sp, rep from * ending with 1dc into top of turning ch, turn.
7th row Ch 3, (2dc, ch 2, 2dc) into next 2ch sp, * skip next 3ch sp, (ch 3, 1sc into next 3ch sp) 10 times, ch 3, (2dc, ch 2, 2dc) into next 2ch sp, rep from * ending with 1dc into top of turning ch, turn.
8th row Ch 3, (2dc, ch 2, 2dc, ch 2, 2dc) into next 2ch sp, * skip 3ch, (ch 3, 1sc into next 3ch sp) 9 times, ch 3, (2dc, ch 2, 2dc, ch 2, 2dc) into next 2ch sp, rep from * ending with 1dc into top of turning ch, turn.
9th row Ch 3, (2dc, ch 2, 2dc) into first 2ch sp, ch 1, (2dc, ch 2, 2dc) into next 2ch sp, * skip next 3ch sp, (ch 3, 1sc into next 3ch sp) 8 times, ch 3, (2dc, ch 2, 2dc) into next 2ch sp, ch 1, (2dc, ch 2, 2dc) into next 2ch sp, rep from * ending with 1dc into top of turning ch, turn.
10th row Ch 3, (2dc, ch 2, 2dc) into next 2ch sp, ch 1, (2dc, ch 2, 2dc) into next 1ch sp, ch 1, (2dc, ch 2, 2dc) into next 2ch sp, * skip next 3ch sp, (ch 3, 1sc into next 3ch sp) 7 times, ch 3, (2dc, ch 2, 2dc) into next 2ch sp, ch 1, (2dc, ch 2, 2dc) into next 1ch sp, ch 1, (2dc, ch 2, 2dc) into next 2ch sp, rep from * ending with 1dc into top of turning ch, turn.
11th row Ch 3, (2dc, ch 2, 2dc) into next 2ch sp, ch 2, (2dc, ch 2, 2dc) into next 2ch sp, ch 2, (2dc, ch 2, 2dc) into next 2ch sp, * skip next 3ch sp, (ch 3, 1sc into next 3ch sp) 6 times, ch 3, (2dc, ch 2, 2dc) into next 2ch sp, ch 2, (2dc, ch 2, 2dc) into next 2ch sp, ch 2, (2dc, ch 2, 2dc) into next 2ch sp, rep from * ending with 1dc into top of turning ch, turn.
12th row Ch 3, (2dc, ch 2, 2dc) into next 2ch sp, ch 3, skip next 2ch sp, (2dc, ch 2, 2dc) into next 2ch sp, ch 3, skip next 2ch sp, (2dc, ch 2, 2dc) into next 2ch sp, * skip next 3ch sp, (ch 3, 1sc into next 3ch sp) 5 times, ch 3, (2dc, ch 2, 2dc) into next 2ch sp, skip next 2ch sp, ch 3, (2dc, ch 2, 2dc) into next 2ch sp, ch 3, skip next 2ch sp, (2dc, ch 2, 2dc) into next 2ch sp, rep from * ending with 1dc into top of turning ch, turn.
13th row Ch 3, (2dc, ch 2, 2dc) into next 2ch sp, ch 4, (2dc, ch 2, 2dc) into next 2ch sp, ch 4, (2dc, ch 2, 2dc) into next 2ch sp, * skip next 3ch sp, (ch 3, 1sc into next 3ch sp) 4 times, ch 3, (2dc, ch 2, 2dc) into next 2ch sp, ch 4.

(2dc, ch 2, 2dc) into next 2ch sp, ch 4, (2dc, ch 2, 2dc) into next 2ch sp, rep from * ending with 1dc into top of turning ch, turn.

14th row Ch 3, (2dc, ch 2, 2dc) into next 2ch sp, ch 5, (2dc, ch 2, 2dc) into next 2ch sp, ch 5, (2dc, ch 2, 2dc) into next 2ch sp, * skip next 3ch sp, (ch 3, 1sc into next 3ch sp) 3 times, ch 3, (2dc, ch 2, 2dc) into next 2ch sp, ch 5, (2dc, ch 2, 2dc) into next 2ch sp, ch 5, (2dc, ch 2, 2dc) into next 2ch sp, rep from * ending with 1dc into top of turning ch, turn.

15th row Ch 3, (2dc, ch 2, 2dc) into next 2ch sp, ch 6, (2dc, ch 2, 2dc) into next 2ch sp, ch 6, (2dc, ch 2, 2dc) into next 2ch sp, * skip next 3ch sp, (ch 3, 1sc into next 3ch sp) twice, ch 3, (2dc, ch 2, 2dc) into next 2ch sp, ch 6, (2dc, ch 2, 2dc) into next 2ch sp, ch 6, (2dc, ch 2, 2dc) into next 2ch sp, rep from * ending with 1dc into top of turning ch, turn.

16th row Ch 3, (2dc, ch 2, 2dc) into next 2ch sp, * ch 3, 13tr into next 2ch sp, ch 3, (2dc, ch 2, 2dc) into next 2ch sp, skip next 3ch sp, ch 3, 1sc into next 3ch sp, ch 3, (2dc, ch 2, 2dc) into next 2ch sp, rep from * ending with ch 3, 13tr into next 2ch sp, ch 3, (2dc, ch 2, 2dc) into last 2ch sp, 1dc into top of turning ch, turn.

17th row Ch 3, (2dc, ch 2, 2dc) into next 2ch sp, * ch 3, (1tr into next tr, ch 1) 12 times, 1tr into next tr, ch 3, (2dc, ch 2, 2dc) into next 2ch sp, ch 3, (2dc, ch 2, 2dc) into next 2ch sp, rep from * ending with ch 3, (1tr into next tr, ch 1) 12 times, 1tr into next tr, ch 3, (2dc, ch 2, 2dc) into last 2ch sp, 1dc into top of turning ch, turn.

18th row Ch 3, (2dc, ch 2, 2dc) into next 2ch sp, * (ch 3, 1sc into next 1ch sp) 12 times, ch 3, (2dc, ch 2, 2dc) into next 2ch sp, ch 2, (2dc, ch 2, 2dc) into next 2ch sp, rep from * ending with (ch 3, 1sc into next 1ch sp) 12 times, ch 3, (2dc, ch 2, 2dc) into last 2ch sp, 1dc into top of turning ch, turn.

19th row Ch 3, (2dc, ch 2, 2dc) into next 2ch sp, * skip next 3ch sp, (ch 3, 1sc into next 3ch sp) 11 times, ch 3, (2dc, ch 2, 2dc) into next 2ch sp, ch 1, skip next 2ch sp, (2dc, ch 2, 2dc) into next 2ch sp, rep from * ending with skip next 3ch sp, (ch 3, 1sc into next 3ch sp) 11 times, ch 3, (2dc, ch 2, 2dc) into last 2ch sp, 1dc into top of turning ch, turn.

20th row Ch 3, (2dc, ch 2, 2dc) into next 2ch sp, *skip next 3ch sp, (ch 3, 1sc into next 3ch sp) 10 times, ch 3, (2dc, ch 2, 2dc) into next 2ch sp, (2dc, ch 2, 2dc) into next 2ch sp, rep from * ending with skip next 3ch sp, (ch 3, 1sc into next 3ch sp) 10 times, ch 3, (2dc, ch 2, 2dc) into last 2ch sp, 1dc into top of turning ch, turn.

21st row Ch 3, (2dc, ch 2, 2dc, ch 2, 2dc) into next 2ch sp, * skip next 3ch sp, (ch 3, 1sc into next 3ch sp) 9 times, ch 3, (2dc, ch 2, 2dc) into next 2ch sp, (2dc, ch 2, 2dc) into next 2ch sp, rep from * ending with skip next 3ch sp, (ch 3, 1sc into next 3ch sp) 9 times, ch 3, (2dc, ch 2, 2dc, ch 2, 2dc) into last 2ch sp, 1dc into top of turning ch, turn.
Rep rows 9-21 until a total of 63 rows have been worked, ending with a 12th row.
Fasten off.

Front
Work as for back.

To finish
Block the pieces, if necessary. Using matching sewing thread, join the two semicircles tog at straight edges, forming the sleeve/shoulder seams.

Cuffs
Mark a distance of 11in along the outer edge (with one seam in the center); using knitting needles with RS facing, pick up and K 72 sts. Work in K1, P1 ribbing for 1½in. Bind off.
Rep for other cuff.

Waistband
Mark a distance of 14in along the center of the lower edge of each semicircle, and similarly pick up and K 112 sts on each section. Work in K1, P1 ribbing for 2¼in. Bind off.
Join the two underarm seams from cuffs to waist.

Neck edging
Using crochet hook with WS facing, join yarn to either shoulder seam.
1st round 1sc into each foundation ch all around.
2nd round 1sc into each sc of first round.
Fasten off.

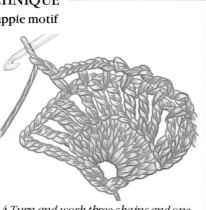

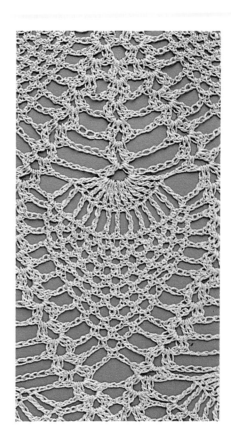

1 *Start with a base of four chains, then work one double crochet, two chains and two doubles all into the fourth chain from the hook.*

4 *Turn and work three chains and one single crochet into the next one-chain space all along. This makes 12 three-chain spaces.*

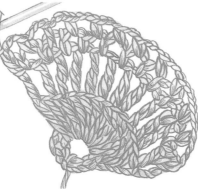

2 *Turn, chain four, then work 12 triples all into the two-chain space. This makes 13 triples, including the turning chain.*

5 *Turn, skip the first three-chain space, and work three chains and one single crochet into the next three-chain space all along to make 11 three-chain spaces.*

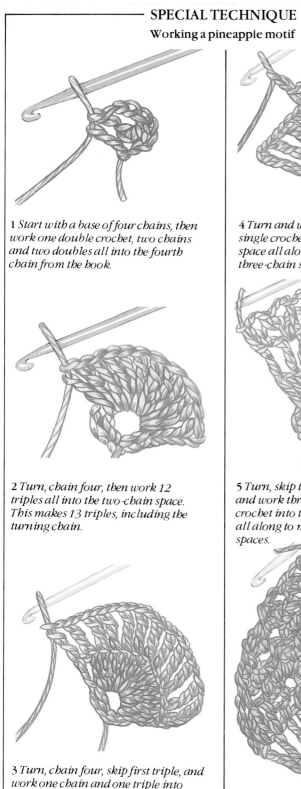

3 *Turn, chain four, skip first triple, and work one chain and one triple into each of the following triples, ending with the last triple worked into the top of the turning chain.*

6 *Repeat step 5 until the number of three-chain spaces in the row is reduced to one. Fasten off.*

BEADED CARDIGAN

This elegant cardigan, made in a mohair yarn and worked with beads, is the perfect light wrap for an evening out.

Sizes
Misses' sizes 8 [10:12:14]
Length from shoulder 21 [21:22:22] in
Sleeve seam 17 in

Note Instructions for larger sizes are in brackets [ ]; where there is only one set of figures it applies to all sizes.

Materials
13 [13:14:15] oz of a pure mohair yarn
Approx 2000 [2000:2200:2200] small pearl beads
Size G crochet hook
10 small buttons

Gauge
13 dc and 8 rows to 4 in over pat worked on size G hook

To save time, take time to check gauge.

Back
Before starting each new ball of yarn, thread approx 200 beads onto it.
Make 56 [60:60:64] ch, 1dc into 4th ch from hook, *bring forward a bead to lie at RS of work, 1dc into each of next 2ch, rep from * to end, turn. 54 [58:58:62] dc.
1st row Ch 3, *bring forward a bead to lie at RS of work, 1dc into each of next 2dc, rep from * to last dc, bring forward a bead, 1dc into last dc, turn.
2nd row Ch 3, 1dc into next dc, *bring forward a bead to lie at RS of work, 1dc into each of next 2dc, rep from * to end, turn.
Rep first and 2nd rows 11 more times.
Shape armholes
Sl st over 3dc, ch 2, skip next dc, still working in bead pat, work 1dc into each of next 46 [50:50:54] dc, 1hdc into next dc, turn.
Next row Sl st over first hdc, ch 2, skip next dc, 1dc into each of next 44 [48:48:52] dc, 1hdc into next dc, turn.
Next row Sl st over first hdc, ch 2, skip next dc, 1dc into each of next 42 [46:46:56] dc, 1hdc into next dc, turn.
Next row Ch 3, skip hdc, 1dc into each dc to end, turn, leaving hdc unworked. 42 [46:46:50] dc.
Work even for 11 [11:13:13] rows in dc bead pat.
Shape shoulders
Next row Ch 2, 1hdc into each dc to end.
Next row Sl st across 11 [12:12:13] hdc, ch 2, skip next hdc, 1hdc into each of next 19 [21:21:23] hdc. Fasten off.

Left front
Make 29 [31:31:33] ch. Work base row as for back. 27 [29:29:31] dc. Cont in pat as for back until front measures same as back to underarm, ending at armhole edge.
Shape armhole
Sl st over 2dc, ch 2, skip next dc, 1dc into each dc to end, turn.
Next row Ch 3, 1dc into each of next 23 [25:25:27] dc, turn.
Next row Sl st over first dc, ch 2, skip next dc, 1dc into each dc to end, turn.
Next row Ch 3, 1dc into each of next 20 [22:22:24] dc, 1hdc into next dc, turn.
Next row Ch 3, 1dc into each dc to end, turn. 21 [23:23:25] dc.
Work 5 [5:7:7] rows in dc bead pat without shaping, ending at armhole edge.
Shape neck
Ch 3, 1dc into each of next 12 [13:13:14] dc, 1hdc into next dc, turn and leave rem sts unworked.
Next row Sl st into hdc, 1hdc into next dc, 1dc into each dc to end, turn.
Next row Ch 3, 1dc into each of next 10 [11:11:12] dc, 1hdc into next dc, turn.
Next row Ch 3, skip hdc, 1dc into each dc to end, turn. 11 [12:12:13] dc. Work 1 more row in pat on these sts.
Next row Ch 2, 1hdc into each dc to end. Fasten off.

Right front
Work as for left front, making sure beads lie on RS of fabric, reversing shaping.

Sleeves
Make 28 [28:32:32] ch and work in pat as for back for 3 rows. 26 [26:30:30] dc.
Next row Inc 1dc at each end of next row, working extra sts into pat. 28 [28:32:32] dc.
Work even for 4 rows. Rep these 5 rows once more. 30 [30:34:34] sts.
Next row Inc 1dc at each end of next row. Work 3 rows without shaping. Rep these 4 rows once more. 34 [34:38:38] dc.
Next row Inc 1dc at each end of next row. Work even for 2 rows. 36

Double crochet with beads

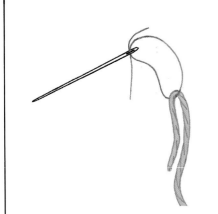

1 *Beads are worked into the fabric of the mohair cardigan. Begin by threading the number of beads specified onto the ball of yarn. Use a fine sewing needle that will slip through the beads. Make a loop of thread through the needle so that both ends pass through the eye as shown. Loop the working yarn through thread.*

2 *Slip the first bead over the needle, along the thread and onto the doubled end of yarn. Thread each bead onto the yarn in the same way. Keep one bead over the doubled yarn at all times to keep the yarn in place over the loop of the thread.*

3 *With the right side of the fabric facing work in double crochet to the position for the first bead. Slip the bead up close to the hook. Take the yarn over the hook, taking the yarn beyond the bead, and holding the bead at the front.*

4 *Insert the hook into the next stitch and complete the double in the usual way, keeping the bead at the front of the work.*

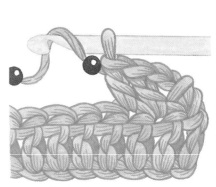

5 *Smaller beads sometimes have a tendency to slip to the back of the work. To prevent this, slip the bead up close to the hook and begin the next double by taking the yarn over the hook from front to back.*

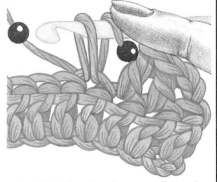

6 *Hold the bead and yarn on the hook at the front of the work with the forefinger of the right hand to prevent the yarn from becoming too tight. Insert the hook into the next stitch and pull the yarn through.*

7 *Complete the double in the usual way. In order to maintain an even tension it is important to hold the yarn and bead on the hook each time while working the stitch.*

[36:40:40] sts.

Next row Inc 1dc at each end of next row. Work 1 row without shaping. Rep these 2 rows once. 40[40:44:44] sts. Inc 1dc at each end of next 4 rows. 48[48:52:52] dc. Work 1 row without shaping.

Shape sleeve cap

Next row Sl st over 2dc, 1hdc into next dc, 1dc into each of next 42[42:46:46] dc. 1hdc into next dc, turn and leave rem sts unworked.

Next row Sl st into hdc, 1hdc into next dc, 1dc into each of next 40[40:44:44] dc, 1hdc into next dc, turn.

Next row Sl st into hdc and first dc, 1hdc into next dc, 1dc into each of next 36[36:40:40] dc, 1hdc into next dc, turn.

Next row Sl st into hdc, 1hdc into next dc, 1dc into each dc to last dc, 1hdc into last dc, turn. Rep last row until there are 14 sts. Fasten off.

To finish

Join shoulder, side and sleeve seams. Set in sleeve, gathering sleeve cap to form puff.

Edging With RS facing join yarn at lower side seam. Work in hdc along bottom edge, up right front, around neck, back down left front and back along lower edge. Join with a sl st. Fasten off.

Sew on buttons down left front, spacing evenly and using spaces between hdc as buttonholes.

Gently brush mohair to raise pile. Press seams lightly, taking care to avoid beads.

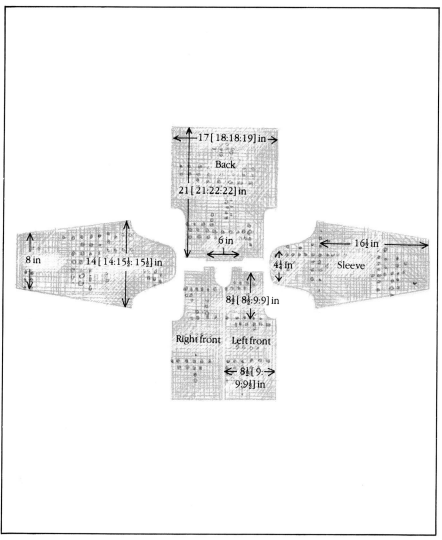

STRIPED CARDIGAN

Glitter yarn adds a bit of sparkle to this versatile striped cardigan.

Sizes

Misses' sizes 12 [14:16]
Length from shoulder 23½ in
Sleeve seam 17 in

Note *Instructions for larger sizes are in brackets [ ]; where there is only one set of figures it applies to all sizes.*

Materials

6 [8:8] oz of a knitting worsted-weight yarn in main color A
4 [6:6] oz in each of four contrasting colors: B, C, D and E
3 oz of a fingering-weight metallic yarn (F)
Size G crochet hook
Pair of size 2 knitting needles
5 buttons

Gauge

16 sc to 4 in worked on size G hook using knitting worsted-weight yarn.

To save time, take time to check gauge.

Pocket linings (make 2)

Using crochet hook and A, make 17ch.
Base row (RS) 1sc into 2nd ch from hook, 1sc into each ch to end. Turn. 16 sts.
Next row Ch 1 to count as first sc, skip first st, 1sc into each st to end. Turn.
Rep last row until work measures 4 in. Fasten off.

Back and fronts

(worked in one piece to armholes)
Using knitting needles and A, cast on 194 [206:216] sts.
Ribbing row *K1, P1, rep from * to end. Rep ribbing row until work measures 4 in.
Bind off in ribbing.
Using crochet hook, join B to last bound-off st.
Next row Ch 1 to count as first sc, skip st at base of joining, work 153 [161:169] sc evenly into bound-off edge. Turn. 154 [162:170] sts.
Beg stripe pat
1st row (WS) Using C and F tog, ch 2, skip first st, 1hdc into each st to end. Turn.
2nd row Using E, ch 3, skip first st, 1dc into each st to end. Turn.
3rd row Using 3 strands of F, ch 1 to count as first sc, skip first st, 1sc into each st to end. Turn.
4th row Using D, as first row.
5th row Using A, as 2nd row.
6th row Using B, as 3rd row.
First-6th rows form stripe pat. Cont in stripe pat until work measures 7 in from cast-on edge, ending with a RS row.
Place pockets
Next row Pat first 8 sts, skip next 16 sts, pat across 16 sts of first pocket lining, pat to last 24 sts, skip next 16 sts, pat across 16 sts of second pocket lining, pat last 8 sts. Turn. Cont in stripe pat until work measures 16 in from cast-on edge, ending with a WS row.

Divide for back and fronts

Next row Sl st across first 2 sts, pat next 35 [37:39] sts, turn. 35 [37:39] sts.
Shape right armhole and front
1st row (WS) Sl st across first 2 sts, pat to end. Turn. 34 [36:38] sts.
2nd row Pat to last st, turn, leaving last st unworked. 33 [35:37] sts.
3rd row Sl st across first 2 sts, pat to last st, turn, leaving last st unworked. 31 [33:35] sts.
4th row As 2nd row. 30 [32:34] sts.
5th row As first row. 29 [31:33] sts.
6th row As 3rd row. 27 [29:31] sts.
Rep first and 2nd rows once more. 25 [27:29] sts.
Keeping armhole edge straight, dec one st at front edge as before on every following 3rd row until 18 [21:24] sts rem.
Work even in stripe pat shaping until right front measures 23½ in from cast-on edge, ending at armhole edge.
Shape shoulder
Next row Sl st across first 7 [8:9] sts, pat to end. Turn. 12 [14:16] sts.
Next row Pat to end.
Rep last 2 rows once more. 6 [7:8] sts.
Pat one row.
Fasten off.
Back
With RS facing, skip next 6 sts left unworked at beg of right front and using crochet hook and keeping stripe pat correct, join yarn to next st.
Next row Pat into same place as joining, pat next 71 [75:79] sts, turn. 72 [76:80] sts.
Shape armholes
Next row Sl st across first 2 sts, pat to last st, turn, leaving last st unworked.
Rep last row 8 [7:6] more times. 54 [60:66] sts.
Work even in stripe pat until back matches right front at armhole edge, ending with a RS row.
Shape shoulders
Next row Sl st across first 7 [8:9] sts,

SPECIAL TECHNIQUE

Inserting a horizontal pocket

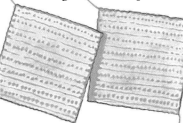

1 The cardigan has a horizontal pocket on each front. Before beginning the back and fronts, work two pocket linings as instructed in the pattern After working the knitted ribbing waistband, work in the stripe pattern until the work is the required length, ending with a right-side pattern row.

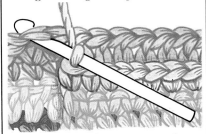

2 Work to the pocket as instructed. Bring the top of the pocket lining up to the front of the work (i.e. on the wrong side) and pattern across the 16 stitches of the pocket lining. Skip the next 16 stitches on the front. Pattern to the position of the other pocket and place the lining as before. Pattern to the end of the row.

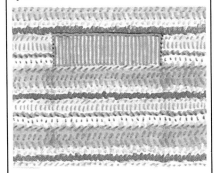

3 When finishing the cardigan, pick up the stitches at the top of the pocket as instructed and work the pocket tops in knit-one, purl-one ribbing. Sew the row ends of the pocket tops to the right side of the fronts using slipstitch. Also using slipstitch, sew the pocket linings in place on the wrong side of each front.

pat to last 6 [7:8] sts, turn.
Next row Pat to end. Rep last 2 rows once more. Fasten off.

Left front

With RS facing, skip next 6 sts left unworked at beg of back and using crochet hook and keeping stripe pat correct, join yarn to next st.
Next row Pat into same place as joining, pat next 34 [36:38] sts, turn. 35 [37:39] sts.
Keeping stripe pat correct, work as for right front, reversing all shaping.

Sleeves (alike)

Using knitting needles and A, cast on 54 sts. Work in K1, P1 ribbing as for back and fronts for 3½ in.
Bind off in ribbing.
Using crochet hook, join B to last bound-off st.
Next row Ch 1 to count as first sc, skip st at base of joining, 1sc into each bound-off st to end. 54 sts.
Cont in stripe pat as for back and fronts until work measures 17 in from cast-on edge, ending with same row as back and fronts to "Divide for back and fronts."

Shape top

Next row Sl st across first 4 sts, pat to last 3 sts, turn. 48 sts.
Next row Sl st across first 2 sts, pat to last st, turn. 46 sts.
Rep last row 11 more times. 24 sts.
Fasten off.

To finish

Block the work. Join shoulder seams.

Button band

Mark positions of 5 buttonholes on right front edge, the first 4 rows from the cast-on edge, the last at the beg of front neck shaping and the rem 3 evenly spaced in between.
Using knitting needles and A, cast on 11 sts.
1st row K1, (P1, K1) to end.
2nd row P1, (K1, P1) to end.
Rep last 2 rows once more.
1st buttonhole row Rib 4, bind off 3 sts, rib to end.
2nd buttonhole row Rib 4, cast on 3 sts, rib to end.
* *Cont in ribbing to position of next buttonhole. Work buttonhole as before over next 2 rows.* *
Rep from * * to * * 3 more times. Cont in ribbing until button band, slightly stretched, fits up right front, around back neck and down left front.
Bind off in ribbing.
Set in sleeves, matching stripes at armhole. Join sleeve seams, matching stripes at edges.
Sew border neatly to fronts and back neck.
Sew buttons to left front to correspond with buttonholes.

Pocket tops (alike)

With RS facing, using knitting needles and A, pick up and K 32 sts from sts at top of pocket opening.
Work in K1, P1 ribbing for 1¼ in.
Bind off in ribbing.
Sew pocket linings neatly in place on WS. Sew row ends of pocket tops to RS.

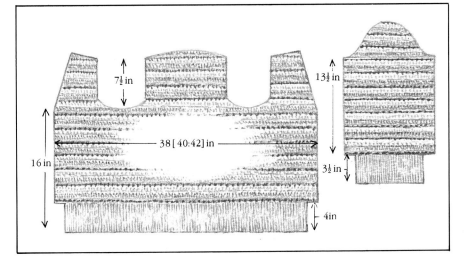

7½ in

13½ in

38 [40:42] in

16 in

3½ in

4in

BOBBLE CARDIGAN

This pretty cardigan is easier to make than it looks. The bobbles are worked in three different colors using a simple technique to create an interesting variation in color and texture.

Size

Misses' sizes 10-12
Length from shoulder 19½ in
Sleeve seam 17 in

Materials

10oz of a fingering-weight cotton yarn in main color A
2oz in contrasting color B
1oz each in contrasting colors C and D
7 buttons
Size E crochet hook

Gauge

16 sts and 9 rows to 4in over pat worked on size E hook

To save time, take time to check gauge.

Note *Use one contrasting color, along with main color A, for each bobble row, alternating colors as instructed and carrying yarn not in use across back of work. Break off each contrasting color at end of row.*

Back

Using A make 75ch.
1st row 1dc into 4th ch from hook, 1dc into each ch to end, turn. 73dc.
2nd row (RS) Ch 3 to count as first dc, 1dc into each of next 8dc joining in B on last dc, (5dc into next dc, drop working loop and re-insert hook from front to back through top of first dc of 5dc group, then back through working loop, drop B, using A draw yarn through and pull 5dc tog – called Bl –, 1dc into each of next 10dc) 5 times, Bl, 1dc into each dc to end, 1dc into top of turning ch, turn.
3rd row Using A, ch 3, 1dc into each dc to end, turn.
4th row Ch 3, 1dc into each of next 3dc, (using C, Bl, 1dc into each of next 10dc) 6 times, Bl, 1dc into dc to end, turn.
5th row As 3rd row.
6th row As 2nd row, using D for bobbles.
These 6 rows form pat. Cont in pat, maintaining color sequence on bobble rows throughout, until 26 rows in all have been worked.
Shape armholes
27th row Sl st over first 4dc, ch 2 to count as first hdc, 1hdc into next st, 1dc into each of next 61dc, 1hdc into next st, turn and leave rem sts unworked.
28th row Ch 2, 1hdc into next st, 1dc into each of next 8dc, (B1, 1dc into each of next 10dc) 4 times, B1, 1dc into each of next 7dc, turn.
29th row Ch 3, 1dc into each of next 61dc, turn. 62dc.
30th row Ch 3, 1dc into each of next 3dc, (B1, 1dc into each of next 10dc) 5 times, B1, 1dc into each of last 2dc, turn. Keeping pat correct work even for another 14 rows.
Shape shoulders
Next row Sl st over first 16 sts, ch 2, 1hdc into each of next 29 sts, turn and leave rem sts unworked. Fasten off.

Right front

Using A, make 37ch. Work first row as for back. 35dc.
2nd row Ch 3 to count as first dc, 1dc into each of next 9dc, (using B, B1, 1dc into each of next 10dc) twice, B1, 1dc into each of next 2dc, turn.

3rd row Ch 3, 1dc into each dc to end, turn. 35dc.
4th row Ch 3, 1dc into each of next 4dc, (using C, B1, 1dc into each of next 10dc) twice, B1, 1dc into each st to end, turn.
5th row As 3rd row.
6th row As 2nd row, using D for bobbles.
Cont in pat as set, maintaining correct color sequence for bobble rows until 26 rows in all have been worked from beg.
Shape armhole
27th row Sl st over first 3 sts, work 1hdc into next st, 1dc into each st to end, turn.
28th row Ch 3, 1dc into each of next 4dc, (B1, 1dc into each of next 10dc) twice, B1, 1dc into each of next 2dc, 1hdc into next st, turn.
29th row Ch 3, skip hdc, 1dc into each dc to end, turn.
Keeping pat correct work even for 9 more rows.
Shape front neck
39th row Ch 3, 1dc into each of next 15 sts, turn and leave rem sts unworked.
Keeping pat correct work 6 more rows on these sts. Fasten off.

Left front

Using A make 37ch. Work first row as for right front. 35dc.
2nd row Ch 3, to count as first dc, 1dc into next dc, (using B, B1, 1dc into each of next 10dc) 3 times, turn.
3rd row Ch 3, 1dc into each st to end. Turn.
4th row Ch 3, 1dc into each of next 6dc, (using C, B1, 1dc into each of next 10dc) twice, B1, 1dc into each dc to end. Cont in pat following color sequence as for right front until 26 rows in all have been worked from beg.
Shape armhole
27th row Ch 3, 1dc into each of next 29dc, 1hdc into next st, turn.
28th row Ch 2, 1hdc into next st, 1dc into next st, (B1, 1dc into each of next 10 sts) twice, B1, dc to end, turn.
29th row Ch 3, 1dc into each of next 29dc, turn. 30dc.
Cont in pat as set, work even for 9 more rows.

Shape front neck

39th row Sl st over first 14 sts, ch 3, 1dc into each dc to end, turn. 16 sts.

40th row Ch 3, 1dc into next dc, B1, 1dc into each of next 10dc, B1, 1dc into each of last 2dc, turn.

Keeping pat correct work even for 5 more rows on these sts.

Fasten off.

Sleeves

Using A, make 40ch.

1st row 1dc into 4th ch from hook, 1dc into each ch to end, turn. 38dc.

2nd row Ch 3 to count as first dc, 1dc into each of next 2dc, (B1, 1dc into each of next 10dc) 3 times, B1, 1dc into last dc, turn.

3rd row Ch 3, 1dc into each st to end, turn.

4th row Ch 3, 1dc into each of next 8dc, (B1, 1dc into each of next 10dc) twice, B1, 1dc into each st to end, turn.

These 4 rows form pat. Cont in pat until 13 rows have been worked, alternating bobble colors as before.

14th row Ch 3 to count as first dc, 1dc into first (edge) st, 1dc into each of next 2dc, (B1, 1dc into each of next 10dc) 3 times, B1, 1dc into next dc, 2dc into last st, turn. 40dc.

15th row Ch 3, 1dc into each dc to end, turn.

16th row Ch 3, 1dc into each of next 9dc, (B1, 1dc into each of next 10dc) twice, B1, 1dc into each st to end. Pat 2 more rows on these sts.

19th row Ch 3, 1dc into first (edge) st, 1dc into each st to last st, 2dc into last st, turn. 42dc.

Keeping bobble pat correct cont increasing one st at each end of row in this way on 22nd, 26th and 32nd rows. 48dc. Work even for 3 more rows.

Shape sleeve top

36th row Ch 1, sl st over next 2 sts, 1hdc into next st, pat to last 4 sts, 1hdc into next st, turn and leave rem 3 sts unworked.

37th row Ch 2, 1hdc into next st, 1dc into each of next 39dc, 1hdc into next st, turn.

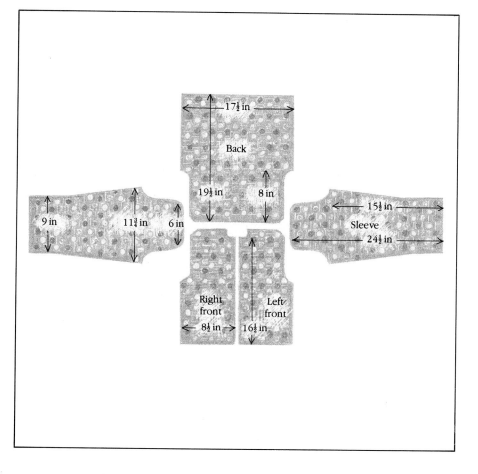

38th row Ch 2, 1hdc into next st, 1dc into each of next 3dc, (B1, 1dc into each of next 10dc) 3 times, B1, 1dc into next st, 1hdc into next st, turn.
39th row Ch 3, 1dc into each of next 39dc, turn. 40dc.
40th row Ch 3, 1dc into each of next 9dc, (B1, 1dc into each of next 10dc) 3times, 1dc into each of next 3dc, turn.
41st row As 39th.
42nd row Ch 3, 1dc into each of next 3dc, (B1, 1dc into each of next 10dc) 3 times, 1dc into each of next 2dc, turn.
43rd row As 39th.
44th row Ch 1, 1dc into next st, 1dc into each of next 8dc, (B1, 1dc into each of next 10dc) twice, B1, 1dc into each of next 5dc, 1hdc into next st, turn.
45th row Ch 2, 1hdc into next st, 1dc into each of next 34dc, 1hdc into next st, turn.
46th row Ch 2, 1hdc into next st, 1dc into each of next 11dc, B1, 1dc into each of next 10dc, B1, 1dc into each of next 9dc, 1hdc into next st, turn.
47th row Ch 2, 1hdc into next st, 1dc into each of next 30dc, 1hdc into next st, turn.
48th row Ch 2, 1hdc into next st, 1dc into each of next 4dc, (B1, 1dc into each of next 10dc) twice, B1, 1dc into next st, 1hdc into next st, turn.
49th row Ch 2, 1hdc into next st, 1dc into each of next 26dc, 1hdc into next st, turn.
50th row Ch 2, 1hdc into next st, 1dc into each of next 7dc, B1, 1dc into each of next 10dc, B1, 1dc into each of next 5dc, 1hdc into next st, turn.
51st row As 49th, working 22dc instead of 26.
52nd row Ch 2, 1dc into each of next 2 sts, B1, 1dc into each of next 10dc, B1, 1dc into each of next 10dc, turn.
53rd row Ch 2, 1dc into each of next 22dc, turn.
54th row Ch 2, 1hdc into next st, 1dc into each of next 4dc, B1, 1dc into each of next 10dc, B1, 1dc into each of next 3dc, 1hdc into next st, turn.
55th row As 51st, working 19dc instead of 23.
56th row Ch 2, 1hdc into next st, 1dc into each of next 19dc, 1hdc into next st. Fasten off.

To finish
Block the work if necessary, but do not press.
Join shoulder, side and sleeve seams.
Set in sleeves, gathering excess on sleeve cap to form puff.
Border
Using D, join yarn to edge of center front at lower corner, ch 3, work 67dc up front edge to neck, ch 3, turn work 90 degrees and work 16dc to first inside corner of neck, * ch 3, rep 90-degree turn, sl st through 3rd dc * to make corner, work 12dc to back neck, rep from * to *, work 28dc across back neck, rep from * to *, work 10dc down side of neck, rep from * to *, work 12dc across front neck, ch 3, turn 90 degrees and work 67dc down left front to lower corner, ch 3, turn and work 144dc along lower edge to beg of edging, join with a sl st. Fasten off. Sew buttons to border, spacing them evenly down right front. Use spaces between dc in opposite border as buttonholes.
Sleeve border
Using D, rejoin yarn at sleeve seam, ch 3, work 27dc around sleeve edge, join with a sl st to 3rd of first 3ch. Fasten off. Press seams.

Working bobbles in different colors

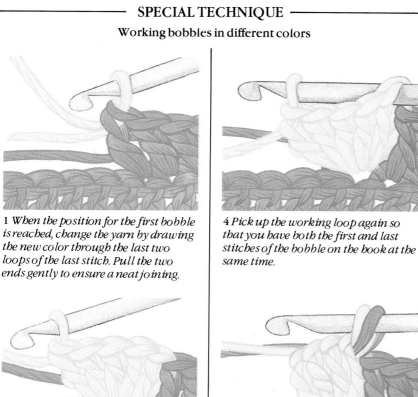

1 *When the position for the first bobble is reached, change the yarn by drawing the new color through the last two loops of the last stitch. Pull the two ends gently to ensure a neat joining.*

4 *Pick up the working loop again so that you have both the first and last stitches of the bobble on the hook at the same time.*

2 *Work five double crochets (or the specified number) into the next stitch, working over the free end of the bobble yarn to avoid having to darn in too many ends when the crochet has been completed.*

5 *Now draw the working bobble loop together with a loop of the main color through the first stitch to complete the bobble. The main color is now ready for use.*

3 *Drop the working yarn and re-insert the hook from front to back through the top of the first double of the bobble. Make sure that the working loop does not slip back through the top of the last stitch.*

6 *Drop the bobble color and continue to work with the first or main color only. Pull the color used for the bobble gently at the back of the work to make a good shape. Break off the yarn. When the fabric is completed, darn in the loose ends on the wrong side.*

WOVEN CROCHET JACKET

Strands of a contrasting mohair blend yarn are woven into the fabric of this attractive jacket.

Sizes
Misses' sizes 12 [14:16]
Length from shoulder before weaving 23 [23¼:23½] in
Sleeve seam edge before weaving 19 in

Note *Instructions for larger sizes are in brackets [ ]; where there is only one set of figures it applies to all sizes.
Measurements given are for completed jacket pieces before weaving, since weaving tends to make pieces shorter and wider.*

Materials
*19 oz of a knitting worsted-weight yarn (A)
3 oz of a medium-weight mohair blend (B)
Size E crochet hook
4 buttons*

Gauge
10 spaces and 10 rows to 4 in over filet mesh worked on size E hook

To save time, take time to check gauge.

Back
Using A, make 102 [106:110] ch.
Base row 1dc into 6th ch from hook, *ch 1, skip 1ch, 1dc into next ch, rep from * to end of ch. Turn. 49 [51:53] 1ch sps – called sp(s).
1st row Ch 4 to count as first dc and sp, * 1dc into next dc, ch 1, rep from * ending with 1dc into top of turning ch. Turn.
First row forms basic filet mesh pat and is rep throughout. Cont in pat until work measures 14in, ending with a WS row.
Shape armholes
Next row Sl st across first 6 sps, ch 4, pat across 39 [41:43] sps. Turn and leave rem sps unworked.
Work even until work measures 23 [23¼: 23½]in, ending with a WS row.
Shape shoulders
Next row Sl st across first 5 sps, ch 4, pat across 31 [33:35] sps. Turn and leave rem sps unworked.
Next row Sl st across first 5 sps, ch 4, pat across next 23 [25:27]sps. Turn and leave rem sps unworked.
Next row Sl st across first 6 [6:7] sps, ch 4, pat across next 13 [15:15] sps. Fasten off leaving rem sps unworked.

Left front
Using A, make 50 [52:54] ch. Work base row as for back. 23 [24:25] sps. Cont in pat as for back for 17 more rows. Break off yarn.
Make pocket lining
Using A, make 34ch. Work base row as for back. 15 sps. Cont in pat as for back for 17 more rows.
Next row Ch 4, 1dc into next dc, (ch 1, 1dc into next dc) twice, ch 1, work next dc through first dc on front section and next dc of pocket lining tog, now cont working mesh across

front section only to end of row. 27 [28:29] sps. Cont in pat until work measures 14in, ending at same side as pocket opening (armhole edge).
Shape armhole
Next row Sl st across first 6sps, ch 4, 1dc into next dc, pat to end of row. 22 [23:24] sps. Work even until work measures 19¾ [20:20½] in, ending at armhole edge.
Shape neck
Next row Pat across 18 [19:20] sps, turn and leave rem 4sps unworked. Dec one sp at neck edge on next and every following row until 13 [13:14] sps rem. Work even until front measures 23 [23¼:23½] in, ending at armhole edge.
Shape shoulder
Dec 4 sps at armhole edge on next 2 rows. Fasten off.

Right front
Make pocket lining as for left front. Break off yarn.
Work as for left front for first 8 rows of filet mesh, ending with RS of work facing.
Buttonhole row Ch 4, 1dc into next dc, ch 1, 1dc into next dc, ch 3, skip next dc, 1dc into next dc, pat to end of row.
Next row Pat to buttonhole, ch 1, 1dc into 2nd of 3ch, ch 1, 1dc into next dc, pat to end of row.
Complete as for left front, reversing all shaping. Insert pocket lining after 18 rows of mesh and work 2 more buttonholes 12 rows apart.

Sleeves (alike)
Using A, make 62ch. Work base row as for back. 29sps. Cont in pat as for back. Work 3 more rows.
Next row (inc) Ch 4, 1dc into dc at base of 4ch, pat to end of row working 1dc into last dc, ch 1, 1dc into same

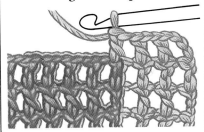

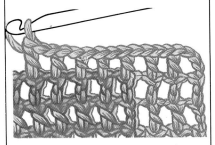

1 *The pocket linings for the woven jacket are made as separate pieces which must be incorporated onto the wrong side of the work while making the front. Hold the pocket at back of the work where indicated in the pattern and work into the stitch on the front piece and on the pocket simultaneously, thus joining the pocket to the front of the garment.*

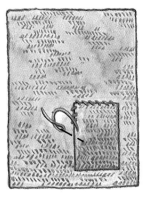

2 *Because of the weaving, the jacket pocket has been joined in only one place, but generally all pocket stitches are worked together with front stitches to hold the pocket in place across the top edge.*

3 *Using matching yarn, sew the pocket lining in place on the wrong side of the garment, making sure that the stitches do not show on the right side of the work. Overcast firmly, but do not pull too tightly or the fabric may pucker.*

place as last dc. Turn.
Work 5 [4:4] rows in pat.
Rep last 6[5:5] rows until there are 43 [45:47]sps. Work even until sleeve measures 19in. Fasten off.

Weaving

Using 3 strands of B tog, weave in and out of mesh holes vertically, alternating the first stitch each time and making sure that weaving is worked evenly. Work color sequence as follows:
Back 5 rows B, 5 rows A, starting by weaving 5 rows B down center of work, then working towards the sides.
Sleeves Work as for back.
Fronts Beg by working 5 rows B down center front, making sure sides match back section.
Pocket lining Use A throughout.

To finish

Join shoulder seams.
Collar
Using A and with RS facing work 2sc into each sp around neck edge.
Turn.

Work another 9 rows sc on these sts. Fasten off.
Cuffs
Using A and with RS facing work 40sc along cuff edge, working * 2sc into first sp, 1sc into each of next 2 sps, rep from * to end. Work 12 more rows sc on these sts. Fasten off.
Pocket edges
Using A and with RS facing, work 2sc into each sp along pocket edge.
Work 4 more rows sc on these sts. Fasten off.
Waistband
Join side seams. Using A and with RS facing, work * 2sc into first sp, 1sc into next sp, rep from * to end. Work 6 rows sc, ending at right front edge.
Buttonhole row 1sc into each of first 2sc, ch 4, skip 4sc, 1sc into next sc, work in sc to end.
Work 5 more rows sc, working 1sc into each of 4ch of buttonhole. Fasten off. Set in sleeves. Join sleeve seams. With RS of work facing and A, work 1 row sc up center front, around collar and down other front. Fasten off. Sew down pocket linings.

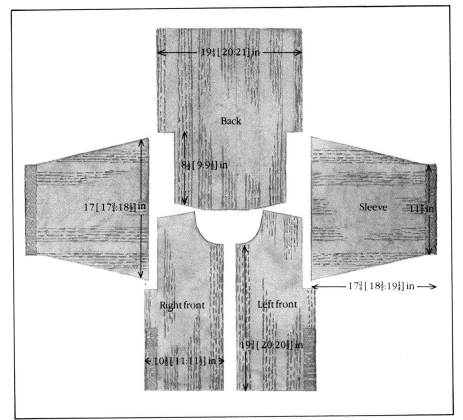

CLASSIC VEST

Two textured patterns – a butterfly crossed stitch and single ribbing – have been used to make this vest.
The pointed fronts, deep V-neck and adjustable half belt complete the essentially classic look.

Sizes

Misses' sizes 12 [14:16]
Length from shoulder 16½ [17¼:18½]in

Note *Instructions for larger sizes are in brackets [ ]; where there is only one set of figures it applies to all sizes.*

Materials

8 [8:9] oz of a sport-weight yarn
Size C crochet hook
5 small buttons
Small buckle to fit completed strap

Gauge

20 sts and 9 rows to 4in over front pat worked on size C hook.
20 sts and 18 rows to 4in over back pat worked on size C hook.

To save time, take time to check gauge.

Left front

**Make 9 [11:11]ch.
Base row 2dc into 5th ch from hook, 1dc into each of next 3 [5:5]ch, (2dc, 1tr) into last ch. Turn. 9 [11:11] sts.
1st row (RS) Ch 4, 2dc into first tr, 1dc into each of next 1 [2:2] sts, inserting hook from front to back and leaving last loop of each st on hook work 2tr around stem of dc on row below and 3 sts to left, yo and draw through all 3 loops on hook – called cluster front –, skip next st behind cluster front, 1dc into each of next 3 sts, cluster front around same st now 3 sts to right, skip next st – called butterfly st over 5 sts or b st over 5 –, 1dc into each of next 1 [2:2] sts, (2dc, 1tr) into top of turning ch. Turn. 13 [15:15] sts.
2nd row Ch 4, 2dc into first tr, 1dc into each st to turning ch, (2dc, 1tr) into top of turning ch. Turn. 17 [19:19] sts.
3rd row Ch 4, 2dc into first tr, 1dc into each of next 1 [2:2] sts, b st over 5, 1dc into each of next 3 sts, b st over 5, 1dc into each of next 1 [2:2] sts, (2dc, 1tr) into top of turning ch. Turn. 21 [23:23] sts.
4th row As 2nd row. 25 [27:27] sts.
5th row Ch 4, 2dc into first tr, 1dc into each of next 1 [2:2] sts, * b st over 5, 1dc into each of next 3 sts, rep from * once more, b st over 5, 1dc into each of next 1 [2:2] sts, (2dc, 1tr) into top of turning ch. Turn. 29 [31:31] sts.
6th row As 2nd row. 33 [35:35] sts.
7th row Ch 4, 2dc into first tr, 1dc into each of next 1 [2:2] sts, * b st over 5, 1dc into each of next 3 sts, rep from * to end, ending last rep with 1dc into each of next 1 [2:2] sts, (2tr, 1tr) into top of turning ch. Turn. 37 [39:39] sts.
8th row As 2nd row. 41 [43:43] sts.
3rd size only
9th row As 7th row. 47 sts.
10th row Ch 3, skip first st, 1dc into each st to end. Turn.
All sizes
Beg pat
1st row (RS) Ch 3, skip first st, 1dc into each of next 1 [2:8] sts, * b st over 5, 1dc into each of next 3 sts, rep from * to end, ending last rep with 1dc into each of next 1 [2:8] sts, 1dc into top of turning ch. Turn.
2nd row Ch 3, skip first st, 1dc into each st to end. Turn.

3rd row Ch 3, skip first st, 1dc into each of next 5 [6:4] sts, * b st over 5, 1dc into each of next 3 sts, rep from * to end, ending last rep with 1dc into each of next 5 [6:4] sts, 1dc into top of turning ch. Turn.
4th row As 2nd row.
Last 4 rows form pat.**
Shape side
Next row Ch 3, skip first st, 2dc into next st – called inc one –, pat to end. Turn. 42 [44:48] sts.
Keeping pat correct, inc one st at beg of following 3 alternate rows. 45 [47:51] sts.
Work even in pat until *front* edge measures 6 [7:7] in from last row of point, ending at front edge.
Shape front
Next row Pat to last 3 sts, work next 2 sts tog, 1dc into top of turning ch. Turn. 44 [46:50] sts.
Next row Ch 3, skip first st, work next 2 sts tog, pat to end. Turn. 43 [45:49] sts.
Rep last 2 rows twice more. 39 [41:45] sts.
Shape armhole
Next row Sl st across first 7 sts, ch 3, skip st at base of 3ch, work next 2 sts tog, pat to last 3 sts, work next 2 sts tog, 1dc into top of turning ch. Turn.
Cont to dec one st at front edge on every following row, *at the same time* dec one st at armhole edge on every row until 21 [23:25] sts rem. Keeping armhole edge straight, cont to dec one st at front edge on next and every following alternate row until 17 [19:20] sts rem.
Work even in pat until armhole measures 8¼ [8¼:9]in, ending at armhole edge.
Shape shoulder
Next row Sl st across first 6 [7:7] sts, ch 3, skip st at base of 3ch, pat to end. Turn.
Next row Pat to last 5 [6:6] sts, turn.
Fasten off.

Right front

Work as for left front from ** to **
Shape side
Next row Pat to last 2 sts, inc one, 1dc into top of turning ch. Turn. 42 [44:48] sts.
Keeping pat correct, inc one st at end

of following 3 alternate rows. 45 [47:51] sts. Work even in pat until front edge matches left-front edge, ending at front edge.

Shape front
Next row Ch 3, skip first st, work next 2 sts tog, pat to end. Turn. 44 [46:50] sts.

Next row Pat to last 3 sts, work next 2 sts tog, 1dc into top of turning ch. Turn. 43 [45:49] sts.

Rep last 2 rows twice more. 39 [41:45] sts.

Shape armhole
Next row Ch 3, skip first st, work next 2 sts tog, pat to last 9 sts, work next 2 sts tog, 1dc into next st, turn. 31 [33:37] sts.

Work as for left front from *** to ***
Work even in pat until armhole measures 8¼ [8¼:9] in, ending at front edge.

Shape shoulder
Next row Pat to within last 5 [6:6] sts, turn.

Next row Sl st across first 6 [7:7] sts, ch 3, skip st at base of 3ch, pat to end. Turn. Fasten off.

Back
Make 87 [91:97]ch.
Base row (RS) 1dc into 4th ch from hook, 1dc into each ch to end. Turn. 85 [89:95] sts.

Next row Ch 1 to count as first sc, skip first st, 1sc into each st to end. Turn.

Next row Ch 2, skip first st, inserting hook from front to back and from right to left work 1dc around next dc on base row – raised dc formed –, *skip next sc behind raised dc, 1dc into next sc, skip next dc on base row, raised dc around next dc on base row, rep from * to end, ending with 1hdc into last sc. Turn. 42 [44:47] raised dc.

Beg pat
1st row (WS) Ch 1 to count as first sc, skip first hdc, 1sc into next raised dc, *1sc between next dc and next raised dc, 1sc into next raised dc, rep from * to end, ending with 1sc into top of turning ch. Turn. 85 [89:95]sc.

2nd row Ch 2, skip first st, raised dc around next raised dc, *skip next sc behind raised dc, 1dc into next sc, raised dc around next raised dc, rep from * to end, ending with 1hdc into last sc. Turn.

First and 2nd rows form pat. Cont in pat until work matches fronts at side edges, ending with a first row.

Shape armholes
Next row Sl st across first 7 sts, ch 2, skip first st at base of 3ch, work next 2

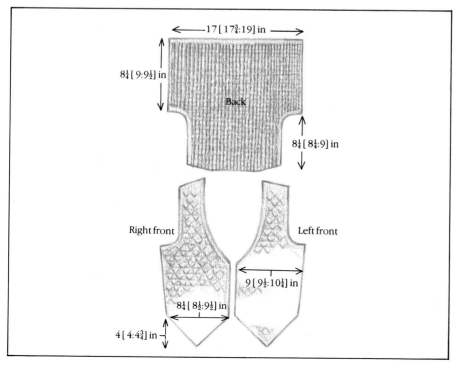

sts tog, pat to last 9 sts, work next 2 sts tog, 1hdc into next st, turn. Keeping pat correct, dec one st at each end of every following alternate row until 61 [65:71] sts rem.

Work even in pat until work matches fronts to shoulder shaping, ending with a first row at armhole edge.

Shape shoulders

Next row Sl st across first 6 [7:7] sts, ch 2, skip st at base of 2ch, pat to last 6 [7:7] sts, 1hdc into next st, turn.

Next row Pat to end.

Rep last 2 rows once more.

Next row Sl st across first 8 [8:9] sts, ch 2, skip st at base of 2ch, pat to last 8 [8:9] sts, 1hdc into next st, turn.

Next row Pat to end. 27 [27:31] sts. Fasten off.

To finish

Join side and shoulder seams. Mark position of 5 buttonholes on left front, one ½in from end of point, one at beg of front neckline shaping and rem 3 evenly spaced in between.

Edging

With RS facing join yarn to side seam on lower edge.

1st round Work a round of sc into outer edge of work, sl st to first sc.

Buttonhole round Work 1sc into each sc to end, working 2sc into each sc at corners and working buttonholes at markers as follows: ch 2, skip next 2sc, 1sc into next sc, sl st into first sc. Turn.

3rd round Work 1sc into each sc to end, working 2sc into each sc at corners and 2sc into each buttonhole, sl st into first sc.

Fasten off.

Armhole borders (alike)

With RS facing join yarn to side seam.

1st round Work a round of sc into armhole edge, sl st into first sc. Turn.

2nd round 1sc into each sc to end, sl st into first sc. Fasten off.

Strap

Make 36 [40:44]ch.

Base row 1sc into 2nd ch from hook, 1sc into each ch to end. Turn. 35 [39:43]sc.

Next row Ch 1 to count as first sc, skip first st, 1sc into each st to end. Turn.

Rep last row twice more. Fasten off.

Buckle strap

Make 22 [26:30] ch.

Work as for Strap.

Sew on buckle.

Sew straps to back approx 2¼in from lower edge and 3in from side seams. Sew on buttons to correspond with buttonholes.

--- SPECIAL TECHNIQUE ---

Alternating rib

1 *The back of the vest has been worked in a form of crochet ribbing which can also be used to make cuffs and waistbands. This alternating ribbing is worked on an odd number of stitches. Work the base row in double crochet and the next row in single crochet as usual. Begin the next row with two chains and skip the first stitch.*

2 *Work a raised double around the stem of the next double on the base row, inserting the hook from front to back and from right to left. Skip the next single crochet lying behind the raised double and work one double into the next single crochet. Skip the next double on the base row. Continue in this way to the last stitch, ending with a half double crochet into the top of the turning chain.*

3 *Begin the next row with one chain to count as the first single crochet and skip the first stitch. Work one single crochet into the next raised double. Work the next single crochet between the next double and the next raised double. Continue in this way, working one single crochet into the top of the turning chain. Work the next row as in step 2, this time working raised doubles around the stems of the previous raised doubles.*

REVERSIBLE VEST

This reversible vest – fluffy on one side and smooth on the other – is made from two rectangular strips of Tunisian crochet, joined at the center back and sides. The buttons are sewn to a separate strip.

Back and front (alike)

Using afghan hook and A, make 106 [112] ch.

Base row (RS) 1 Ttr into 4th ch from hook, 1 Ttr into each ch to end. Join in B.

1st row Yo, draw through first st, *yo, draw through 2 sts, rep from * to end of row.

2nd row Tdst to end of row, join in A.

3rd row As first row.

4th row Ch 1, Ttr to end of row, join in B.

5th row As first row.

Rep first-5th rows 4 [5] more times. Work first row once more. Fasten off. Make another piece in the same way.

Right front edging

Using ordinary crochet hook and A, make 15ch, working first ch into last Tst (RS).

Base row Work 1sc into second st from hook, 1sc into each ch and along the long side of the Tunisian crochet rectangle. Turn.

1st row Ch 1, skip first st, 1sc into each sc of previous row, turn.

2nd row (buttonhole row) Ch 1, 2sc into 2sc of previous row, * ch 2, 1sc into third sc, 4sc*. Rep from * to * twice more and work 1sc into each sc of previous row to end, turn.

3rd row Ch 1, 1sc into each sc and ch of previous row, turn.

4th row Ch 1, 1sc into each sc of previous row.

Fasten off.

Left front edging

Using ordinary hook and A, make 15ch, working first ch into last Tst (RS) of

Sizes

Misses' sizes 10-12 [14-16]
Length 20 [21¼] in

Note *Instructions for the larger size are in brackets [ ]; where there is only one set of figures it applies to both sizes.*

Materials

16oz of a bulky mohair blend yarn in main color A
4oz in contrasting color B
Size K afghan hook
Size I ordinary crochet hook
3 brass or plastic rings, approximately 1 in in diameter

Gauge

13 sts and 10 rows to 4in over Tunisian triple st worked on size K afghan hook

To save time, take time to check gauge.

Note *Instructions for working Tunisian double stitch (Tdst) and Tunisian triple stitch (Ttr) are on pages 161 and 162*

lower front corner of left front. Fasten off.

Starting at the center back of the lower edge of the left front rectangle work sc along to the center front and along the 15ch. Turn.

Complete left front edging to match right front edging including the three buttonholes (to make the vest completely reversible).
Fasten off.

To finish

Block the work if necessary.
Armhole edging and side seams
Using ordinary hook and A, work one row of sc along the other long side of the rectangle. Fold rectangle in half. Picking up one sc from each side, work 30 [33] sc through two sts at a time, starting at the opposite end from the fold.
Fasten off.
Join center back seam from lower edge up to about half-way from shoulder.

Waistband

Using ordinary hook and A work one sc into every sc of the 15sc on right front edging, picking up the back loop of every sc of previous row. Make the waistband 27 [30] in long. Join it to left front edging with a row of sc. Sew rest of waistband invisibly to main body.

Buttons

Using B, make three Dorset crosswheel buttons as shown below, left.

Button strip

Using ordinary hook and A, make 16ch.
Base row 1sc into second ch from hook, 1sc into each ch to end, 6sc into last ch, sc along other edge to first ch.
Fasten off.
Sew buttons to the strip 2¼ in apart. To fasten vest, lap right front edge over left and pull buttons through both sets of buttonholes from wrong side.

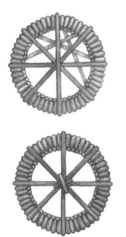
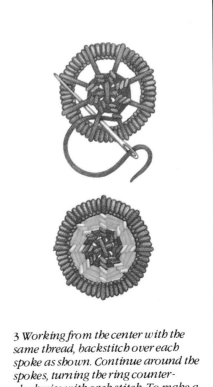
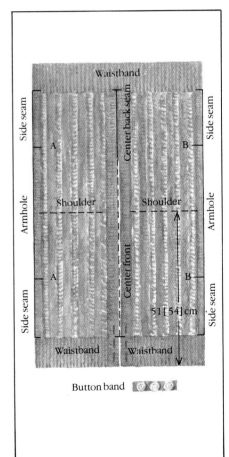

Button band

PUFF STITCH VEST

Make this attractive vest in shades to coordinate with a favorite skirt or pair of pants.

Sizes
Misses' sizes 10 [12:14:16]
Length from shoulder *21 [22:23:24] in*

Note *Instructions for larger sizes are in brackets [ ]; where there is only one set of figures it applies to all sizes.*

Materials
4 [4:6:6] oz of a knitting worsted-weight yarn in each of two colors, A and B
4 oz in each of colors C and D
Size F crochet hook
Pair of size 3 knitting needles

Gauge
16 sts and 16 rows to 4 in over pat worked on size F hook

To save time, take time to check gauge.

Back
Using A make 61 [65:69:73] ch.
1st row 1sc into 2nd ch from hook, 1sc into each ch to end, turn.
2nd row (RS) Ch 1 to count as first sc, * 2sc into next st, skip next st, rep from * to last st, 1sc into last st changing to A, turn.
3rd row Ch 1, 1sc into each of next 2 sts, * yo, insert hook into next st and pull loop through loosely, (yo, insert hook into same st and pull loop through loosely) twice, yo and pull through 6 loops on hook, yo and pull through rem 2 loops – 1 puff st formed –, 1sc into each of next 3 sts, rep from * to last st, 1sc into last st, changing to C, turn.
4th row Ch 1, 1sc into next st, * insert hook into sp between sts on row below next st and pull loop through to height of row being worked, insert hook into next st as usual and pull loop through, yo and pull through 3 loops on hook – 1 spike st formed –, 1sc into each of next 3 sts, rep from * to last st, 1sc into last st changing to D, turn.
5th row Ch 1, * (1sc, 1dc) into next st, skip next st, rep from * to last st, 1sc into last st changing to A, turn.
6th row Ch 1, 1dc into same place as ch, * skip 1dc, (1sc, 1dc) into next sc, rep from * to last 2 sts, 1sc into each st, changing to B on last st, turn.
7th row Ch 1, * 1sc into next sc, 1 puff st into next dc, rep from * to last st, 1sc into last st, changing to C, turn.
8th row Ch 1, * 1sc into top of puff st, 1 spike st over next sc, rep from * to last st, 1sc into last st, changing to D, turn.
9th row Ch 1, * 2sc into next st, skip next st, rep from * to last st, 1sc into last st, changing to A, turn.
Rep 2nd-9th rows throughout for stitch and color pat.

Work even until 47 [49:51:53] rows have been completed.
Shape armholes
Next row Skip 5 [5:6:6] sts, join new color with a sl st to next st, ch 1, work in pat to last 6 [6:7:7] sts, 1sc into next st, fasten off.
Next row Join next color with a sl st to 2nd st, ch 1, work in pat to last 2 sts, 1sc into next st, changing color, turn.
Next row Work in pat to end.
Fasten off.
Rep last 2 rows 2 [3:3:4] times, then work even until 27 [29:31:33] rows from beg of armhole shaping have been completed.
Shape shoulder
Next row Join new color with a sl st to 6th [7th:7th:7th] st, ch 1, pat to last 6 [7:7:7] sts, 1sc into next st, fasten off.
Next row Join next color to 7th [7th:7th:8th] st, ch 1, pat to last 7 [7:7:8] sts, 1sc into next st, fasten off.

Front
Work as for back to armhole.
Shape neck and armhole
Next row Skip 5 [5:6:6] sts, join next color with a sl st to next st, ch 1, work in pat for 24 [26:28:30] sts, changing color on the last st, turn.
Next row Work in pat to last 2 sts; 1sc into next st, changing color, turn. Rep last row 4 [6:6:8] more times, then cont keeping armhole edge straight and dec one st as before at neck edge on every 2nd row until 11 [12:12:13] sts rem.
Work even until 27 [29:31:33] rows from beg of armhole shaping have been completed.
Shape shoulder
Next row Join in new color to 6th [7th:7th:7th] st, ch 1, work in pat to end, fasten off.

Return to first row of neck shaping and rejoin yarn with a sl st to next st at center of neck, ch 1, work in pat to last 6 [6:7:7] sts, 1sc into next st, fasten off. Complete to correspond with first side, reversing all shapings.

To finish

Using knitting needles and A, pick up and K 60 [64:68:72] sts along foundation ch of back. Work in K1, P1 ribbing for 10 rows. Bind off loosely in ribbing. Rep for front. Darn in all ends at the back of the work.
Join shoulder and side seams.

Armhole edging

With RS facing, join in A with a sl st to seam at underarm. Ch 1, work in sc all around armhole, working 1sc into each row end, join with a sl st to first ch, turn.

Next round Ch 1, 1sc into each sc all around, join with a sl st to first ch, turn.
Next round Sl st into each st to end, join with a sl st to first sl st.
Fasten off.
Rep on other armhole.

Neck edging

With RS facing, join in A with a sl st to edge of first neck row, work in sc all around neck edge, turn.
Next row Ch 1, leaving last loop of each st on hook work 1sc into each of next 2 sts, yo and pull through all loops on hook – called sc2tog –, 1sc into each st to last 3 sts, sc2tog, 1sc into last st, turn. Rep this row twice more.
Next row Sl st into each st all around. Fasten off.
Join short seam at point of neck.

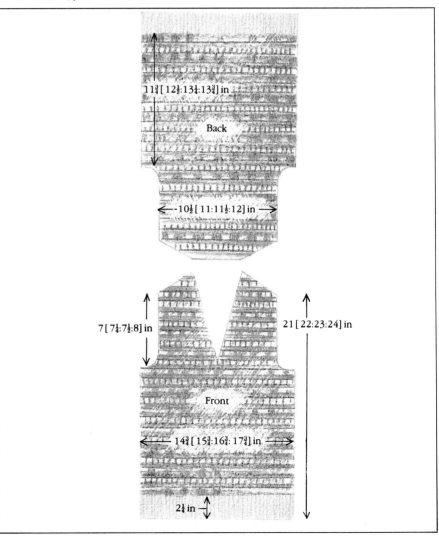

11¾ [12½:13¼:13¾] in

Back

10½ [11:11½:12] in

7 [7¼:7½:8] in

21 [22:23:24] in

Front

14¾ [15¾:16¾:17¾] in

2¼ in

Working puff stitches

1 *To work the puff, take the yarn over the hook, insert the hook into the next stitch in the previous row and pull yarn through. Three loops are on the hook.*

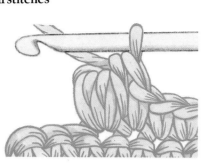

4 *Complete the puff stitch by taking the yarn around the hook and drawing it through the two remaining loops to form a flat loop at the top of the stitch.*

2 *Repeat step 1 twice more, extending the yarn each time to create a longer loop. Seven loops are on the hook.*

5 *Work one single crochet into each of the next two stitches.*

3 *Take the yarn over the hook and draw it through six of the seven loops so that the extended loops are pulled together. Two loops are on the hook.*

6 *On the next row, work into the top of the puff stitch. Take care to draw stitches together to maintain correct gauge.*

PATCHWORK VEST

This unusual vest is made of hexagons and half hexagons worked separately and then crocheted together with single crochet.

Sizes
Misses' sizes 12-14
Length from shoulder *16½in approx*

Materials
6oz of a knitting worsted-weight yarn in main color A
4oz in each of two contrasting colors, B and C
2oz of a mohair yarn in contrasting color D
Size F crochet hook
3 buttons

Gauge
Each motif measures 3⅛in between two opposite sides worked on size F hook.

To save time, take time to check gauge.

Hexagon motifs (make 43)
1st round Using B, make 4ch. Join into a ring with a sl st.
2nd round Ch 3 to count as first dc, work 11dc into ring. Join with a sl st to 3rd of first 3ch. 12dc.
3rd round Using C, ch 3 to count as first dc, * 3dc into next dc, 1dc into next dc, rep from * 4 more times, 3dc into next dc. Join with a sl st to 3rd of first 3ch.
4th round Ch 3 to count as first dc, * 1dc into next dc, 3dc into next dc (center dc of 3dc group worked in previous round), 1dc into each of next 2dc, rep from * 4 more times, 1dc into next dc, 3dc into next dc, 1dc into next dc. Join with a sl st to 3rd of first 3ch. Fasten off.
To make motif larger, work each round in same way, working two more dc between each 3dc group each time.

Make 42 more motifs in same way, using B, C and D at random for each motif.

Half hexagon motif (make 12)
1st round Using C, make 4ch. Join into a ring with a sl st.
2nd round Using C, ch 3 to count as first dc, 1dc into st at base of ch, * 1dc into next dc, 3dc into next dc, rep from * once more, 1dc into next dc, 2dc into top of turning ch. Turn.
3rd round Using B, ch 3 to count as first dc, 1dc into st at base of ch, *1dc into each of next 3dc, 3dc into next dc, rep from * once more, 1dc into each of next 3dc, 2dc into top of turning ch. Turn.
4th round Using C, ch 3 to count as first dc, 1dc into st at base of ch, * 1dc into each of next 5dc, 1dc into next dc, rep from * once more, 1dc into each of

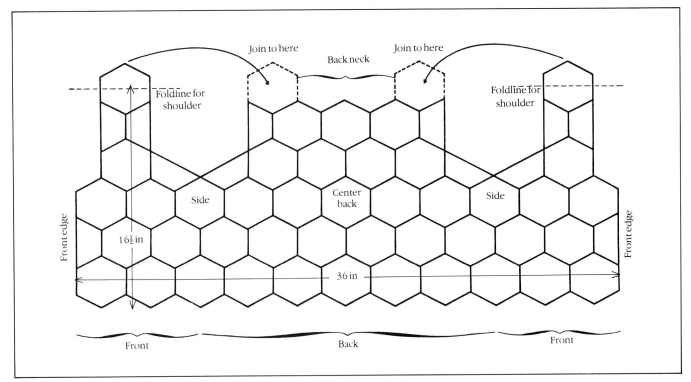

next 5dc, 2dc into top of turning ch. Fasten off.

To make motif larger cont working in same way, working 2 extra dc between 3dc groups and 2dc into st at each end of row.

Make 11 more motifs in same way, using B, C and D at random on each motif.

To finish

Block or press motifs, as appropriate for yarn used. Using A and with RS tog, join motifs and half motifs into horizontal strips with sc as in diagram. Then fold shoulder motifs and join to back as indicated.

Using A and with RS facing, work 5 rows sc around back neck, then down one front and around lower edges, and then up the other front. On every round at lower edge work 3sc into motif points and omit 2sc where motifs join.

Mark positions for 3 buttonholes, spaced evenly, on right front, and make buttonholes on 3rd row of sc as markers are reached by working ch 2, skip next 2dc, cont working in dc until next marker is reached. On the next row work 1dc into each ch worked in previous row to complete buttonholes. Sew buttons to left front edge to correspond with buttonholes. Work armhole edging in same way, starting at underarm.

SPECIAL TECHNIQUE

Working a half hexagon motif

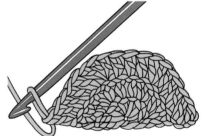

1 The half hexagons used at the armholes of this vest are essentially the same as the whole hexagon motifs, but, of course, use fewer stitches. Make four chains, slip stitch to the first chain to form a ring. Work three chains and six doubles into the ring; turn.

*3 Chain three, work one double into the stitch at the base of the chains. *One double into each of the next three doubles, three doubles into the next double*. Repeat from * to *. Work one double into each of the next three doubles, two doubles into the top of the turning chain; turn.*

*2 Chain three, work one double into the stitch at the base of the chain. * Work one double into the next double and three doubles into the next double*. Repeat from * to * once. Work one double into the next double and two doubles into the top of the turning chain; turn.*

4 Continue to work as for step 3, working 2 extra doubles between each group of three doubles (or two doubles at the ends of the row) until the motif is the required size.

MULTI-TEXTURED JACKET

A subtle blending of yarns and Tunisian crochet stitches give this jacket real fashion flair.

Sizes

Misses' sizes 10-12 [14]
Length from shoulder $20\frac{1}{2}$ [$22\frac{1}{2}$] in
Sleeve seam 18 [$19\frac{1}{4}$] in

Note *Instructions for the larger sizes are in brackets [ ]; where there is only one set of figures it applies to both sizes.*

Materials

*8 oz of an Icelandic-type yarn in color A
4 oz of a bulky mohair blend in color B
6 [8] oz of a mohair yarn with glitter in color C
4 [6] oz of a pure mohair yarn in color D
4 oz of a knitting worsted-weight yarn in color E
11 [13] oz of a bulky mohair blend in color F
Size K afghan hook
Size I ordinary hook*

Gauge

12 Ttr to 4 in worked on size K afghan hook

To save time, take time to check gauge.

Note: *Instructions for working Basic Tunisian stitch (Tst), Tunisian double stitch (Tdst), Tunisian triple (Ttr), Tunisian triple triple (Ttrtr), Tunisian purl (Tp) and Tunisian bobble stitch (Tb) are on pages 161-163.*

Note *Cut off each color as it is used and run ends in. The color is always changed on the left side of the work for the return row.*

Back and fronts (Jacket is worked in one piece to armholes.)

Using afghan hook and A, make 111 [119] ch.

1st row Tdst, work first st into 2nd ch.
2nd row With B, work as for row 2 of Tst – called "return row."
3rd row Ch 3, Ttr into 2nd st, Ttr to end of row.
4th row With C, work return row.
5th row * 1 Ttrtr into vertical loop of 2nd row. 1 Tdst into 4th row *. Rep from * to * to end.
6th row With D, return row.
7th row Tp.
8th row With E, return row.
9th row Tdst.
10th row With F, return row.
11th row Ch 3, Ttr into 2nd st, Ttr to end.
12th row With A, return row.
13th row Into 2nd st 1 Tdst, * 1 Tp, 1 Tdst*.
Repeat from * to * to end of row.
14th row With E, return row.
15th row Working into 2nd loop, 3 [7] Tdst, * 5 Tdst, 1 Tb*. Repeat from * to * to end of row, finishing with 4 [8] Tdst.
16th row With B, return row.
17th row Ttr into 2nd loop, Ttr to end of row.
18th row With D, return row.
19th row 1 Tdst into 2nd loop, 3 [7] Tdst, *yo 3 times, place hook into loop 2 rows down and 3 sts to right, complete Ttrtr, 1 sc, yo 3 times, hook into loop 2 rows down and 3 sts to left, complete Ttrtr, yo, and pull through 1 Ttrtr, 1 Tdst, 1 Ttrtr, making an inverted V from Tdst, 5 Tdst, rep from * to end of row, finishing with 4 [8] Tdst.
20th row With A, return row. Slip last row onto a hook and leave while pockets are worked.

Pockets (make 2)

Using afghan hook and B, make 15 [17] ch.

1st row Ttr.
2nd row With C, return row.
3rd row Tdst.
4th row With D, return row.
5th row Tdst.
6th row With E, return row.
7th row Tdst.
8th row With F, return row.
9th row Tdst.
10th row With A, return row.
11th row Tdst.
12th row With E, return row.
13th row Tdst.
14th row With B, return row.
15th row Tdst.
16th row With D, return row.
17th row Tdst.
18th row With A, return row.
19th row Tdst.
Place both pockets on hooks and return to the main garment.
21st row 1 Tdst into 2nd st, 11 Tdst, sl st over 15 [17] Tdst, 57 [61] Tdst, sl st over 15 [17] Tdst, 12 Tdst.
22nd row Pin pocket linings into place behind 15 [17] sl st. With F, work a return row over 11 Tdst of garment, 15 [17] Tdst of right pocket, 57 [61] Tdst across back, 15 [17] Tdst of left pocket and finish with 12 Tdst to left front.
23rd row Tdst.
24th row With C, return row.
25th row 1 [2] Tdst, * 1 Tdst, ch 3, 2 Tdst* to end of row, finishing with 2 Tdst.
26th row With E, return row.
27th row Tp.
28th row With B, return row. 3rd-28th rows form pat. Using either rows 3 to 28 or any preferred combination of colors and rows, cont until work measures 13 [14] in, ending with a return row.
Divide for back and fronts: 1 Tdst into 2nd st, 21 [23] Tdst, sl st 8 [9] sts, Tdst 49 [51] sts, sl st 8 [9] sts, Tdst 23 [25] sts.

Back yoke

The center 49 [51] sts form back. Work in sequence already selected for $7\frac{1}{2}$ [$8\frac{1}{2}$] in. End with 1 row of sl st, working from right to left.
Fasten off.

Right front

Work on right front for 4 [5] in. Sl st along 6 sts. Cont on rem sts until right front is the same length as back. Work left front to match right front, but leave 6 sts at end of row to shape neck instead of sl st as on right front. Place right front shoulder against back. With ordinary hook and F, crochet tog with 1 row of sc. Complete left shoulder in the same way.

Sleeves

With afghan hook and A, make 28 [32] ch.

Work in pat to match main garment, starting with row 1. Inc 1 st each side, every 2in, until there are 44 [52] sts. Work in chosen sequence until sleeve measures 18 [19¼] in. End with a row of sl st. Fasten off.

Pocket edging

With ordinary hook and F, work 2 rows of sc on front edge of pocket. Join D to left front. Inserting hook into front loop only of each st, work a row of crab st (sc worked from left to right).

4th row With F, work 1 row sc on back loops of sc of 2nd row. Fasten off. Sew down each side of facing. Sew pocket linings in place.

Jacket edging

With RS facing, join F to neck edge.

1st row With ordinary hook and F, work sc down left front, across bottom and up right front to neck edge. Turn.

2nd row Work in sc to neck edge of left front, inc 2sts at each front corner. Turn.

3rd row As row 2, but ending at right neck edge. 2sl st on each side of sc.

4th row Work along neck to first row of sc, making 1dc in each neck curve. Turn.

5th row 1 row sc. Turn.

Rep 5th row 4 times. Fasten off.

Next row Join D to center back of neckband and from left to right work crab st on front loop of sts along neckband, and all around jacket, finishing off at center back of neck.

Next row Join F to center back on back loop of sc, behind crab st, and work all the way around jacket on back loops of sc.

Sleeve and armhole edgings

Join F to corner of armhole and work 44 [52] sc along straight armhole edge. Pin top of sleeve to armhole edge. Work 1 row of sc, taking hook through sl st on top of sleeve and sc of jacket for each st.

With F, sew 2 sides of sleeve to lower edge of armhole. Sew sleeve seams.

Sleeve band

With F, work 2 rows of sc, 1 row of crab st and 1 row sc to match band on jacket.

To finish

Lightly press seams, using a dry cloth on wrong side of garment.

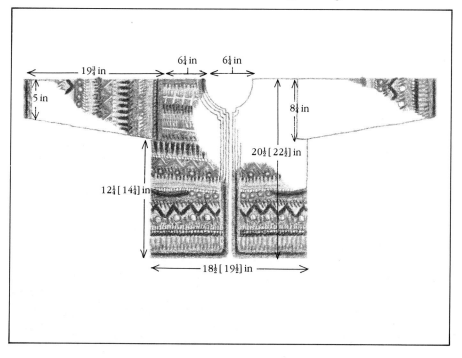

CASUAL PLAID CARDIGAN

This attractive plaid cardigan is made by weaving different colors through a striped filet background.

Sizes
Misses' sizes 12 [14:16]
Length from shoulder *21 [21½:22½]in*
Sleeve seam *17¾ [18½:19¼]in*

Note: *Instructions for larger sizes are in brackets [ ]; where there is only one set of figures it applies to all sizes.*

Materials
15 [16:16] oz of a sport-weight yarn (yarn used is a wool-silk blend) in main color A
8 [9:9] oz in contrasting color B
1oz in each of contrasting colors C and D
Size F crochet hook
Size H crochet hook
8 buttons
Large tapestry needle

Gauge
10 sps and 10 rows to 4in over pat worked on size H hook

To save time, take time to check gauge.

Back
Using smaller hook and A make 23ch.
1st row 1sc into 2nd ch from hook, 1sc into each ch to end, turn. 22 sts.
2nd row Ch 1 to count as first sc, working into back loop only of each st, work 1sc into each st to end, turn. Rep 2nd row 88 [92:96] more times to complete ribbing.
Beg pat
Turn ribbing sideways. Using larger hook cont working along side edge of ribbing.
Next row Using A, ch 4 to count as first dc and 1ch sp, 1dc into top of 2nd row end, * ch 1, skip 1 row end, 1dc into top of next row end, rep from * to end of ribbing, working last dc into edge of last row end. 45 [47:49] 1ch sps.
2nd row Using A, ch 4 to count as first dc and 1ch sp, 1dc into next dc, * ch 1, 1dc into next dc, rep from * to end of row working last dc into 3rd of first 4 turning ch and joining in C at end of row, turn.
3rd row Using C, ch 1 to count as first sc, *1sc into next 1ch sp, 1sc into next dc, rep from * to end of row, working last sc into 3rd of 4 turning ch and changing to A at end of row, turn.
4th row Using A, ch 4 to count as first dc and 1ch sp, skip next sc, 1dc into next sc, *ch 1, skip one sc, 1dc into next sc, rep from * to end of row, working last dc into turning ch, turn.
5th-16th rows Work as for 2nd row, working in color sequence of 1 row A, 1 row B, 1 row A, 2 rows B, 1 row A, 2 rows B, 1 row A, 1 row B, 2 rows A.
17th row Using D, as third row.
4th-17th rows These form pat and are rep throughout, noting that C and D are used alternately when sc row is reached. Cont working in pat and color sequence until 31 [33:35] rows in all

have been worked from waistband. Fasten off.
Shape armholes
Next row With RS facing, rejoin correct color in sequence to 9th [11th:11th] st from side edge, pat to last 8 [10:10] sts, turn and leave rem sts unworked. Cont working in pat and color sequence on rem sts for 22 [23:24] rows. Fasten off.

Right front
Using smaller hook and A, make 23ch. Work 45 [47:49] rows ribbing as for back waistband.
Beg pat
Using larger hook and A, turn ribbing and work in pat as for back across edge of ribbing. 22 [23:24] 1ch sps. Cont in pat as for back until 31 [33:35] rows have been worked from waistband.
Shape armholes
Next row Pat to last 8 [10:10] sts, turn and leave rem sts unworked. Cont in pat on these sts for 14 rows. Fasten off.
Shape neck
Next row With RS facing, rejoin correct color to 10th [10th:12th] st at front edge, counting each dc and each 1ch sp as one st, pat to end. Cont in pat on rem sts, work 7 [8:9] rows from beg of neck shaping. Fasten off securely.

Left front
Work as for right front, reversing armhole and neck shaping.

Sleeves
Using smaller hook and A, make 23ch. Work in ribbing as for back for 45 [49:53] rows.
Beg pat
Turn ribbing sideways. Using larger hook cont working along side edge of ribbing.

SPECIAL TECHNIQUE

Weaving a filet crochet fabric

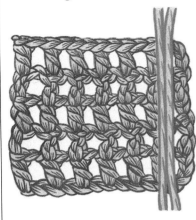

1 *The basic fabric used for the cardigan is a 1 double, 1 chain mesh. To begin the weaving, cut lengths of yarn equivalent to the length of the background, plus at least 4in. You can use two or more strands together, depending on the thickness of the yarn.*

2 *Thread the strands onto a large tapestry needle, making sure that they are exactly the same length. Pull yarn through the middle of the foundation chain, leaving a short end. Take the yarn under the first bar of the background mesh, then weave the strands up the vertical line of spaces, weaving in and out of each space. Do not pull the strands too tightly. If the yarn is too thick for a needle, use a crochet hook to pull the strands through.*

Next row Using A, ch 4 to count as first dc and 1ch sp, 1dc into first row end, ch 1, (1dc into next row end, ch 1) twice, skip next row end, * 1dc into next row end, ch 1, skip next row end, rep from * to last 3 row ends, (1dc into next row end, ch 1) twice, 1dc into last row end, turn. 51 [57:59] sts. (25 [27:29] 1ch sps.) Cont in st and color pat starting at 4th row of color sequence as for back, using C for first sc stripe and inc one sp at each end of 4th and every following 4th row by working (1dc, ch 1) into first sp at beg of row and last sp at end of row, until there are 83 [87:91] sts. (41 [43:45] 1ch sps.) Cont in pat until 45 [47:49] rows have been worked from cuff. Fasten off.

Neckband

Using smaller hook and A, make 8ch. Work in ribbing as for back until strip measures 13 [13¾:14½]in. Fasten off.

To work the weaving

Weave each piece separately before sewing pieces tog. Work weaving vertically with the yarn used double, working 2 lines of weaving into each ch sp. Measure length of yarn needed for each vertical row, adding 8in, then cut several lengths at once. When working weaving, leave a loop of 2¼in at edge so that fabric and checks can be adjusted once weaving has been completed.

Weaving sleeves

Using C, start at cuff and center 1ch sp of sleeve. Weave in and out of each 1ch sp to top of sleeve. Work another line of weaving into same 1ch sp. (2 lines of weaving up center of sleeve.) Cont working out to each side of center, working 2 lines of weaving into each vertical row of 1ch sps and using colors as follows: 2 lines A, 1 line B, 1 line A, 2 lines B, 1 line A, 1 line B, 2 lines A, 1 line D, cont weaving to side of sleeve on each side of center stripe in this way, noting that you should alternate C and D when they occur in weaving as in crochet stripe pat.

Weaving back and fronts

Join shoulder seams. Beg at center sp at center of back and using C double work 2 lines weaving from ribbing to top of back. Using yarn double throughout and working 2 lines of weaving up each vertical row of 1ch sps, work weaving in color sequence as given for sleeve, working from center back to each side and working back and fronts tog by taking weaving across shoulder seam and down fronts to waistband.

3 *To secure the yarn at the top, take it through the center of the top chain. Leave a short end, as at the bottom.*

4 *On the next row, alternate the weaving so that the yarn is taken over the first bar of the background fabric. Work the lines of weaving alternately across the mesh fabric until all the spaces have been filled. If necessary, adjust weaving by pulling gently at the top or bottom so that the fabric lies smoothly.*

To finish

Block garment to size, then press lightly if appropriate for yarn used. Darn all loose ends to WS. Set in sleeves along straight edge. Join sleeve and side seams, working from cuff, up sleeve, along bodice to waistband. Sew neckband in place.

Button band

Using smaller hook and A, work as for neck edging until strip is long enough to fit from neck to hem, slightly stretched. Sew to left front.

Buttonhole band

Mark positions for 8 buttons on button band, the first $\frac{3}{4}$ in from beg, another $\frac{5}{8}$ in from the top, and the rest evenly spaced between. Work buttonhole band as for button band, making buttonholes as markers are reached as follows:

Next row Ch 1, 1sc into back loop of next st, ch 3, skip next 3 sts, 1sc into back loop of each st to end, turn.

Next row Work in sc, working into back loop of each st and working 1sc into each ch made in previous row, turn. Sew buttonhole band to right front. Sew on buttons to correspond with buttonholes.

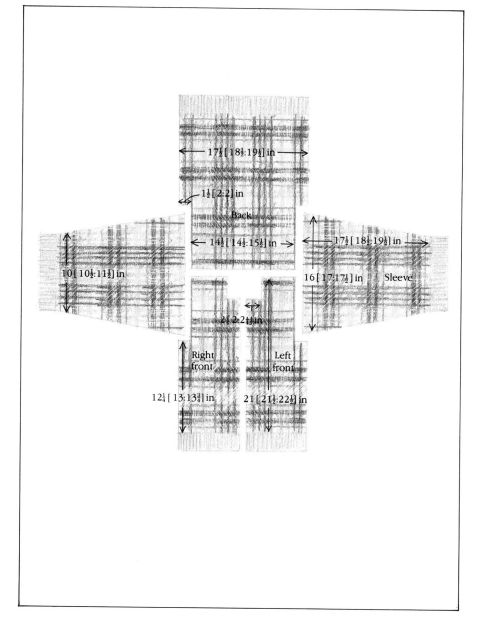

ARAN-STYLE CARDIGAN

Inspired by knitted Aran garments, this cardigan is a classic style you'll enjoy wearing for years.

Sizes
Misses' size 38 [woman's size 42]
Length from shoulder *25 [26] in*
Sleeve seam *18 in*

Note: *Instructions for the larger size are in brackets []; where there is only one set of figures it applies to both sizes.*

Materials
37 [40] oz of a fisherman yarn
Size H crochet hook
Size I crochet hook
6 buttons

Gauge
12 sts and 16 rows to 4 in over pat worked on size I hook

To save time, take time to check gauge.

Back
Using smaller hook make 7 ch for waistband.
1st row 1 sc into 3rd ch from hook, 1 sc into each ch to end. Turn. 6 sc.
2nd row Ch 1, * 1 sc into horizontal loop below next sc, rep from * to end. Turn.
Rep 2nd row 59 [65] more times. 61 [67] rows. Do not break off yarn. Change to larger hook, turn and work along long edge of waistband: ch 1, 1 sc into each row end. Turn. 61 [67] sts.
Next row (WS) Ch 1, (1 hdc into next sc, sl st into next sc) 4 [5] times, 1 sc into each of next 10 sc, sl st into next sc, (1 hdc into next sc, sl st into next sc) 11 [12] times, 1 sc into each of next 10 sc, sl st into next sc, (1 hdc into next sc, sl st into next sc) 4 [5] times. Turn.
Next row Ch 2, (sl st into hdc, 1 hdc into sl st) 4 [5] times, 1 sc into each of next 10 sc, 1 hdc into next sl st, (sl st into hdc, 1 hdc into sl st) 11 [12] times, 1 sc into each of next 10 sc, 1 hdc into next sl st, (sl st into hdc, 1 hdc into sl st) 4 [5] times. Turn.
Next row Ch 1, (1 hdc into sl st, sl st into hdc) 4 [5] times, 1 sc into each of next 10 sc, sl st into hdc, (1 hdc into sl st, sl st into hdc) 11 [12] times, 1 sc into each of next 10 sc, sl st, into hdc, (1 hdc into sl st, sl st into hdc) 4 [5] times. Turn.
Rep last 2 rows until work measures 16 in, ending with a WS row.
Shape armholes
Next row Sl st over first 5 sts, ch 2, pat to last 4 sts, turn.
Keeping pat correct, dec one st at each end of next 3 [4] rows. 47 [51] sts.
Work even until armholes measure 8 [9] in, ending with a WS row.
Shape neck and shoulders
Next row Sl st over first 6 sts, ch 1, pat over next 10 [11] sts, turn. Complete this side first.
Next row Sl st over first 3 sts, ch 1, pat over next 3 [4] sts, turn. 4 [5] sts. Fasten off. Return to where work was left, skip first 15 [17] sts, using larger hook rejoin yarn into next st, ch 1, pat to last 5 sts, turn.
Next row Sl st over first 6 sts, ch 1, pat to last 2 sts, turn. 4 [5] sts. Fasten off.

Left front
Using smaller hook make 7 ch for waistband and work first 2 rows as for back. 6 sts.
Rep 2nd row 27 [30] more times. 29 [32] rows.
Change to larger hook, turn and work along top of waistband as for back. 29 [32] sts. * *.
Next row (WS) Ch 2, [ch 1, 1 hdc into next sc], sl st into next sc, (1 hdc into next sc, sl st into next sc) 4 times, 1 sc into each of next 10 sc, sl st into next sc, (1 hdc into next sc, sl st into next sc) 4 [5] times. Turn.
Cont in pat as set until work measures same as back to underarm, ending at armhole edge.
Shape armhole and front edge
Next row Sl st over first 5 sts, ch 2, pat to last st, turn.
Dec one st at armhole edge on next 3 [4] rows and *at the same time* cont to dec one st at front edge on every 4th row 7 [8] more times. 14 [15] sts.
Work even until armhole measures same as back to shoulder, ending at armhole edge.
Shape shoulder
Next row Sl st over first 6 sts, ch 1, pat to end. Turn.
Next row Pat to last 5 sts, turn. 4 [5] sts. Fasten off.

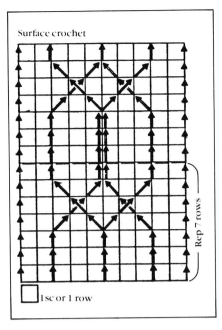

Surface crochet

Rep 7 rows

☐ 1sc or 1 row

Right front

Work as for left front to * *
Next row (WS) Ch 1, (1hdc into next sc, sl st into next sc) 4 [5] times, 1sc into each of next 10sc, sl st into next sc, (1hdc into next sc, sl st into next sc) 4 [5] times, 1hdc into last st on first size only. Turn.
Complete to match left front, reversing all shaping.

Sleeves

Using smaller hook make 13ch. Work first 2 rows as instructed for back. 12 sts.
Rep 2nd row 25 [29] more times. 27 [31] rows.
Change to larger hook and work along top edge of cuff as for back inc one st in center. 28 [32] sts.
Next row (WS) Ch 1, (1hdc into next sc, sl st into next sc) 4 [5] times, 1sc into each of next 10sc, sl st into next sc, (1hdc into next sc, sl st into next sc) 4 [5] times. Turn.
Cont in pat as set, inc one st at each end of 7th and every following 6th row, working extras sts into edge pat, until there are 44 [48] sts. Work even until sleeve measures 18in, ending with a WS row.

Shape top

Next row Sl st over first 5 sts, ch 2, pat to last 4 sts, turn.
Dec one st at each end of next and following 5 [6] alternate rows, then at each end of next 8 rows. 8 [10] sts.
Fasten off.

Front band

Using smaller hook make 7ch and work first 2 rows as for back. Rep 2nd row twice more. 6 sts.
5th row (buttonhole row) Ch 1, 1sc, ch 2, skip 2sc, 1sc into last 2sc. Turn.
6th row Ch 1, 1sc, 2sc into 2ch sp, 1sc into last 2sc. Turn.
Cont in pat, making 5 more buttonholes at intervals of 2½in, then cont until band is long enough to reach up front edge, around back neck and down other front. Fasten off.

To finish

Press or block, as appropriate.
Join shoulder seams.
Using smaller hook work surface slip stitch (see page 19) over each panel of 10sc as shown in diagram.
Join side and sleeve seams. Set in sleeves. Sew on front band. Press seams. Sew on buttons.

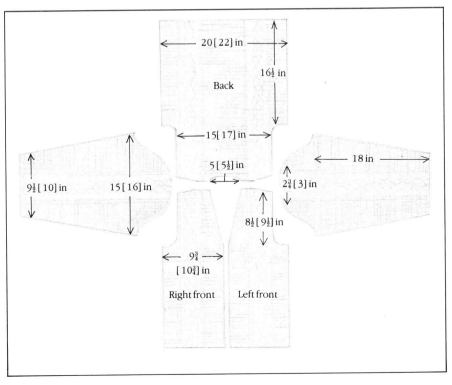

SHAWL-COLLARED JACKET

This stylish edge-to-edge jacket has turn-back cuffs and an unusual shawl collar.

Sizes

Misses' sizes 10 [12:14]
Length from shoulder 27 [28:28½] in
Sleeve seam (with cuff turned back) 17 in

Note Instructions for larger sizes are in brackets [ ]; where there is only one set of figures it applies to all sizes.

Materials

48 [51:53] oz of a bulky yarn
Polyester batting for shoulder pads
¼ yd of lining fabric for pockets
Size I crochet hook
Size K crochet hook

Gauge

15 sts and 15 rows to 4 in over pat worked on size K hook

To save time, take time to check gauge.

Back pocket linings

Using smaller hook, make 19 [23:23] ch.
Base row 1sc into 2nd ch from hook, 1sc into each ch to end. Turn. 18 [22:22] sts.
Next row Ch 1 to count as first sc, skip first st, 1sc into each st to end. Turn.
Rep last row until work measures 4¾in. Fasten off and break yarn. Work a 2nd pocket lining in the same way. *Do not break yarn.*

Back

Using larger hook and new ball of yarn, make 73 [77:83] ch.
Base row (WS) 1sc into 2nd ch from hook, 1sc into each ch to end. Turn. 72 [76:82] sts.
Pat row Inserting hook from front to back work 1sc around stem of first 0 [2:2] sts – raised sc formed –, *1sc into each of next 3 sts, 1 raised sc into each of next 3 sts, rep from * to last 0 [2:2] sts, 1sc into each of last 0 [2:2] sts. Turn.
Rep pat row until work measures 8in, ending with a WS row.
Fasten off and place a marker at the end of last row.
Join in back pocket linings
Next row Using larger hook and yarn left on 2nd pocket lining and beg at first st of 2nd pocket lining, work (1sc into each of first 3 sts, 1 raised sc into each of next 3 sts) 3 times, (1sc into each of next 3 sts, 1 raised sc into next st) 0 [1:1] time, pat across 72 [76:82] sts of back (with RS facing), (1 raised sc into first st of other pocket lining, 1sc into each of next 3 sts) 0 [1:1] time, (1sc into each of next 3 sts, 1 raised sc into each of next 3 sts) 3 times. Turn. 108 [120:126] sts.
Pat one row.
Shape pocket linings
Keeping pat correct, dec one st at each end of next and every following 5 [1:1] alternate row. 96 [116:122] sts.
Dec one st at each end of next 6 [14:14] rows, ending with a RS row. 84 [88:94] sts.
Next row Sl st across first 7 sts, pat to last 6 sts, turn. 72 [76:82] sts.
Place a marker at each end of last row.
Cont in pat until work measures 19in, ending with a WS row.

Shape armholes
Next row Keeping pat correct, sl st across first 4 sts, pat to last 3 sts, turn. 66 [70:76] sts.
Next row Sl st across first 3 sts, pat to last 2 sts, turn. 62 [66:72] sts. Dec one st at each end of next 3 [4:5] rows. 56 [58:62] sts.
Work even in pat until armhole measures 8¼ [9:9½] in, ending with a WS row.
Shape shoulders
Next 2 rows Sl st across first 6 [6:7] sts, pat to last 5 [5:6] sts, turn.
Next row Sl st across first 6 [7:7] sts, pat to last 5 [6:6] sts. 26 sts. Fasten off.

Front pocket linings

Using back pocket linings as a guide and allowing ¾in for turning under on all edges, cut out 2 front pocket linings from lining fabric.

Left front

Using larger hook, make 37 [39:43] ch. Work base row as for back. 36 [38:42] sts.
1st row (RS) 1 raised sc into each of first 0 [2:2] sts, * 1sc into each of next 3 sts, 1 raised sc into each of next 3 sts, rep from * to last 0 [0:4] sts, (1sc into each of next 3 sts, 1 raised sc into last st) 0 [0:1] time. Turn.
2nd row (1sc into first st, 1 raised sc into each of next 3 sts) 0 [0:1] time, * 1sc into each of next 3 sts, 1 raised sc into each of next 3 sts, rep from * to last 0 [2:2] sts, 1sc into last 0 [2:2] sts. Turn.
Last 2 rows form left-front pat. Rep left-front pat until work matches back to first marker, ending with a WS row.
Make pocket extension
Next row Ch 7, 1sc into 2nd ch from hook, 1sc into each of next 5ch, pat to end. 42 [44:48] sts.
Cont in left-front pat until work matches back to 2nd marker, ending with a RS row.
Next row Pat to last 6 sts, turn. 36 [38:42] sts.
Cont in left-front pat until 10 rows less than on back have been worked to beg of armhole shaping, ending with a WS row.
Shape collar
Keeping pat correct, inc one st at front

edge on next and every following 4 alternate rows. 41 [43:47] sts.
Pat one row.

Shape armhole
Next row Sl st across first 4 sts, pat to last st, inc 1 into last st. Turn.
Next row Pat to last 2 sts, turn. 37 [39:43] sts.
Keeping pat correct, dec one st at armhole edge on next 3 [4:5] rows and *at the same time* cont to shape collar by inc one st at front edge on every following 4th row from last inc 4 [4:5] times. 38 [39:43] sts.
Pat 5 rows.
Inc one st at front edge on next and following 6th row. 40 [41:45] sts.
Work even in left-front pat until work matches back to beg of shoulder shaping, ending with a WS row.

Shape shoulder
Next row Sl st across first 6 [6:7] sts, pat to end. 35 [35:39] sts.
Next row Pat to last 5 [5:6] sts, turn. 30 [29:33] sts.
Next row Sl st across first 7 sts, pat to end. 24 [25:27] sts.

Collar extension
Work 14 more rows in left-front pat.
Fasten off.

Right front
Using larger hook, make 6ch for pocket extension.
Fasten off.
Using larger hook, make 37 [39:43] ch. Work base row as for back. 36 [38:42] sts.
1st row (RS) (1 raised sc into first st, 1sc into each of next 3 sts) 0 [0:1] time, * 1 raised sc into each of next 3 sts, 1sc into each of next 3 sts, rep from * to last 0 [2:2] sts, 1 raised sc into each of last 0 [2:2] sts. Turn.
2nd row 1sc into first 0 [2:2] sts, * 1 raised sc into each of next 3 sts, 1sc into each of next 3 sts, rep from * to last 0 [0:4] sts, (1 raised sc into each of next 3 sts, 1sc into last st) 0 [0:1] time. Turn.
Last 2 rows form right-front pat. Rep right-front pat until work matches back to first marker, ending with a WS row.

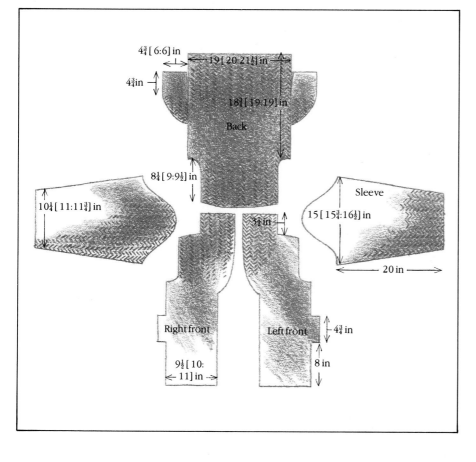

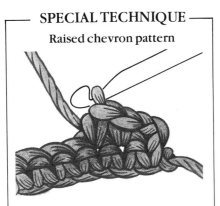

1 *The reversible pattern on the jacket shown here is formed by working around the stems of groups of single crochet. Begin with a base row of single crochet. If working the first size of the jacket, begin the next row with one single crochet worked into each of the first three stitches, beginning with one chain. (The number of stitches to be worked for larger sizes is specified in the pattern.)*

2 *Insert the hook from front to back and from right to left around the stem of the next stitch and work one single crochet. Repeat twice more to form a ridge of raised single crochet on the back of the work. On following rows work raised single crochet of the last row and vice versa.*

3 *When a row begins with raised single crochet, do not work a turning chain to count as the first stitch as usual; instead work a raised single crochet around the stem of the first stitch. When a row begins with single crochet, work one chain to count as the first stitch.*

Outer edging

With RS facing and using smaller hook, beg at beg of collar shaping on right front and work a row of sc and then a row of crab st (sc worked from left to right) around front and lower edges of jacket to beg of collar shaping on left front. Fasten off.

With WS facing (i.e. RS of collar), beg at start of collar shaping on right front and work a row each of sc and crab st along edge of collar to beg of shaping on left front. Fasten off.

Sleeve edging

With WS facing, work a row each of sc and crab st along lower edge of sleeves. Fasten off.

Press seams very lightly.

Shoulder pads (make 2)

Join 2 sections of shoulder pads, leaving one straight edge open. Insert batting, grading thickness from a thin layer at the shaped edge to a thicker layer at flat edge.

Close open edge.

Sew shoulder pads in place.

Fold 3in of sleeves to RS and catch loosely in place at sleeve seam.

Make pocket extension

Next row Pat to end, keeping pat correct work across 6ch formed at beg. Turn. 42 [44:48] sts. Cont in pat and complete to correspond with left front, reversing all shaping.

Sleeves (alike)

Using larger hook, make 41 [43:47] ch and work base row (WS) as for back. 40 [42:46] sts.

Pat row 1 raised sc into first 2 [0:2] sts, * 1sc into each of next 3 sts, 1 raised sc into each of next 3 sts, rep from * to last 2 [0:2] sts, 1sc into each of last 2 [0:2] sts. Turn.

Rep pat row until work measures 5½in, ending with a WS row.

Shape sleeve

Keeping pat correct, inc one st at each end of next and every following 6th row until there are 58 [60:64] sts. Work even in pat until work measures 20in, ending with a WS row.

Shape top

Next row Sl st across first 4 sts, pat to last 3 sts, turn. 52 [54:58] sts.

Next row Sl st across first 3 sts, pat to last 2 sts, turn. 48 [50:54] sts.

Keeping pat correct, dec one st at each end of next and every following 7 [8:8] alternate rows. 32 [32:36] sts.

Keeping pat correct, dec one st at each end of next 6 [6:8] rows. 20 sts.

Next 2 rows Sl st across first 4 sts, pat to last 3 sts, turn.

Fasten off.

Shoulder pads (make 4)

Using smaller hook, make 31ch and work base row as for back pocket linings. 30 sts.

Work 3 rows in sc.

Shape top

Next row Ch 1, skip first 2 sts, 1sc into each st to last 2 sts, skip next st, 1sc into last st. Turn. 28 sts.

Next row Work in sc.

Rep last 2 rows twice more. 24 sts.

Next row Sl st across first 3 sts, work in sc to last 2 sts, turn. 20 sts.

Next 3 rows As last row. 8 sts. Fasten off.

To finish

Block or press lightly, as appropriate for yarn used.

Using a zigzag machine st, or overcasting, finish edges of front pocket linings.

With WS facing, sew front pocket linings to front pocket extensions at side edges.

Join shoulder and sleeve seams.

Join side seams, leaving seams open between markers.

Join front and back pocket linings.

Set in sleeves.

Join collar extensions neatly at center back and sew in place around neck.

AUTUMN STRIPES

Four shades of brown have been used for this warm jacket, perfect for a cool autumn day.

Sizes

Misses' sizes 10-12 [14-16]

Length from shoulder *29 [30] in*

Sleeve seam *15¾ [16½] in*

Note *Instructions for the larger size are in brackets []; where there is only one set of figures it applies to both sizes.*

Materials

21 [23] oz of a bulky yarn in main color A (cinnamon)

8 [10] oz in contrasting color B (old gold)

6 oz in contrasting color C (pale gold)

6 [8] oz in contrasting color D (cocoa brown)

Size H crochet hook

Size K crochet hook

Gauge

18 sts and 16 rows to 6 in over seed st pat worked on size H hook.

To save time, take time to check gauge.

Back

Using smaller hook and A, make 55 [63] ch.

Base row (RS) Using A, 1sc into 2nd ch from hook, 1sc into each ch to end. Turn. 54 [62] sts.

1st row Using A, ch 1 to count as first sc, skip first st, 1sc into each st to end.

2nd and 3rd rows Using A, as first row.

4th row Using B, ch 1 to count as first sc, skip first st, 1sc into next st, insert hook into next st 2 rows below, yo and draw through a long loop, insert hook into same st of working row, yo and draw through first loop on hook, yo and draw through rem 2 loops on hook – spike st formed –, * 1sc into each of next 3 sts, spike st into next st, rep from * to last 3 sts, 1sc into each of last 3 sts. Turn.

5th row Using D, ch 1 to count as first sc, skip first st, 1sc into each of next 2 sts, (insert hook into next st, yo and draw through a loop, yo) 3 times, draw through first 5 loops on hook, yo and draw through rem 2 loops on hook – bobble formed –, *1sc into each of next 3 sts, bobble into next st, rep from * to last 2 sts, 1sc into each of last 2 sts. Turn.

6th row Using B, ch 1 to count as first sc, skip first st, * 1sc into each of next 3 sts, spike st into next st, rep from * to last st, 1sc into last st. Turn.

7th row Using D, ch 1 to count as first sc, skip first st, * bobble into next st, 1sc into each of next 3 sts, rep from * to last st, 1sc into last st. Turn.

8th-10th rows Rep 4th-6th rows once more.

11th row Using A, ch 2, skip first st, * 1sc into next st, 1dc into next st, rep from * to last st, 1sc into last st. Turn. Last row forms seed st pat.

12th-16th rows Using A, work in seed st pat.

17th row Using C, work in seed st pat.

18th, 20th, 22nd, 24th rows Using A, work in seed st pat.

19th row Using B, work in seed st pat.

21st row Using D, work in seed st pat.

23rd row Using B, work in seed st pat.

25th row Using C, work in seed st pat.

26th-32nd rows Using A, work in seed st pat.

Rep 17th-32nd rows once more, then rep 17th-27th rows once more.

Shape armholes

60th row Using A, sl st across first 5 [7] sts, ch 1 to count as first st, skip sl st at base of first ch, pat to last 4 [6] sts, turn. 46 [50] sts.

61st-64th rows Using A, work in seed st pat.

65th-73rd rows Work as for 17th-25th rows.

74th row Using A, work in seed st pat.

2nd size only

Using A, work 2 rows in seed st pat.

All sizes

75th [77th] row Using A, ch 1 to count as first sc, skip first st, 1sc into each st to end. Turn.

76th [78th] row Using B, ch 1 to count as first sc, skip first st, 1sc into each st to end. Turn.

77th [79th] row Using D, ch 1 to count as first sc, skip first st, * bobble into next st, 1sc into each of next 3 sts, rep from * to last st, 1sc into last st. Turn.

78th [80th] row Using B, ch 1 to count as first sc, skip first st, 1sc into next st, * spike st into next st, 1sc into each of next 3 sts, rep from * to end. Turn and fasten off.

Shape shoulders

Skip first 14 [16] sts and rejoin D to next st.

Next row Using D, ch 1 to count as first sc, skip first st, 1sc into each of next 0 [2] sts, bobble into next st, * 1sc into each of next 3 sts, bobble into next st, rep from * twice, 1sc into each of next 4 [2] sts, turn.

Next row Using B, ch 1 to count as first sc, skip first st, 1sc into each of next 1 [3] sts, * spike st into next st, 1sc into each of next 3 sts, rep from * twice, spike st into next st, 1sc into each of last 3 [1] sts.

Fasten off.

Left front

Using smaller hook and A, make 27 [31] ch. Work base-11th rows as for back. 26 [30] sts.

Make pocket

12th row Using A, work 6 [8] sts in seed st pat, then, working into *back* loop only of each st, pat next 16 sts, turn. 22 [24] sts.

Keeping stripe sequence correct, cont in seed st pat on these sts only until 30th row has been worked. Fasten off.

Return to 12th row and rejoin A to front loop of 7th [9th] st, working into *front* loop only of each st pat 16 sts, working into both loops of each st pat to end. Turn. 20 [22] sts. Keeping stripe sequence correct, cont in seed st pat on these sts only for 7 more rows.
20th row Sl st across first 2 sts, ch 1 to count as first sc, skip first st, work in seed st pat to end. Turn.
21st row pat to last st, skip last st, turn. Keeping stripe sequence correct, cont in seed st pat, dec 1 st at pocket edge on each row until 10 [12] sts rem. Keeping stripe sequence correct, work even in seed st pat until 30th row has been worked.
31st row Pat first 4 [6] sts, bring up other part of pocket, pat next 6 sts through both parts of pocket, pat to end. 26 [30] sts.
32nd-59th rows Work as for back.
Shape armhole
60th row Using A, sl st across first 5 [7]

sts, ch 1 to count as first sc, skip sl st at base of 1ch, pat to end. Turn. 22 [24] sts.
61st-72nd rows Work as for back.
Shape neck
73rd row Sl st across first 4 sts, ch 2, skip sl st at base of 2ch, pat to end. Turn.
74th row Pat to last 3 sts, turn. 16 [18] sts.
75th row Sl st across first 3 [3] sts, pat to end. Turn. 14 [16] sts.
Work even for 3 [5] more rows as for back. Fasten off.

Right front
Work as for left front to pocket.
Make pocket
12th row Using A, pat 4 [6] sts, working into front loop only of each st, pat next 16 sts, turn.
Keeping stripe sequence correct, cont in seed st pat on these sts only until 19th row has been worked.

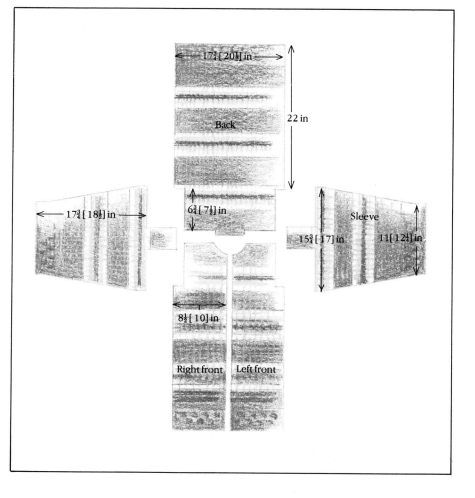

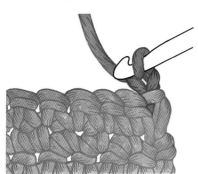

1 *Spiked stitches are used with bobbles to form the patterned bands at the lower edges and shoulders on the jacket. Work a few rows of single crochet. Change to a contrasting color and work one chain to count as the first single crochet. Skip the first stitch.*

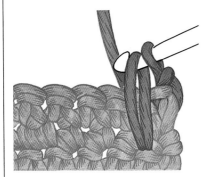

2 *Insert the hook into the next stitch two rows below. Wind the yarn around the hook and draw through a long loop, extending the yarn so that the previous rows do not curl and spoil the work.*

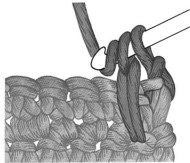

3 *Insert the hook into the same stitch of the current row, wind the yarn around the hook and draw through the first loop on the hook. Wind the yarn around the hook and draw through the remaining two loops to complete the spiked stitch.*

20th row Pat to last st, skip last st, turn.
21st row Sl st across first 2 sts, ch 1 to count as first sc, skip first st, work in seed st pat to end. Turn. Keeping stripe sequence correct, cont in seed st pat, dec 1 st at pocket edge on each row until 10 [12] sts rem.
Work even in seed st pat until 30th row has been worked. Fasten off.
Return to 12th row and rejoin A to back loop of 5th [7th] st, working into *back* loop only of each st, pat 16 sts, working into both loops of each st, pat to end. Turn. Cont in seed st pat until 30th row has been worked.
31st row Pat first 16 [18] sts, bring up other piece of pocket, pat next 6 sts through both parts of pocket, pat to end. Turn. 26 [30] sts.
Complete to match left front, reversing all shaping.

Sleeves (alike)
Using smaller hook and A, make 35 [39] ch.
Base-5th rows Work as for back. 34 [38] sts.
6th row Work as for back, inc 1 st at each end of row. Turn.
Cont as for back, inc 1 st at each end of every following 5th [4th] row until there are 46 [54] sts.
Cont in seed st pat until 43 [45] rows have been worked from beg.
Next row Work as for 75th [77th] row of back.
Next row Work as for 76th [78th] row of back.
Next row Work as for 77th [79th] row of back.
Next row Work as for 78th [80th] row of back. Fasten off and turn.

Sleeve extension
Next row Skip first 19 [23] sts and rejoin D to next st, ch 1 to count as first sc, skip first st, 1sc into each of next 3 sts, bobble into next st, 1sc into each of next 3 sts, turn.
Next row Using B, ch 1 to count as first sc, skip first st, spike st into next st, 1sc into each of next 3 sts, spike st into next st, 1sc into each of last 2 sts. Turn.
Next row Using D, ch 1 to count as first sc, skip first st, 1sc into next st, bobble into next st, 1sc into each of next 3 sts, bobble into next st, 1sc into last st. Turn.
Next row Using B, ch 1 to count as first sc, skip first st, 1sc into each of 2 sts, spike st into next st, 1sc into each of next 4 sts. Turn.
Work 18 [20] more rows in this way. Fasten off.

To finish
Block or press lightly, as appropriate for yarn used. Join side and sleeve seams, leaving 1¼in open at top of sleeve to set into armhole.
Set in the sleeves, then join the shoulder seams.
Sew sides of pockets to fronts on WS.
Front band
Using larger hook and one strand each of A, B, C and D, make a length of ch to fit around neck and down both fronts. Work 2 rows of sc into ch. Fasten off. Sew band to front and neck edges.
Cuffs (both alike)
Using larger hook and one strand each of A, B, C and D, make a length of ch to fit around lower edge of sleeve. Work 1 row of sc into ch. Fasten off. Sew cuffs to lower edges of sleeves.

RED-EDGED BEACH CARDIGAN

This cool filet crochet jacket is the perfect light wrap over swimsuit or sun top.

Back

Using A make 122 [130:138:146:154] ch.

Base row 1dc into 6th ch from hook * Ch 1, skip 1ch, 1dc into next ch, rep from * to end. Turn. 119 [127:135:143:151] sts.

1st row Ch 4 to count as first dc and 1ch sp, 1dc into next dc, *ch 1, 1dc into next dc, rep from * to end, working last dc into 4th of first 5ch. Turn.

2nd row As first row, working last dc into 3rd of first 4ch.

2nd row forms pat and is rep throughout.

Cont in pat until work measures 15in. Mark each end of last row with contrasting thread to denote armholes.

Cont in pat until work measures 23 [23½:24:24½:25] in.

Fasten off.

Left front

Using A make 62 [66:70:74:78] ch. Work base row as for back. 59 [63:67:71:75] sts.

Cont in pat as for back until front measures 2½ [2½:3:3:3] in less than back to shoulder, marking armhole as for back and ending at armhole edge.

Shape neck

Next row Pat to last 16 [18:18:20:22] sts, turn.

Next row Ch 3 to count as first dc, skip first dc and 1ch sp, 1dc into next dc, * ch 1, 1dc into next dc, rep from * to end. Turn.

Next row Pat to last 3ch, turn.

Rep last 2 rows 2 [2:3:3:3] more times. 37 [39:41:43:45] sts.

Work even until front measures same as back to shoulder.

Fasten off.

Right front

Work as for left front, noting that fabric is reversible.

Sleeves

Using A make 114 [122:130:138:146] ch. Work base row as for back. 111 [119:127:135:143] sts. Cont in pat as for back until work measures 16½ [17:17:17½:17½]in.

Fasten off.

Neck band

Join shoulder seams. Using knitting needles, A and with RS facing, pick up and K 109 [117:125:137:145] sts around neck, picking up one st from each crochet st and 2 sts from each row end.

1st row (WS) P1, * K1, P1, rep from * to end.

2nd row K1, * P1, K1, rep from * to end.

Work 3 more rows of ribbing in A, then K 1 row in B, rib 1 row in B, K1 row in A, then rib 5 rows in A. Alternatively, rib a total of 13 rows in A. Bind off in ribbing.

Lower edge

Join side seams as far as armhole markers. Using knitting needles, A and with RS facing, pick up and K 153 [167:183:197:213] sts along lower edge, picking up (one st from each of next 2 crochet sts, skip one st), ending with pick up one st from each of last 2 sts. Work in K1, P1 ribbing as for neckband.

Cuffs

Using knitting needles, A and with RS facing, pick up and K sts around cuff edge of sleeves, picking up every

Sizes

Misses' sizes 10 [12:14:16:18] Length from shoulder 24 [24½:25:25½:26]in Sleeve seam 18 [18½:18½:19:19]in

Note: *Instructions for larger sizes are in brackets [ ]; where there is only one set of figures it applies to all sizes.*

Materials

1600 [1800:1800:2000:2200:] yd (approx 13 [15:15:16:17] oz) of a size 5 pearl cotton in main color A Small amount of contrasting color B Size 0 steel crochet hook Pair of size 2 knitting needles A 24 [24:24:26:26]in open-ended zipper

Gauge

28 sts and 13 rows to 4in over pat worked on size 0 steel hook

To save time, take time to check gauge.

alternate crochet st. Work in K1, P1 ribbing as for neckband.
Then K1 row in B, rib 1 row in B, K1 row in A, rib 5 rows in A. Alternatively, rib a total of 21 rows in A. Bind off in ribbing.

Front bands
Using knitting needles, A and with RS of right front facing, beg at lower edge of ribbed waistband and pick up and K sts up front edge to top of ribbed neckband, picking up one st from each ribbed row end and 3 sts from each crochet row end. Work 3 rows K1, P1 ribbing. Bind off firmly in ribbing. Work along left front edge in same way, beg at top of ribbed neckband.

To finish
Press each piece lightly under a damp cloth with a warm iron, omitting ribbing. Join sleeve seams. Set in sleeves between markers, with underarm seam at side seam of jacket. Sew zipper to front opening from lower edge of ribbed waistband to top of neckband. Press seams.

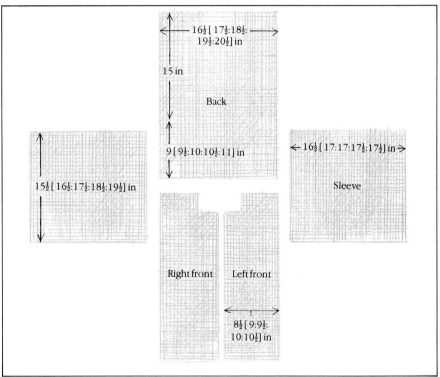

16½ [17½ : 18½ : 19½ : 20½] in

15 in

Back

9 [9½ : 10 : 10½ : 11] in

16½ [17 : 17 : 17½ : 17½] in

Sleeve

15½ [16½ : 17½ : 18½ : 19½] in

Right front   Left front

8½ [9 : 9½ : 10 : 10½] in

118

BABY'S JACKET

This simple jacket for a baby is worked all in one piece.

Sizes

B-1 [B-2]

Length from center back $8\frac{1}{2}$ [9]*in*

Sleeve seam $6\frac{3}{4}$ [7]*in*

Note *Instructions for larger size are in brackets [ ]; where there is only one set of figures it applies to both sizes.*

Materials

4 [5] oz of a sport yarn in main color A
1 [1] oz in contrasting color B
Size C crochet hook
1 button

Gauge

24 dc to 4 in worked on size C hook

To save time, take time to check gauge.

Back

Beg at lower edge. Using A, make 60 [66] ch.

Foundation row (RS) 1dc into 4th ch from hook, 1dc into each ch to end, turn. 58 [64] sts.

1st pat row Ch 1, skip 1dc, 1sc into each dc to end, working last sc into top of turning ch, turn.

2nd pat row Ch 3, skip 1sc, 1dc into each sc to end, working last dc into turning ch, turn. These 2 rows, with dc rows on RS, form the pat. Rep until work measures 5 [$5\frac{1}{2}$]in, ending after a sc row, turn.

Shape sleeves

Using a separate length of A, make 34 [36] ch, fasten off and leave aside until end of next row.

Return to main piece.

Next row Work 36 [38] ch, 1dc into 4th ch from hook, 1dc into each of next 32 [34] ch, 1dc into each sc of back, working last dc into turning ch; do not turn but work 1dc into each of 34 [36] separate ch. 126 [136] sts. Cont in pat

on all sts until work measures $8\frac{3}{4}$ [9]in at center, ending with a sc row. Mark both ends of this row (fold line) with a short piece of contrasting yarn.

Divide for fronts

Next row (RS) Ch 3, skip 1sc, 1dc into each of next 50 [54]sc, turn and work on these sts only for right front and sleeve. 51 [55] sts.

Work 4 rows pat, ending at front edge, turn.

Shape neck

Next row Ch 12 [13], 1sc into 2nd ch from hook, 1sc into each of next 10 [11]ch, 1sc into each dc to end, working last sc into top of turning ch, turn. 62 [67] sts. Work even in pat until front sleeve matches back sleeve, working the same number of rows to the marked row and ending with a dc row, at front edge; turn.

Shape sleeve

Next row Ch 1, skip 1dc, 1sc into each dc to last 34 [36]dc, turn. Cont in pat on rem 28 [31] sts until right front measures $8\frac{3}{4}$ [9]in from marked

shoulder row, ending with dc row. Fasten off.

Return to front dividing row. Skip center 24 [26] sts, join A to next st, ch 3, do not skip next st, but work 1dc into each sc to end, turn and cont in pat on these 51 [55] sts for left front and sleeve.

Work 4 rows pat, thus ending at cuff edge, turn.

Using a separate length of A, make 11 [12] ch. Fasten off and leave aside until end of next row. Return to main piece.

Next row Work in sc to end; do not turn but work 1sc into each of separate ch, turn. Cont in pat until left sleeve matches right sleeve, ending at cuff edge. Fasten off.

Shape sleeve
With WS facing, skip first 34 [36] sts, join A to next st, 1sc into each st to end, turn. Cont in pat on rem 28 [31] sts until left front matches right front. Fasten off.

To finish

Join side and sleeve seams. With RS facing, using A and beg at lower edge of right front, work 1 row sc evenly up front edge, around neck and down left front edge, working a multiple of 3 sts plus 1. With RS facing, join B to first st, ch 1, 1sc into each st to end, turn. Ch 1, (ch 2, skip 2sc, 1sc into next sc) to end, turn. Ch 1, (3dc into 2ch sp, 1sc into next sc) to end. Fasten off. Join A to first cuff st and work 1 row sc around cuff edge and join to first st with a sl st, making this round a multiple of 3 sts. Fasten off A and join in B. Ch 1, 1sc into each sc to end, join with a sl st to first sc, 1sc, (ch 2, skip 2 sts, 1sc into next st) to end, ending with a sl st into first st.

1sc, (3dc into next 2ch sp, 1sc into next sc) to end, joining with a sl st as before.
Fasten off.

Press or block, as appropriate. Using 2 strands of B tog, work 18in ch for each cuff. Fasten off. Insert tie through ch sps of cuff borders to tie. Sew button to neck edge; use top 2 ch sp as buttonhole.

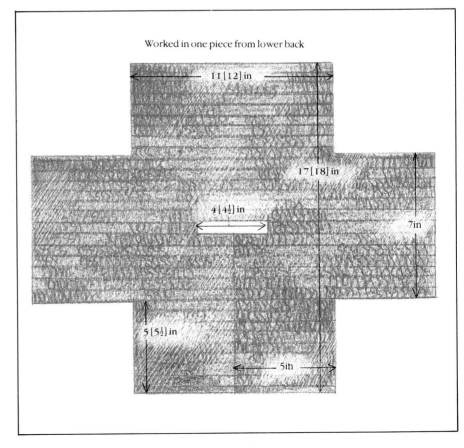

Worked in one piece from lower back

11 [12] in

17 [18] in

4 [4½] in

7 in

5 [5½] in

5 in

BABY'S SWEATER AND BLANKET

A sweater and matching blanket, worked in bold navy and white checks, make a smart outfit for a baby.

Blanket

Using size H hook and A, make 90ch.
Base row (WS) 1sc into 2nd ch from hook, 1sc into each ch to end. Turn. 89sc.
1st row Using B, ch 1, 1sc into first sc, *(yo, insert hook from front of work, from right to left around stem of next sc and work 1dc – 1dc front worked –, 1sc into next sc) 4 times, 1sc into each of next 8sc, rep from * to end, omitting 8sc at end of last rep. Turn.
2nd row Using B, ch 1, 1sc into first sc, 1sc into each dc and sc to end. Turn.
3rd row Using A, ch 1, 1sc into first sc, * (skip next sc of last row, 1dc front around stem of next dc of row before last, 1sc into next sc of last row) 4 times, 1sc into each of next 8sc, rep from * to end, omitting 8sc at end of last rep. Turn.
4th row Using A, as 2nd row.
5th row Using B, as 3rd row.
6th-10th rows Rep 2nd-5th rows once, then 2nd row again.
11th row Using A, ch 1, 1sc into first sc, 1sc into each of next 8sc, *(skip next sc to last row and work 1dc front around stem of corresponding sc of last A row, 1sc into next sc of last row) 4 times, 1sc into each of next 8sc, rep from * to end. Turn.
12th row Using A, as 2nd row.
13th row Using B, ch 1, 1sc into first sc, 1sc into each of next 8sc, * (skip next sc of last row and work 1dc front around stem of next dc of row before last, 1sc into next sc of last row) 4 times, 1sc into each of next 8sc, rep from * to end. Turn.
14th row As 2nd row.
15th row Using A, as 13th row.
16th-20th rows Rep 12th – 15th rows once, then 12th row again.
21st row Using B, ch 1, 1sc into first sc, * (skip next sc of last row, 1dc front around stem of corresponding sc of last B row, 1sc into next sc of last row) 4 times, 1sc into each of next 8sc, rep from * to end, omitting 8sc at end of last rep. Turn. Rep 2nd-21st rows 5 times, then 2nd-10th rows again.
Fasten off.

Edging

1st round With RS facing, join A to corner of long side at end of base row, work sc evenly into row-ends to next corner, 1sc into each st to next corner, work sc evenly into row-ends to next corner.
2nd round Working into other side of foundation ch, work 2sc into first ch, 1sc into each ch to last ch, 2sc into last ch, (2sc into first sc of next side, 1sc into each sc to last sc before corner, 2sc into next sc) 3 times sl st to first sc.
Fasten off.

Sweater
Front

Using size F hook and A, make 43ch.
Base row 1dc into 4th ch from hook, 1dc into each ch to end. Turn. 41 sts.
1st row (RS) Ch 2, skip first dc, (yo, insert hook from front of work, from right to left around stem of next dc and work 1dc – 1dc front worked –, yo, insert hook from back of work, from right to left around stem of next dc and work 1dc – 1dc back worked –) to end, working last dc around stem of turning ch. Turn.
2nd row Ch 2, skip first dc, (1dc back around stem of next dc, 1dc front around stem of next dc) to end, working last dc around stem of turning ch. Turn.
Rep first and 2nd rows once more, then first row again. Change to size G hook.
Next row Ch 1, 1sc into first st, 1sc into each st to end, working last sc into top of turning ch. Turn**. Work first-21st rows of blanket, then 2nd-19th rows again. Cont with A only. Change to size F hook.
Buttonhole row Ch 1, 1sc into first sc, 1sc into each of next 2sc, (ch 1, skip next sc, 1sc into each of next 4sc) twice, ch 1, skip next sc, 1sc into each of next 13sc, (ch 1, skip next sc, 1sc into each of next 4sc) twice, ch 1, skip next sc, 1sc into each of last 3sc. Turn.
Next row Ch 1, 1sc into first sc, 1sc into each st to end.
Fasten off.

Back

Work as for front to **. Cont in pat:
1st row Using B, ch 1, 1sc into first sc, 1sc into each of next 8sc, (1dc front around stem of next sc, 1sc into next sc) 4 times, 1sc into each of next 8sc)

twice. Turn.
2nd row As 2nd row of blanket.
3rd row As 15th row of blanket.
4th row As 4th row of blanket.
5th row As 13th row of blanket.
6th-10th rows Rep 2nd-5th rows once, then 2nd row again.
11th row Using A, ch 1, 1sc into first sc, * (skip next sc of last row, 1dc front around stem of corresponding sc of last A row, 1sc into next sc of last row) 4 times, 1sc into each of next 8sc, rep from * twice, omitting 8sc at end of last rep. Turn.
12th row As 4th row of blanket.
13th row As 5th row of blanket.
14th row As 2nd row of blanket.
15th row As 3rd row of blanket.
16th-20th rows Rep 12th-15th rows once, then 12th row again.
21st row Using B, ch 1, 1sc into first sc, 1sc into each of next 8sc, * (skip next sc of last row and work 1dc front around stem of corresponding sc of last B row, 1sc into next sc of last row) 4 times, 1sc into each of next 8sc, rep from * to end. Turn. Rep 2nd-21st rows once, then 2nd-10th rows again.
Front extensions
Next row Pat across 13 sts, turn. Keeping pat correct, work 9 more rows on these 13 sts.
Change to size F hook and using A work 2 rows of sc.
Fasten off.
2nd side
Next row With RS facing and using size G hook, skip center 15 sts for back neck and rejoin A to next st. Keeping pat correct, work 10 rows on these 13 sts.
Change to size F hook and using A work 2 rows of sc.
Fasten off.

Sleeves
Using size F hook and A, make 25ch. Work as for front to ** on 23 sts. Cont in sc in stripes of 2 rows B and 2 rows A, inc 1 sc at each end of 4th row and every following 6th row until there are 31sc. Work even until sleeve measures 8in, ending after a 2-row stripe.
Fasten off.

Neck edging
1st row With RS of back facing, using

size F hook and A, work 9sc evenly down row-ends of inner edge of first front extension, work 1sc into each sc across back neck and 9sc evenly up row-ends of second front extension. Turn.
2nd row Ch 1, 1sc into first sc, 1sc into each of next 7sc, skip next 2sc, 1sc into each of next 13sc, skip next 2sc, 1sc into each of last 8sc.
Fasten off.

To finish
With side edges even, lap last 2 rows of front over last 2 rows of front extensions on back. Catch-stitch row-ends neatly at side edges. Sew buttons to front extensions to correspond with buttonholes. With center of sleeve top even with first row of front extensions, sew in sleeves. Join side and sleeve seams with invisible seams.

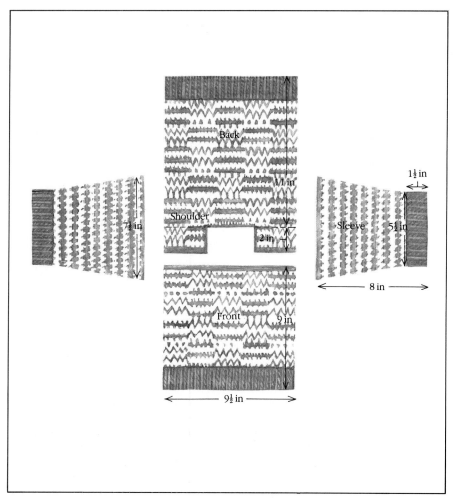

COAT OF MANY COLORS

Make this brightly-striped, reversible quilted jacket in an assortment of soft or bright colors, using one of the colors for the terry cloth lining.

Size
B1-2
Length from shoulder *10¼in*
Sleeve seam 5¾in

Materials
2oz of knitting worsted-weight yarn in main color A
1oz in each of seven contrasting colors: B, C, D, E, F, G and H (you can mix varieties of yarn, provided they are all of approximately the same weight)

Size E crochet hook
Size 4 steel crochet hook
1yd of stretch terry cloth
⅓ yd of medium weight polyester batting
Matching sewing thread

Gauge
18sc and 22 rows to 4in worked on size E hook.

To save time, take time to check gauge.

Note *Jacket is worked sideways in one piece, starting at left cuff.*

First sleeve (started at cuff)
Using size E hook and A, make 51ch.
1st row 1sc into 2nd ch from hook, 1sc into each ch to end, turn. 50sc. Cont working in sc throughout. Work 7 more rows A, changing to B at end of last row. Cont in stripe pat, working 3 rows B, 4 rows C, 1 row D, 7 rows E, 1 row F, 8 rows A, 1 row G.
Shape sleeve
Next row Using G, ch 1, 2sc into first st, sc to last st, 3sc into last st, turn. (2sc inc at each end of row.) 54sc. Work 1 row G, changing to H at row end.
Next row Using H, ch 1, 2sc into first st, 1sc into each sc to last st, 3sc into last st, turn. 58sc.
Fasten off.

Main body
Using D, make 20ch for back; with RS facing, work 1sc into each sc across sleeve, ch 21 for left front, turn.
Next row Using D, 1sc into 2nd ch from hook, 1sc into each of next 19ch, 1sc into each of next 58sc across sleeve, 1sc into each ch to end, turn. 98sc.
Work 1 more row in D on these sts. Cont in stripe pat on these sts working 2 rows E, 1 row F, 5 rows A, 8 rows B, 3 rows C, 1 row H and 3 rows C, changing to A at end of last row.
Next row Using A, ch 1, 1sc into each of next 44 sts, turn and leave next 8sts for neck edge, placing marker at each end to mark neck opening, then leave rem 45 sts for front.

Back
Cont working in stripe pat on rem sts for back, working 5 more rows A, 6 rows D, 2 rows B, 4 rows H, 7 rows E, 1 row F and 2 rows G.

Right front and neck edge
Next row Using G, pat across 45 sts for back, make 54ch for neck edge and right front, placing markers at each end of first 8ch for neck opening; turn.
Next row Using G, 1sc into 2nd ch from hook, 1sc into next 52ch, 1sc into each sc to end of back, turn. 98sc. Work 4 more rows G. Cont in stripe pat on all sts for right front and back, working 8 rows A, 5 rows C, 3 rows D, 1 row F, 3 rows B, 1 row E. Fasten off.

Second sleeve
With RS of body facing, skip first 20 sts, rejoin E to next sc.
Next row Using E, ch 1 to count as first sc, 1sc into each of next 57sc, turn and leave rem 20sc unworked. 58sc.
Shape sleeve
Next row Using E, ch 1, skip next 2sts, 1sc into each sc to last 2sc, turn and leave rem sts unworked. 54sc. Work 1 row E without shaping, then work 1 row E dec 2 sts at each end of row as before. 50sc. Cont in stripe pat on these sts working 5 rows G, 4 rows H, 8 rows D, 1 row C, 5 rows F and 8 rows A. Fasten off.

Left front
Using F and with WS facing, rejoin yarn at hem of left front. Work in pat across first 45sc, to neck edge. Turn and work one more row F on these sts. Cont in stripe pat on these 45 sts for left front working 4 rows G, 4 rows E and 4 rows A. Fasten off.

Right front
With RS of front facing, rejoin A to hem of right front and work as for left front, working 3 rows A and 11 rows H. Fasten off.

To finish

Lay crochet flat, WS down, on WS of terry cloth. Pin all around without stretching. Cut out terry cloth leaving 1in seam allowance all around.

Place crochet on batting and pin, then cut out batting in same way, again allowing 1in margin.

Place three layers tog with WS of crochet and terry cloth facing inside and batting in between them.

Quilting

With RS of crochet facing upward, pin all three layers tog, working from center outward and placing pins parallel to work along edges of stripes. Turn work over and make sure that terry cloth has not become stretched. Smooth out any creases and pin again if necessary.

Work quilting by machine, using a medium length straight stitch, with thread matching terry cloth in the bobbin and appropriate colors in the needle. Stitch along stripes, starting and finishing $\frac{1}{2}$in in from edge each time and keeping work flat without pulling or stretching it. Alternatively, quilt by hand, using short running stitches.

Trim batting to measure $\frac{3}{8}$ in less than crochet all around. Turn terry cloth seam allowance inside between batting and crochet; trim off excess fabric to prevent bulk and facilitate working crochet edging. Pin in place all around.

Edging

Using steel hook and A, and with terry cloth side of right front facing, work sc evenly down right front, working through terry cloth and crochet, 3sc into corner, sc up side and sleeve seam, 3sc into corner, sc around cuff, 3sc into corner, sc across hem, 3sc into corner, cont to work around other side of sleeve and side seam. Cont all around jacket in same way, making sure that sc are not worked too closely tog to prevent uneven, stretched edging. Starting at hem, join side and sleeve seam with 1 row sc. Work other side to match. Steam press lightly.

Ties

Using A and with RS of front facing, rejoin yarn at left front neck edge. Using smaller hook make 50ch, turn and work 1sc into 2nd ch from hook, 1sc into each ch to end, join with a sl st to left front. Fasten off. Work 2 more ties in same way, spacing them evenly down left front. Work 3 ties to correspond on right front.

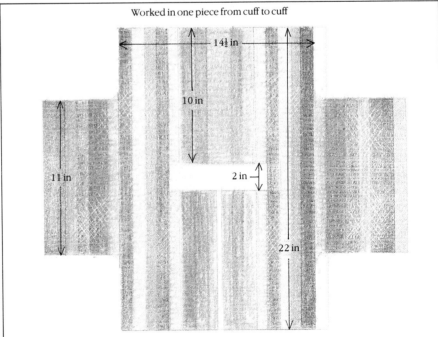

Worked in one piece from cuff to cuff

14½ in

10 in

11 in

2 in

22 in

Quilting a crocheted fabric

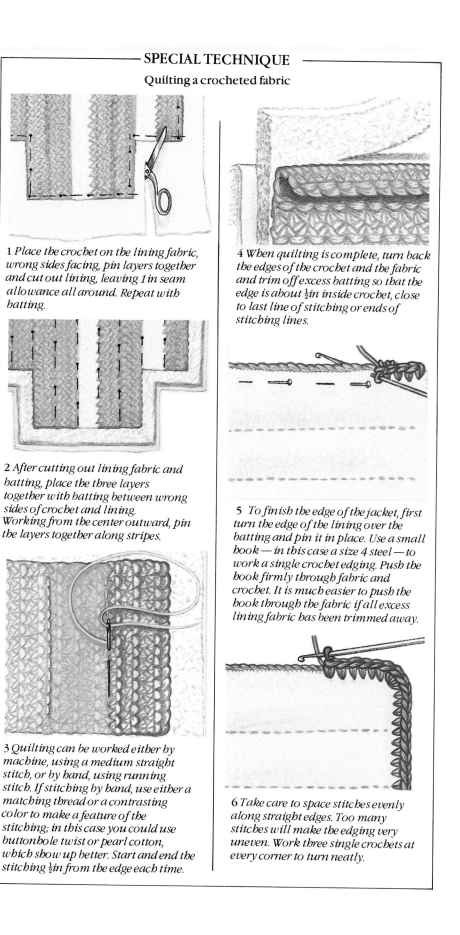

1 *Place the crochet on the lining fabric, wrong sides facing, pin layers together and cut out lining, leaving 1 in seam allowance all around. Repeat with batting.*

2 *After cutting out lining fabric and batting, place the three layers together with batting between wrong sides of crochet and lining. Working from the center outward, pin the layers together along stripes.*

3 *Quilting can be worked either by machine, using a medium straight stitch, or by hand, using running stitch. If stitching by hand, use either a matching thread or a contrasting color to make a feature of the stitching; in this case you could use buttonhole twist or pearl cotton, which show up better. Start and end the stitching ½in from the edge each time.*

4 *When quilting is complete, turn back the edges of the crochet and the fabric and trim off excess batting so that the edge is about ½in inside crochet, close to last line of stitching or ends of stitching lines.*

5 *To finish the edge of the jacket, first turn the edge of the lining over the batting and pin it in place. Use a small hook — in this case a size 4 steel — to work a single crochet edging. Push the hook firmly through fabric and crochet. It is much easier to push the hook through the fabric if all excess lining fabric has been trimmed away.*

6 *Take care to space stitches evenly along straight edges. Too many stitches will make the edging very uneven. Work three single crochets at every corner to turn neatly.*

BUTTONED-NECK
SWEATER

Crocheted buttons provide the finishing touch on this little sweater. They're comfortable for baby and washable, too.

Front

**Using larger hook and A, make 50ch.
Base row 1dc into 4th ch from hook, 1dc into each ch to end. Turn. 48 sts.
1st row Ch 3, skip first dc, 1dc into each st to end. Turn.
Break off A. Join in B.
2nd row Ch 3, skip first dc, * skip 1dc, 1dc into next dc, 1dc into dc just skipped, rep from * to turning ch, 1dc into turning ch. Turn.
Break off B. Join in A.
3rd row As first row.
Break off A. Join in C.
4th row As 2nd row.
Break off C. Join in A.
5th row As first row.
Work 19 more rows in dc. Turn.
Next row Ch 1, skip first dc, 1sc into each st to end. Turn.**
Shape neck
Next row Ch 1, skip first sc, 1sc into next 14sc, turn. 15 sts.
Work 2 more rows in sc on these 15 sts. Fasten off.
Skip next 18sc on neck edge and rejoin A to next sc, ch 1, skip first sc, 1sc into next 14 sts. Turn. 15 sts.
Work 2 more rows in sc on these 15 sts. Fasten off.

Back

Work as front from ** to **

Shape neck

Next row Ch 1, skip first sc, 1sc into next 14sc, turn. 15 sts.
Buttonhole row Ch 1, skip first sc, 1sc into next sc, (ch 2, skip next 2sc, 1sc into each of next 3sc) twice, ch 2, skip next 2sc, 1sc into last st. Turn.
Next row Ch 1, skip first sc, (1sc into each of next 2ch, 1sc into each of next 3sc) twice, 1sc into each of next 2ch, 1sc into each of next 2 sts. Fasten off.
Skip next 18sc on neck edge and rejoin A to next sc, ch 1, skip first sc, 1sc into next 14sc. Turn. 15 sts.
Buttonhole row Ch 3, skip first 3sc, (1sc into each of next 3sc, ch 2, skip next 2sc) twice, 1sc into each of last 2 sts.
Next row Ch 1, skip first sc, 1sc into next sc, (1sc into each of next 2ch, 1sc into each of next 3sc) twice, 1sc into each of last 3ch. Fasten off.

Sleeves (alike)

With RS tog and with crossed double rows corresponding, sew back to front at side seams, beg at lower edge and ending after 14th row. Pin sc rows at shoulder tog with buttonholes on top. With RS facing, join A to underarm, ch 3, 16dc into row ends to sc rows at shoulder, 3dc into shoulders working through both thicknesses, 16dc into

Size

B-1
Length from shoulder 8½in
Sleeve seam 4½in

Materials

3oz of a baby yarn in main color A
1oz in each of two contrasting colors B and C
Size E crochet hook
Size 4 steel crochet hook
¾yd of gathered eyelet lace edging

Gauge

19dc and 12 rows to 4in worked on size E hook

To save time, take time to check gauge.

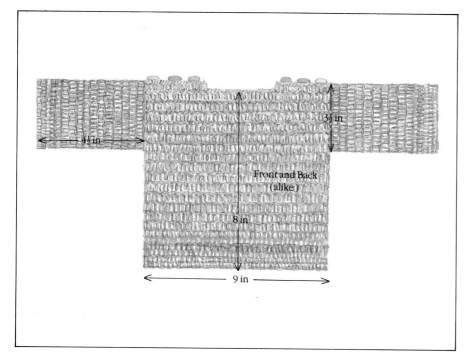

Crossed double crochet

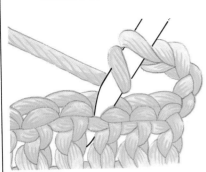

1 *Make three chains to count as the first double crochet and skip the first stitch. Then skip the next stitch. Take the yarn over the hook and insert the hook into the next stitch. Work the double in the usual way.*

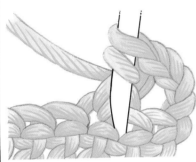

2 *Take the yarn over the hook and, working from the front, insert the hook into the last stitch just skipped. Work the double in the usual way. One pair of doubles has now been crossed.*

3 *Continue in this way to the turning chain, crossing doubles by working into the stitch just skipped. At the end of the row, work one double in the usual way into the top of the turning chain.*

Working an invisible seam

1 *This flat seam is often used on babies' clothing, since it does not produce a hard ridge. It also makes it easier to match patterns. Place the pieces right side up, and edge to edge, matching patterns, if any.*

2 *Using a matching yarn (here a contrasting color is shown for clarity) and a tapestry needle, fasten the yarn to one lower edge. Take the needle over to the other side edge and pass it under one stitch.*

3 *Take the needle back to the first side edge and under the next stitch. Pull the yarn through firmly to make the stitch invisible, but not so tightly that the fabric puckers. Continue catching one stitch on each edge, until the seam is complete.*

row ends to underarm. Turn. 36 sts.
Next row Ch 3, skip first dc, 1dc into each st to end. Turn.
Work 8 more rows in dc.
Break off A. Join in C.
Next row As 2nd row of front.
Break off C. Join in A.
Work 1 row in dc.
Break off A. Join in B.
Next row As 2nd row of front.
Break off B. Join in A.
Work 1 row in dc.
Fasten off.

Buttons
Make 2 in A, 2 in B and 2 in C as follows:
Using smaller hook, ch 3, sl st to first ch to form a ring.
1st round Ch 2, 7hdc into ring, join with a sl st to first ch.
2nd round Working *from left to right* and into front loops only, ch 1, skip first st, 1sc into each st to end, join with a sl st to first ch.
3rd round Working from right to left and into back loops only of first round, ch 1, 1sc into each st to end, join with a sl st to first ch.
4th round Ch 1, * dec 1sc over next 2 sts, rep from * to end, join with a sl st to first ch. Fasten off.

To finish
Join sleeve seams.
Sew buttons to shoulders to correspond with buttonholes, placing buttons in A at neck edge, buttons in B at shoulder edge and buttons in C in between.
Cut lengths of eyelet lace to fit front and back neck edges and lower edges of sleeves, allowing $\frac{1}{2}$in extra on each piece. Turn under $\frac{1}{4}$in at each end of neck pieces and topstitch. Slipstitch lace to underside of neck edge. Join ends of sleeve lace, taking $\frac{1}{4}$in seam allowance. Slipstitch lace under edges of sleeves.

CLUSTER-STITCH VEST

Clusters give a pleasing texture to this attractive little vest. Make it in pretty pastel stripes or all in one color.

Size
C-5
Length from shoulder *13½in*

Materials
2oz of a knitting worsted-weight yarn in each of five colors: A, B, C, D and E
Size F crochet hook
Pair of size 5 knitting needles
4 buttons

Gauge
8 clusters and 8 rows to 4in worked on size F hook

To save time, take time to check gauge.

Note *Change color while working the last st of each row.*

Main part (worked in one piece to armholes)
Using crochet hook and A, make 103ch.
Base row (RS) Leaving last loop of each dc on hook, work 3dc into 3rd ch from hook, yo and draw through all 4 loops – 1 cluster worked –, * ch 1, skip next ch, 1 cluster into next ch, rep from * to end. Turn. 51 clusters.
Working in stripes of 1 row each B, C, D, C, B, A, D and A, cont in pat:
1st row Ch 2, * 1 cluster into next 1ch sp, ch 1, rep from * to end, ending 1hdc into top of turning ch. Turn. 50 clusters.
2nd row Ch 2, * 1 cluster into next 1ch sp, ch 1, rep from * to end, ending 1 cluster into sp formed by turning ch. Turn. 51 clusters.
Rep first and 2nd rows for pat. Cont in stripes and pat until a total of 12 rows has been worked from beg.
Shape front
Next row Ch 2, skip first 1ch sp, * 1 cluster into next 1ch sp, ch 1, rep from * to last 1ch sp, 1 cluster into 1ch sp, ch 1, 1dc into top of turning ch. Turn. 49 clusters.
Rep last row once.
48 clusters.

Shape right front
1st row Ch 2, skip first 1ch sp, (1 cluster into next 1ch sp, ch 1) 8 times, 1hdc into next 1ch sp, turn. 8 clusters.
2nd row As first row of pat. 8 clusters.
3rd row Ch 2, skip first 1ch sp, * 1 cluster into next 1ch sp, ch 1, rep from * to end, 1hdc into top of turning ch. Turn. 7 clusters.
4th row As first row of pat. 7 clusters.
5th row As 3rd row. 6 clusters.
6th row As first row of pat. 6 clusters.
7th row As 3rd row. 5 clusters.
8th row As first row of pat. 5 clusters.
9th row As 3rd row. 4 clusters.
10th row As 2nd row of pat. 5 clusters.
11th row As first row of pat. 4 clusters.
12th row As 10th row. Fasten off.
Shape back
1st row With RS facing, skip next three 1ch sps after right front and join A to next 1ch sp, ch 2, (1 cluster into next 1ch sp, ch 1) 21 times, 1dc into next 1ch sp. 21 clusters. Work even in pat until the same number of rows have been worked as on right front. Fasten off.
Shape left front
1st row With RS facing, skip next three 1ch sps after back and join A to next 1ch sp, ch 2, (1 cluster into next 1ch

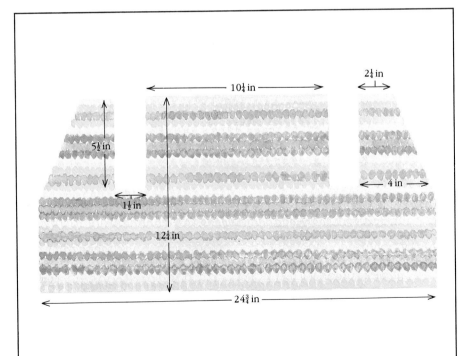

sp, ch 1) 8 times, 1hdc into top of turning ch. Turn. 8 clusters. Complete to match right front, reversing shapings.**Waistband**
With RS facing, using knitting needles and E, pick up and K 103 sts evenly along other side of foundation ch.
Work 1¼in of K1, P1 ribbing, beg RS rows P1.
Bind off in ribbing.

Armbands
With RS facing, using knitting needles and E, pick up and K 81 sts evenly around armhole.
Rib 4 rows as for waistband.
Bind off in ribbing.
Join shoulder and armband seams.

Front band
1st row With RS facing, using knitting needles and E, pick up and K 201 sts evenly up right front, across back neck and down left front.
2nd row P1, (K1, P1) to end.
3rd row K1, (P1, K1) to end.
4th row Rib 152sts, (bind off 2 sts, rib 12sts including st remaining on needle after bind-off) 3 times, bind off 2 sts, rib to end.
5th row Rib to end, casting on 2sts over those bound off on previous row.
Rib 2 rows.
Bind off in ribbing.
Sew on buttons.

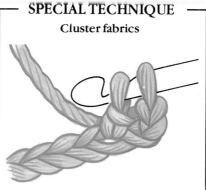

1 *Clusters are simply formed by working a number of doubles together. Make an even number of chains. Yarn over hook, insert the hook into the fourth chain from the hook, yarn over hook and draw through the first two loops on the hook.*

2 *Working into the same chain, repeat step 1 until there are four loops on the hook; yarn over hook and draw through all four loops —one cluster worked. Work one chain, skip the next chain and work a cluster into the next chain. Continue in this way, working one cluster and one chain alternately.*

3 *Turn, work four turning chains and one cluster into the next one-chain space. Work one chain. Continue in this way to the end of the row, working one cluster into the space formed by the turning chain. To vary the size of the cluster simply work fewer or more doubles together.*

PINEAPPLE-STITCH PULLOVER

Diamond-shaped motifs using pineapple stitch decorate the front and sleeves of this V-neck pullover.

Back

Using larger hook, make 57 [59:61:63] ch.

Base row 1sc into 2nd ch from hook, 1sc into each ch to end. Turn. 56 [58:60:62] sc.

Pat row Ch 1 to count as first sc, skip first st, 1sc into each st to end. Turn.

Rep pat row until 44 [46:50:52] rows have been worked.

Shape armholes

Next row Sl st across first 6 sts, ch 1 to count as first sc, skip sl st at base of first ch, pat to last 5 sts, turn. 46 [48:50:52] sts.

Next row Ch 1 to count as first sc, skip first st, work next 2sc tog, pat to last 3 sts, work next 2sc tog, 1sc into last st. Turn. 44 [46:48:50] sts.

Next row Pat to end.

Rep last 2 rows 3 more times. 38 [40:42:44] sts.

Work even in pat until 29 [31:33:35] rows have been worked from beg of armhole shaping.

Shape shoulders

Next row Sl st across first 7 [7:7:8] sts, ch 1 to count as first sc, skip sl st at base of first ch, pat to last 6 [6:6:7] sts, turn. 26 [28:30:30] sts.

Next row Sl st across first 6 [7:8:8] sts, Ch 1 to count as first sc, skip sl st at base of first ch, pat to last 5 [6:7:7] sts. 16 sts. Fasten off.

Front

Work as for back until 28 [30:34:36] rows have been worked.

Beg pineapple band

1st row (RS) Sl st into each st to end. Turn.

2nd row Ch 1 to count as first sc, skip first st, inserting hook into front loop only of each st, work in sc to end. Turn.

3rd and 4th rows Rep last 2 rows once more.

5th row Ch 1 to count as first sc, skip first st, 1sc into each of next 4 [5:6:7] sts, * ch 1, draw up loop to approx $\frac{3}{8}$ in (yo, insert hook into side of last sc, yo, draw through loop to same height as first loop) 4 times, skip next st, insert hook into next st, yo and draw through all 9 loops on hook, ch 1 – pineapple st or ppst formed –, 1sc into each of next 7 sts, rep from * 5 times more, ending last rep with 4 [5:6:7] sc. Turn.

6th row Ch 1 to count as first sc, skip first st, 1sc into each of next 3 [4:5:6] sts, *2sc into top loop of next ppst, 1sc into each of next 7sc, rep from * 5 more times, ending last rep with 5 [6:7:8] sc. Turn.

7th row Ch 1 to count as first sc, skip first st, 1sc into each of next 3 [4:5:6] sts, * 2ppsts, 1sc into each of next 5 sts, rep from * 5 more times, ending last rep with 3 [4:5:6] sc. Turn.

8th row Ch 1 to count as first sc, skip first st, 1sc into each of next 2 [3:4:5] sts, * (2sc into top loop of next ppst) twice, 1sc into each of next 5sc, rep from * 5 more times, ending last rep with 2 [3:4:5] sc. Turn.

9th row Ch 1 to count as first sc, skip first st, 1sc into each of next 2 [3:4:5] sc, * 3ppsts, 1sc into each of next 3 sts, rep from * 5 more times, ending last rep with 2 [3:4:5] sc. Turn.

10th row Ch 1 to count as first sc, skip first st, 1sc into each of next 1 [2:3:4] sts, * (2sc into top loop of ppst) 3 times, 1sc into each of next 3 sts, rep from * 5 more times, ending last rep with 3 [4:5:6] sc. Turn.

11th row Work as for 7th row.

12th row Work as for 8th row.

13th row Work as for 5th row.

14th row Work as for 6th row.

15th row Work as for first row.

16th row Work as for 2nd row.

17th row Work as for first row.

18th row Work as for 2nd row.

Shape armhole and neck

Next row Sl st across first 6 sts, ch 1 to count as first sc, skip first st, pat 22 [23:24:25] sts, turn. 23 [24:25:26] sts.

Next row Ch 1 to count as first sc, skip first st, work next 2sc tog, pat to last 3 sts, work next 2sc tog, 1sc into last st. Turn. 21 [22:23:24] sts.

Cont to dec at armhole edge as for back, then work even while *at the same time* dec 1 st at neck edge on every following 3rd row until 11 [12:13:14] sts rem.

Work even until 29 [31:33:35] rows have been worked from beg of armhole shaping.

Shape shoulder

Next row Sl st across first 7 [7:7:8] sts, ch 1 to count as first sc, skip first st at

Sizes

C-6 [C-7:C-8:C-9]

Length from shoulder $15\frac{3}{4}$ [$16\frac{1}{2}$:$17\frac{3}{4}$:18]in

Sleeve seam $10\frac{1}{4}$ [$11\frac{1}{2}$:$12\frac{1}{4}$:$13\frac{1}{4}$]in

Note *Instructions for larger sizes are in brackets [ ]; where there is only one set of figures it applies to all sizes.*

Materials

8 [9:10:10] oz of a knitting worsted-weight yarn

Size E crochet hook

Size F crochet hook

Gauge

16 sc and 20 rows to 4 in worked on size F hook

To save time, take time to check gauge.

base of sl st, pat to end. Turn.
Next row Pat to end. Fasten off.

Sleeves (both alike)
Using larger hook, make 25 [27:29:29]ch.
Base row Work as for back. 24 [26:28:28] sts.
Pat 2 [2:3:3] rows as for back.
Shape sleeve
Next row Ch 1 to count as first sc, skip first st, 2sc into next st, pat to last 2 sts, 2sc into next st, 1sc into last st. Turn. 26 [28:30:30] sts. Cont in pat, inc 1 st at each end of every following 4th [4th:5th:5th] row, until there are 40 [42:44:46] sts.
Work even in pat until 32 [36:42:50] rows have been worked.
Beg pineapple band
1st-4th rows Work as for first-4th rows of front pineapple band.
5th row Ch 1 to count as first sc, skip first st, 1sc into each of next 5 [6:7:8] sc, * ppst, 1sc into each of next 7 sts,

rep from * 3 times, ending last rep with 5 [6:7:8] sc. Turn.
6th row Ch 1 to count as first sc, skip first st, 1sc into each of next 4 [5:6:7] sts, * 2sc into top loop of next ppst, 1sc into each of next 7 sts, rep from * 3 times, ending last rep with 6 [7:8:9] sc. Turn.
7th row Ch 1 to count as first sc, skip first st, 1sc into each of next 4 [5:6:7] sts, * 2ppsts, 1sc into each of next 5 sts, rep from * 3 times, ending last rep with 4 [5:6:7] sc. Turn.
8th row Ch 1 to count as first sc, skip first st, 1sc into each of next 3 [4:5:6] sts, * (2sc into top loop of next ppst) twice, 1sc into each of next 5 sts, rep from * ending last rep with 5 [6:7:8] sc. Turn.
9th row Ch 1 to count as first sc, skip first st, 1sc into each of next 3 [4:5:6] sts, * 3ppsts, 1sc into each of next 3 sts, rep from * 3 times, ending last rep with 3 [4:5:6] sc. Turn.
10th row Ch 1 to count as first sc, skip

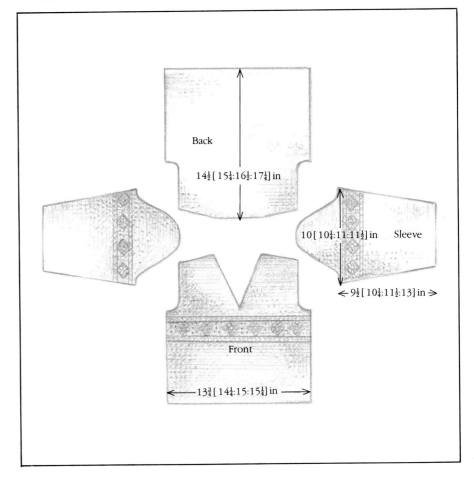

Back

$14\frac{1}{2}$ [$15\frac{1}{4}$:$16\frac{1}{2}$:$17\frac{1}{4}$] in

10 [$10\frac{1}{4}$:11:$11\frac{1}{2}$] in   Sleeve

← $9\frac{1}{2}$ [$10\frac{1}{4}$:$11\frac{1}{2}$:13] in →

Front

← $13\frac{3}{4}$ [$14\frac{1}{4}$:15:$15\frac{1}{4}$] in →

first st, 1sc into each of next 2 [3:4:5] sts, * (2sc into top loop of next ppst) 3 times, 1sc into each of next 3 sts, rep from * 3 times, ending last rep with 4 [5:6:7] sc. Turn.

11th row Work as for 7th row.
12th row Work as for 8th row.
13th row Work as for 5th row.
14th row Work as for 6th row.
15th-18th rows Work as for 15th-18th rows of front pineapple band.
Shape sleeve top
Next row Sl st across first 6 sts, ch 1 to count **as** first sc, skip first sl st at base of first ch, pat to last 5 sts, turn. 30 [32:34:36] sts.
Next row Ch 1 to count as first sc, skip first st, work next 2sc tog, pat to last 3 sts, work next 2sc tog, 1sc into last st. Turn. 28 [30:32:34] sts.
Next row Pat to end.
Rep last 2 rows until 10 sts rem.
Next row Sl st across first 3 sts, ch 1 to count as first sc, skip first st, pat to last 2 sts. Fasten off.

To finish

Do not press. If necessary, spray each piece lightly with water and pin out to correct shape to dry. Join shoulder, side and sleeve seams. Set in sleeves.
Neck edging
With RS facing and using size E hook, join yarn to first row of neck at front,

ch 1 to count as first sc, skip first st, work in sc evenly around neck edge. Turn.
Next row Ch 1 to count as first sc, skip first 2 sts, 1sc into each st to last 2 sts, skip next st, 1sc into last st. Turn.
Next row Sl st into each st to end. Fasten off. Join seam at V.
Cuffs
With RS facing and using size E hook, join yarn to sleeve seam.
Next row Ch 3 to count as first dc, skip first st, work 1dc into each loop of foundation ch, sl st to 3rd of first 3ch. 24 [26:28:28] sts.
Next row Ch 3 to count as first dc, skip first st, * inserting hook from front to back work 1dc around stem of next dc – 1dc front worked –, inserting hook from back to front work 1dc around stem of next dc – 1dc back worked –, rep from * to last st, 1dc front into last st, sl st to 3rd of first 3ch.
Rep last row once more.
Fasten off.
Waistband
With RS facing and using larger hook, join yarn to lower edge at a side seam.
Next row Ch 3 to count as first dc, skip first st, work 1dc into each loop of foundation ch, sl st to 3rd of first 3ch. 112 [116:120:124] sts.
Work 5 rows of dc front and back as for cuff. Fasten off.

┌── **SPECIAL TECHNIQUE** ──┐
Working pineapple stitch

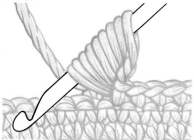

1 *Pineapples are formed from several loops worked together. Those on the sweater shown here are worked on a background of single crochet. Pattern to the position of the first pineapple. Make one chain. Draw the loop on the hook up to a height of just under half an inch.*

2 *Wind the yarn over the hook and insert the hook into the vertical loop at the side of the previous stitch. Wind the yarn over the hook and draw through a loop to the same height as the long loop in step 1. Repeat this step three more times, keeping the loops fairly high up the shaft and making sure that they are the same height.*

3 *Skip the next stitch and insert the hook into the next stitch. Wind the yarn over the hook and draw through all nine loops on the hook. Work one chain to complete the pineapple. On the following row work two single crochets into the top loop of the pineapple.*

CLASSIC CARDIGANS

Two classic cardigans for children. The girl's version has a crocheted lace collar.

Both cardigans
Back
Using size C hook, make 11ch.
Base row (RS) 1sc into 2nd ch from hook, 1sc into each ch to end. Turn. 10sc.
Ribbing row Ch 1 to count as first sc, skip first st, working into *back* loops only work 1sc into each st to end. Turn. Rep ribbing row until there are 35 [37:41] ridges on RS of work, ending with an RS row. Fasten off.
With RS facing and using size E hook, rejoin yarn to first row end on long edge of ribbed band.
Inc row (RS) Ch 3, 1dc into base of 3ch, * 1dc into row end of next ridge, 2dc into row end of next ridge, rep from * to end. Turn. 53 [56:62] sts.
Pattern row Ch 3, skip first st, 1dc into each st to end. Turn.
Rep pat row until work measures 9½ [10¼:11]in.
Shape armholes
Next row Sl st over first 4 sts, ch 3, skip first st, 1dc into each of next 46 [44:55]dc, turn. 47 [50:56] sts.
Dec 1 st at each end of next 3 rows. 41 [44:50] sts.
Work even in dc until work measures 14½ [15¾:17] in.
Shape shoulders
Next row Sl st over first 3dc, 1sc into each of next 2dc, 1hdc into each of next 2dc, 1dc into each of next 27 [30:36]dc, 1hdc into each of next 2dc, 1sc into each of next 2dc, turn. 35 [38:44] sts.
Next row Sl st over first 2sc, 2hdc and 2 [3:5]dc, 1sc into each of next 2dc, 1hdc into each of next 2dc, 1dc into each of next 15 [16:18]dc, 1hdc into each of next 2dc, 1sc into each of next 2dc. Fasten off.

Sleeves (alike)
Using size C hook, make 11ch and work in ribbing as for back until there are 14 [15:17] ridges on RS of work, ending with RS row. Fasten off. With RS facing and using size E hook, rejoin yarn to first row end on long edge of ribbed band.
Inc row Ch 3, skip first row end, 2dc into each ridge to end. Turn. 29 [31:35] sts.

Work 3 rows in pat as for back. Inc 1 st at each end of next row. Cont to inc 1 st at each end of every 4th row in this way until there are 37 [41:45] sts. Work even in dc until work measures 11½ [13:14]in.
Shape top
Next row Sl st across first 4dc, ch 3, skip first st, 1dc into each of next 30 [34:38]dc, turn. 31 [35:39] sts. Dec 1 st at each end of next and every following row until 19 [23:27] sts rem.
Next row Ch 1 to count as first sl st, skip first dc, 1sc into each of next 2dc, 1hdc into each of next 2dc, 1dc into each of next 9 [13:17]dc, 1hdc into each of next 2dc, 1sc into each of next 2dc, sl st into last st. Fasten off.

V-neck cardigan only
Right front
Using size C hook, make 11ch and work in ribbing as for back until there are 15 [17:19] ridges on RS of work, ending with RS row. Fasten off. With RS facing and using size E hook, rejoin yarn to first row end on long edge of ribbed band.
Work inc row as for back. 23 [26:29] sts.
Rep pat row as for back until work measures 9½ [10¼:11]in, ending at front edge.**
Shape armhole and neck
Next row Ch 3, skip first st, work next 2dc tog, 1dc into each of next 17 [20:23]dc, turn.
Dec 1dc at armhole edge on next 3 rows and *at the same time* dec 1dc at neck edge on every following alternate row until 13 [14:16] sts rem.
Work even until work measures same as back from beg. Fasten off.

Left front
Work as for right front, reversing all shaping.
Neckband
Join shoulder seams. Mark position of 4 buttonholes on left front, one at beg of neck shaping, one ¾in from lower edge and two spaced equally between. With RS facing and using size C hook, rejoin yarn to first st on ribbed band of right front.
Work one row of sc up right front, across back neck and down left front,

Sizes
C-3 [C-5:C-7]
Length from shoulder 15½ [16½:17¾]in
Sleeve seam 11½ [13:14]in

Note *Instructions for larger sizes are in brackets [ ]; where there is only one set of figures it applies to all sizes.*

Materials
V-neck cardigan 8 [10:13]oz of a knitting worsted-weight yarn
4 buttons
Round-neck cardigan
8 [10:13]oz of a knitting worsted-weight yarn
6 buttons
Size C crochet hook
Size E crochet hook
Collar
2oz of a size 5 pearl cotton
1 small button
Size B crochet hook

Gauge
Cardigans 17dc and 10 rows to 4in worked on size E hook
Collar measures 6in at its widest point.

To save time, take time to check gauge.

working 1sc into each st on ribbed bands, 2sc into each row end of fronts and 1sc into each st on back neck. Work 2 more rows in sc.

Buttonhole row (WS) Ch 1 to count as first sc, skip first st, (work in sc to position of buttonhole, ch 3, skip next 3sc) 4 times, 1sc into each st to end. Turn.

Next row Ch 1 to count as first sc, skip first st, (work in sc to next 3ch sp, 3sc into next 3ch sp) 4 times, 1sc into each st to end. Turn.

Work 2 more rows in sc. Fasten off.
Note To make a girl's version of this V-neck cardigan, mark buttonholes on right front and work buttonholes on neckband to correspond.

Round-neck cardigan only
Right front
Work as for V-neck cardigan to **.
Shape armhole
Next row Ch 3, skip first st, 1dc into each of next 19 [22:25]dc, turn. 20 [23:26] sts.
Dec 1dc at armhole edge on next 3 rows.
Work even in dc until work measures 13 [14:15¼]in, ending at armhole edge.
Next row Ch 3, skip first st, 1dc into each of next 14 [15:17]dc, turn. 15 [16:18] sts.
Dec 1 st at neck edge on next 2 rows. 13 [14:16] sts.
Work even until work measures same as back to shoulders, ending at neck.
Shape shoulder
Next row Ch 3, skip first st, 1dc into each of next 5 [6:8]dc, 1hdc into each of next 2dc, 1sc into each of next 2sc, turn.
Next row Sl st across first 2sc, 2hdc and 2 [3:5]dc, 1hdc into each of next 2dc, 1dc into each of last 2 sts. Fasten off.

Left front
Work as for right front, reversing all shaping.

Neckband
Join shoulder seams. With RS facing and using size C hook, rejoin yarn to first st on right front neck shaping.
Work a row of sc up right neck, across back neck and down left neck, working 1sc into top of each dc and 2sc into

each dc row end.
Work 4 more rows in sc. Fasten off.

Button band
With RS facing and using size C hook, rejoin yarn to first sc row end of neckband of left front.
Work a row of sc down left front, working 1sc into each sc row end of neckband, 2sc into each dc row end and 1sc into each st of ribbed band.
Work 6 more rows in sc. Fasten off.

Buttonhole band
Mark positions of 6 buttonholes on right front, one ¾in from top edge, one ¾in from lower edge and 4 equally spaced in between.
With RS facing and using size C hook, rejoin yarn to first st on ribbed band of right front.
Work a row of sc up right front, working 1sc into each st of ribbed band, 2sc into each dc row end and 1sc into each sc row end of neckband.
Work 2 more rows in sc.
Buttonhole row (WS) Ch 1 to count as first sc, skip first st (work in sc to position of buttonhole, ch 3, skip next 3sc) 6 times, 1sc into each st to end. Turn.
Next row Ch 1 to count as first sc, skip first st, (work in sc to next 3ch sp, 3sc into next 3ch sp) 6 times, 1sc into each st to end. Turn.
Work 2 more rows in sc. Fasten off.
Note To make a boy's version of this round-neck cardigan, mark buttonholes on left front and reverse position of button and buttonhole bands.

To finish (both cardigans)
Press or block, according to yarn used. Set in sleeves. Join side and sleeve seams. Sew on buttons to correspond with buttonholes.
Collar
Foundation braid Using size B hook, make 2ch. Holding ch between finger and thumb of LH work 1sc into 2nd ch from hook, turn, inserting hook into back of loop work 1sc into foundation loop of 2nd ch, turn, * insert hook into 2 vertical loops on the LH side, yo and draw through 2 loops on hook, yo and draw through rem 2 loops on hook,

turn, rep from * until braid measures approx 11in and has a multiple of 9 loops plus 7 extra on the LH long edge.
1st row (RS) Sl st into first loop, ch 5, 1dc into same loop, *ch 4, skip next 2 loops, (1tr, ch 4, 1tr) into next loop, ch 4, skip next 2 loops, (1dc, ch 2, 1dc) into next loop, ch 1, skip next 2 loops, (1dc, ch 2, 1dc) into next loop, rep from * omitting ch 1, (1dc, ch 2, 1dc) at end of last rep. Turn.
2nd row Ch 5, 1dc into base of 5ch, *ch 5, (leaving last loop of each st on hook work 3tr into next 4ch sp between 2tr, yo and draw through all 4 loops on hook – tr cluster formed –, ch 3) 3 times into next 4ch sp between 2tr, 1tr cluster into same sp, ch 5, (1dc, ch 2, 1dc) into next 1ch sp, rep from * to end. Turn.

3rd row Ch 4, tr cluster into next 2ch sp, *skip next 5ch sp, (ch 4, leaving last loop of each st on hook work 2tr into 4th ch from hook, yo and draw through all 3 loops on hook – small cluster formed –, tr cluster into next 3ch sp) 3 times, ch 4, small cluster into 4th ch from hook, skip next 5ch sp, tr cluster into next 2ch sp, rep from * to end. Fasten off.
Button loop With WS facing and using size B hook rejoin yarn to first loop on top RH loop of braid, ch 4, sl st into top of last st on first row, turn, 6sc into 4ch loop, sl st into same place as joining. Fasten off.
Pin out collar to correct size and spray lightly with water. Allow to dry naturally. Sew button to braid to correspond with button loop.

1 *The lacy collar shown on the girl's cardigan is worked on a special braid. Detailed instructions for working the braid edging are given with the pattern. Shown here is the hook being inserted into two loops on the left-hand side, ready to draw a new loop through.*

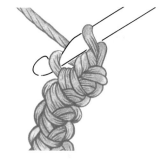

2 *When calculating how much braid to work, treat it as a foundation chain — work for the length required so that the total number of loops on one edge is a multiple of the pattern repeat plus any loops required for edge stitches. Always begin the first row of the lace by slip stitching into the first loop on the left-hand long edge.*

3 *Then follow the instructions to work the first row into the loops of the braid. Insert the hook from front to back as usual. Work following rows into the first row. The braid forms a decorative edge which provides a firm base for heavy edgings such as collars.*

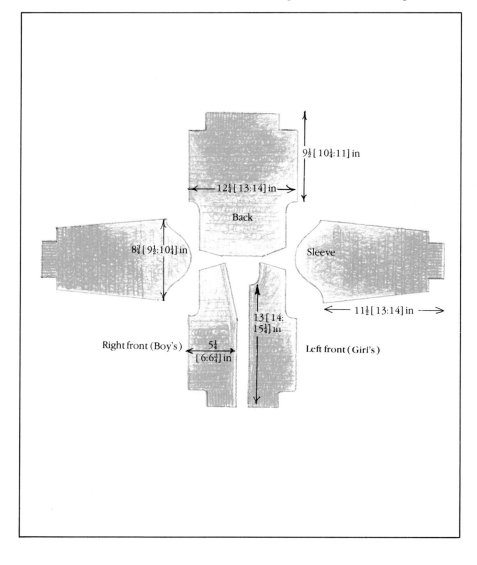

9½ [10¼:11] in

12¼ [13:14] in

Back

8¾ [9½:10¼] in

Sleeve

13 [14: 15¼] in

11½ [13:14] in

Right front (Boy's)   5¼ [6:6¾] in   Left front (Girl's)

DUFFLE COAT

Surface single crochet and puff stitches form the attractive design on this hooded duffle coat, which can be made for a boy or a girl.

Sizes
C-3 [C-5]
Length from back neck *16½ [17¼] in*
Sleeve seam *8½ [9½] in*

Note *Instructions for the larger size are in brackets [ ]; where there is only one set of figures it applies to all sizes.*

Materials
13 [15] oz of a sport-weight yarn in main color A
2oz in contrasting color B
Size C crochet hook
4 toggles

Gauge
21 sc and 30 rows to 4in worked on size C hook

To save time, take time to check gauge.

Back
Using A, make 71 [77] ch.
Base row (RS) 1sc into 2nd ch from hook, 1sc into each ch to end. Turn. 70 [76] sts.
1st row Ch 1 to count as first sc, skip first st, 1sc into each of next 20 [23] sts, (yo, insert hook into next st and draw through a loop) 4 times, yo and draw through first 8 loops on hook, yo and draw through rem 2 loops on hook – puff st formed –, 1sc into each of next 5 sts, puff st, 1sc into each of next 14 sts, puff st, 1sc into each of next 5 sts, puff st, 1sc into each of next 21 [24] sts. Turn.
2nd row Ch 1 to count as first sc, skip first st, 1sc into each st to end. Turn.
3rd row Ch 1 to count as first sc, skip first st, 1sc into each of next 11 [14] sts, puff st, 1sc into each of next 11 sts, puff st, 1sc into each of next 20 sts, puff st, 1sc into each of next 11 sts, puff st, 1sc into each of next 12 [15] sts. Turn.
4th row As 2nd row.
5th row Ch 1 to count as first sc, skip first st, 1sc into each of next 9 [12] sts, puff st, 1sc into each of next 12 sts, puff st, 1sc into next st, puff st, 1sc into each of next 18 sts, puff st, 1sc into next st, puff st, 1sc into each of next 12 sts, puff st, 1sc into each of next 10 [13] sts. Turn.
6th row As 2nd row.
7th row As 3rd row.
8th row As 2nd row.
9th row As first row.
10th row As 2nd row.
11th row Ch 1 to count as first sc, skip first st, 1sc into each of next 7 [10] sts, puff st, 1sc into each of next 15 sts, puff st, 1sc into each of next 20sc, puff st, 1sc into each of next 15 sts, puff st, 1sc into each of next 8 [11] sts. Turn.
12th row As 2nd row.
13th row As 5th row
14th row As 2nd row.
15th row As 11th row.

16th row As 2nd row.
First-16th rows form back pat. Cont in back pat until 115 [121] rows in all have been worked, ending with a RS row.

Shape shoulders
Next row Sl st across first 8 sts, ch 1 to count as first sc, skip st at base of first ch, pat to last 7 sts, turn.
56 [62] sts.
Rep last row twice more.
Fasten off.

Right front
Using A, make 43 [46]ch.
Base row (RS) 1sc into 2nd ch from hook, 1sc into each ch to end. Turn. 42 [45] sts.
1st row Ch 1 to count as first sc, skip first st, 1sc into each of next 20 sts, puff st, 1sc into each of next 5 sts, puff st, 1sc into each of next 14 [17] sts. Turn.
2nd row Ch 1 to count as first sc, skip first st, 1sc into each st to end. Turn.
3rd row Ch 1 to count as first sc, skip first st, 1sc into each of next 11 sts, puff st, 1sc into each of next 11 sts, puff st, 1sc into each of next 17 [20] sts. Turn.
4th row As 2nd row.
5th row Ch 1 to count as first sc, skip first st, 1sc into each of next 9 sts, puff st, 1sc into each of next 12 sts, puff st, 1sc into next st, puff st, 1sc into each of next 16 [19] sts. Turn.
6th row As 2nd row.
7th row As 3rd row.
8th row As 2nd row.
9th row As first row.
10th row As 2nd row.
11th row Ch 1 to count as first sc, skip first st, 1sc into each of next 7 sts, puff st, 1sc into each of next 15 sts, puff st, 1sc into each of next 17 [20] sts. Turn.
12th row As 2nd row.
13th row As 5th row.
14th row As 2nd row.
15th row As 11th row.
16th row As 2nd row.

144

First-16th rows form front pat. Cont in front pat until 100 [106] rows in all have been worked, ending with a WS row.

Shape neck

Next row Sl st across first 13 sts, ch 1 to count as first sc, skip st at base of first ch, pat to end. Turn. 30 [33] sts.

Next row Pat to end. Turn.

Next row Sl st across first 4 sts, ch 1 to count as first sc, skip st at base of first ch, pat to end. Turn. 27 [30] sts.

Next row Pat to end. Turn.

Next row Ch 1 to count as first sc, skip first st, work next 2sc tog, pat to end. Turn. 26 [29] sts.

Rep last 2 rows until 115 [121] rows in all have been worked.

Shape shoulder

Next row Sl st across first 8 sts, ch 1 to count as first sc, skip st at base of first ch, pat to end. Turn.

Next row Pat to last 6 sts, turn. Fasten off.

Left front

Work base row as for right front. Cont as for right front, reversing all shaping *and* reversing all front pat rows as follows:

1st row (WS) Ch 1 to count as first sc, skip first st, 1sc into each of next 13 [16] sts, puff st, 1sc into each of next 5 sts, puff st, 1sc into each of next 21 sts. Turn.

2nd row Ch 1 to count as first sc, skip first st, 1sc into each st to end. Turn.

3rd row Ch 1 to count as first sc, skip first st, 1sc into each of next 16 [19] sts, puff st, 1sc into each of next 11 sts, puff st, 1sc into each of next 12 sts. Turn.

Sleeves (alike)

Using A, make 57 [61]ch.

Base row (RS) 1sc into 2nd ch from hook, 1sc into each ch to end. Turn. 56 [60] sts.

1st row Ch 1 to count as first sc, skip first st, 1sc into each of next 13 [15] sts, puff st, 1sc into each of next 5 sts, puff st, 1sc into each of next 14 sts, puff st, 1sc into each of next 5 sts, puff st, 1sc into each of next 14 [16] sts. Turn.

2nd row Ch 1 to count as first sc, skip first st, 1sc into each st to end. Turn.

3rd row Ch 1 to count as first sc, skip

first st, 1sc into each of next 16 [18] sts, puff st, 1sc into each of next 20 sts, puff st, 1sc into each of 17 [19] sts. Turn.

4th row As 2nd row.

5th row Ch 1 to count as first sc, skip first st, 1sc into each of next 15 [17] sts, puff st, 1sc into next st, puff st, 1sc into each of next 18 sts, puff st, 1sc into next st, puff st, 1sc into each of next 16 [18] sts. Turn.

6th row As 2nd row.

7th row As 3rd row.

8th row As 2nd row.

First-8th rows form sleeve pat. Cont in sleeve pat until 62 [68] rows in all have been worked. Fasten off.

Hood

Using A, make 33 [37] ch.

Base row (RS) 1sc into 2nd ch from hook, 1sc into each ch to end. Turn. 32 [36] sc.

1st row Ch 1 to count as first sc, skip first st, 1sc into each of next 17 sts, puff st, 1sc into each of next 5 sts, puff st, 1sc into each of next 7 [11] sts. Turn.

2nd row Ch 1 to count as first sc, skip first st, 1sc into each st to end. Turn.

3rd row Ch 1 to count as first sc, skip first st, 1sc into each of next 20 sts, puff st, 1 sc into each of next 8 [12] sts, 2sc into next st, 1sc into last st. Turn. 33 [37] sts.

4th row As 2nd row.

5th row Ch 1 to count as first sc, skip first st, 1sc into each of next 19 sts, puff st, 1sc into next st, puff st, 1sc into each of next 8 [12] sts, 2sc into next st, 1sc into last st. Turn. 34 [38] sts.

6th row As 2nd row.

7th row As 3rd row. 35 [39] sts.

8th row As 2nd row.

First-8th rows form hood pat. Cont in hood pat, but omit incs (i.e. 2sc into one st at end of every alternate row) when there are 38 [42] sts.

Work even in hood pat until 66 rows in all have been worked, ending with a WS row.

Shape top

Next row Ch 1 to count as first sc, skip first st, work next 2sc tog, pat to end. Turn.

Next row Ch 1 to count as first sc, skip first st, pat to last 3 sts, work next 2sc tog, 1sc into last st. Turn. Rep last 2

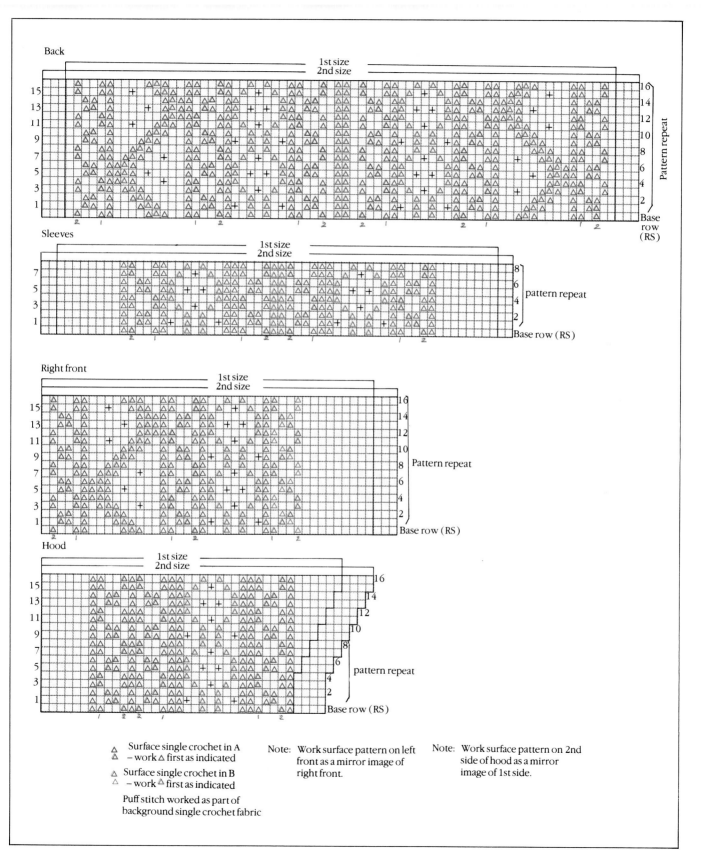

Back

Sleeves

Right front

Hood

△ Surface single crochet in A
△ – work △ first as indicated

△ Surface single crochet in B
△ – work △ first as indicated

Puff stitch worked as part of
background single crochet fabric

Note: Work surface pattern on left
front as a mirror image of
right front.

Note: Work surface pattern on 2nd
side of hood as a mirror
image of 1st side.

Crochet frogging

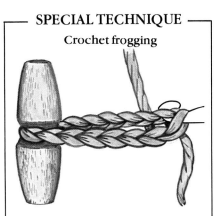

1 *Make 16 chains. Fold the chain in half around the toggle so that the toggle lies at the fold. Holding the toggle in your left hand, work a slipstitch into the first chain to form a ring as shown.*

2 *Work one chain to count as the first single crochet. Skip the first two chains joined in step 1. Work one single crochet into the next chain and into the next corresponding chain on the other side of the ring. Continue in this way until the toggle is held tightly. Fasten off.*

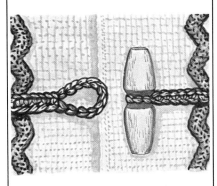

3 *Work the frogging loops in the same way until the toggle slips easily through the loop. When all the toggle and loop frogging has been completed, sew them as required to the fronts of the coat.*

rows once more. 34 [38] sts.
Next row Sl st across first 4 sts, ch 1 to count as first sc, skip st at base of first ch, pat to end. Turn. 31 [35] sts.
Next row Ch 1 to count as first sc, skip first st, pat to last 3 sts, turn. 28 [32] sts.
Rep last 2 rows once more. 22 [26] sts.
Next row Sl st across first 4 sts, ch 1 to count as first sc, skip st at base of first ch, pat to end. Turn. Fasten off. Work 2nd side of hood to match first, reversing all shaping and reversing all hood pat rows as follows:
1st row (WS) Ch 1 to count as first sc, skip first st, 1sc into each of next 6 [10] sts, puff st, 1sc into each of next 5 sts, puff st, 1sc into each of next 18 sts.
2nd row Ch 1 to count as first sc, skip first st, 1sc into each st to end. Turn.
3rd row Ch 1 to count as first sc, skip first st, 2sc into next st, 1sc into each of next 8 [12] sts, puff st, 1sc into each of next 21 sts. Turn. 33 [37] sts.

To finish

Following charts on page 147 and using A or B as directed, work surface sc on back, fronts, sleeves and hood, beg at lower edge and rep pat to top edge of background fabric.
Join shoulder and sleeve seams.
Set in sleeves.
Join side seams.
Sew halves of hood tog and sew in place on neck edge.
Toggle frog fastenings (make 4)
Using B, make 16 ch, fold in half around toggle, sl st into first ch to form a ring.
Next row Ch 1 to count as first sc, skip first 2 joined ch, * 1sc into each of next corresponding 2ch on each side of toggle, rep from * to toggle so that it is firmly held.
Fasten off.
Frog loops (make 4)
Work as for fastenings, leaving loop large enough to slip over toggle. Sew toggle frog fastenings in place on left front (for girl) or right front (for a boy), the first ¾in from neck edge, the 4th 4¾[5] in from lower edge and the rem 2 evenly spaced in between.
Sew frog loops to other front edge to correspond with toggles.
Edging
With RS facing, using A, work a row of sc around outer edge of coat, beg and ending at a side seam.
Work a row of sc around cuff edge in the same way.
Press seams very lightly.

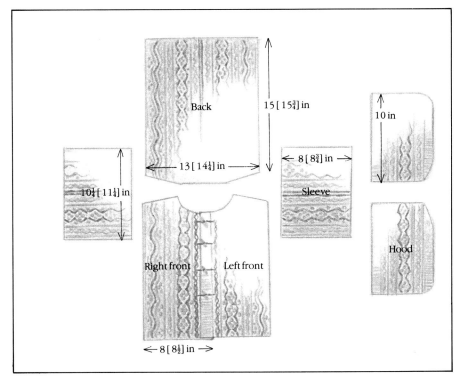

HOODED COAT

Patch pockets, frog fastenings and crab stitch edging give extra style to this comfortable coat.

Sizes

C-7 [C-10: C-12: C-14]
Length from shoulder 24¾ [26:29:32]in
Sleeve seam 10¼ [13:15:17]in

Note: *Instructions for larger sizes are in brackets [ ]; where there is only one set of figures it applies to all sizes.*

Materials

26 [27:30:33] oz of a knitting worsted-weight yarn
Size G crochet hook
Size H crochet hook
6 toggles
3 large snaps (optional)

Gauge

16sc and 16 rows to 4in worked on size H hook

To save time, take time to check gauge.

SPECIAL TECHNIQUE

Single chain braid

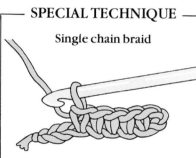

1 *The fastenings on the child's hooded coat are made of this simple braid. Begin with a length of chain. Turn and work a single crochet into each chain to make the braid. Make sure that you work each stitch into the lower loop of the base chain to make a firm edge. Fasten off yarn at the ends and sew them to the wrong side.*

2 *Sew the braid to the garment using a finer, matching thread if a thick yarn has been used for the braid. To make a toggle fastening, join the ends of the single braid to form a ring. Bend the ring into the shape shown, then sew the edges together using sewing thread and slipstitch, from the wrong side.*

Back skirt

Using larger hook, make 84 [88:92:96] ch.

1st row 1sc into 2nd ch from hook, 1sc into each ch to end, turn.
2nd row Ch 1, 1sc into each sc to end, turn. 83 [87:91:95] sts.
The 2nd row forms pat; rep until work measures 4¾ [5½:8:9¾]in.
Next row Ch 1, 1sc into each of first 3sc, * (insert hook into next sc and draw through loop) twice, yo and draw through all loops on hook – dec made – 1sc into each of next 6sc, dec over next 2sc*, 1sc into each st to last 13sc, rep from * to *, 1sc into each of last 3sts, turn. 79 [83:87:91]sc.
Work even for 7 rows.
Rep last 8 rows 5 more times. 59 [63:67:71] sts.
Work even until back measures 19 [19¾:22:24]in. Fasten off.

Left front skirt

Using larger hook, make 45 [47:49:51] ch. Work first and 2nd rows as for back. 44 [46:48:50]sc.
Work even until work measures 4¾ [5½:8:9¾]in.
Next row Ch 1, 1sc into each of first 3sc, work from * to * as for back, 1sc into each sc to end, turn. Work even for 7 rows. Rep last 8 rows 5 more times 32 [34:36:38] sts.
Work even until front skirt measures same length as back. Fasten off.

Right front skirt

Work as for left front skirt, reversing all shapings by working dec row as follows: ch 1, 1sc into each st to last 13sc, work from * to * as on back, 1sc into each of the last 3sc, turn.

Back yoke

Using larger hook, make 44 [48:50:54] ch.
Work first and 2nd rows as for back skirt. 43 [47:49:53] sc. Work even until armhole measures 6 [6¼:6¾:7]in.
Shape shoulders
Sl st over 6sc, work in sc to end, turn. Rep last row once more.
3rd and 4th rows Sl st over 6 [7:7:8] sc, work in sc to end of row.
Fasten off.
19 [21:23:25] sc rem for back neck.

Left front yoke

Using larger hook, make 25 [27:29:31] ch. Work first and 2nd rows as for back skirt. 24 [26:28:30] sts.
Work even until yoke measures 4½ [4¾:5:5½]in, ending at front edge.
Shape neck
Sl st over 9 [10:11:12] sc, work in sc to end, turn.
2nd row Work in sc to last 3 sts, dec over next 2sc, 1sc into last st, turn.
3rd row Ch 1, 1sc into first sc, dec over next 2sc, work in sc to end, turn.
4th row As 2nd row.
3rd and 4th sizes only Rep 3rd row.
All sizes Work a few more rows until armhole measures same as back armhole, ending at side edge.
Shape shoulder
Sl st over 6sc, work in sc to end of row. 6 [7:7:8] sc rem. Fasten off.

Right front yoke

Work as left, reversing all shapings.

Sleeves

Using larger hook, make 49 [53:55:57] ch. Work first and 2nd rows as for back skirt. 48 [52:54:56] sts.
Work even until sleeve measures 10¼ [13:15:17] in. Mark both ends of last row, work another 2in. Fasten off.

Hood

Using larger hook and beg at side edge, make 32 [34:36:38] ch, work first and 2nd rows as for back skirt. 31 [33:35:37] sts.
Work even until work measures 9 [9¾:10¼:10¾]in.
Next row Beg at front edge, work in sc to last 3 sts, dec over next 2sc, 1sc into last sc, turn. Work 1 row straight.
Rep last 2 rows 3 more times. This marks the end of first half of hood.
Work the 2nd half to match first, working incs at end of next and following 3 alternate rows as follows: work in sc to last 2sc, work 2sc into next st, 1sc into last sc, turn.
Work even until work measures same length as first half of hood. Fasten off.

Pockets

Using larger hook, make 19ch. Work first and 2nd rows as for back skirt. 18 sts. Work even for 4¼in. Fasten off.

Braids (make 3)
Using smaller hook, make 16ch. Sl st to first ch, make another 28ch, 1sc into 16th ch from hook, 1sc into each of next 12ch.

To finish
Join shoulder seams. Using smaller hook, and with RS facing, work 1 row of sc down left front yoke edge, along lower edge, left armhole edge, back lower edge, right armhole edge, right lower edge, and up right front edge, working 3sc into corners. Do not turn. Work 1 row of crab st (sc worked from left to right) along previous row of sc. Fasten off.
Sew upper edge of sleeve to armhole, overlapping crab st edging to RS. Join back and front skirt to yoke, placing yoke at center and sewing skirt extensions to rows above sleeve markers. Join side and sleeve seams.

With RS facing, using smaller hook and beg at top front edge of left skirt, work 1 row of sc down left front edge, along lower edge of skirt and up right front to yoke, working 3sc into corner. Do not turn. Work 1 row of crab st into row of sc. Fasten off.
Join back seam of hood. Sew hood to neck edge, beg and ending 5 sts from front edge. With RS facing, using smaller hook, work 1 row of sc around front edge of hood. Without turning, work 1 row of crab st into previous row of sc. Fasten off.
With RS facing, using smaller hook, work 1 row of sc all around pocket edges, working 3sc into corners. Without turning, work 1 row of crab st into previous row of sc. Fasten off. Sew on pockets in positions shown.
Shape and stitch fastenings as shown opposite.
Sew in place on coat fronts.

V-NECK VEST

Two shades of a Shetland yarn are used for this V-neck sweater.

Back

Note *Strand yarn not in use* loosely *up side of work.*

Using crochet hook and A, make 84 [88:92] ch.

Base row 1dc into 4th ch from hook, * skip next ch, 1sc into next ch, skip next ch, 3dc into next ch, rep from * to end, ending last rep with 2dc into last ch. Turn. 81 [85:89] sts.

Beg pat

1st row Ch 1, 1sc into first dc, *3dc into next sc, 1sc into 2nd of next 3dc, rep from * to end, working last sc into top of turning ch. Turn.

2nd row Ch 3, 1dc into first sc, *1sc into 2nd of next 3dc, 3dc into next sc, rep from * to end, ending last rep with 2dc into last sc.

First and 2nd rows form back pat. Cont in back pat until work measures 12¼in, ending with a 2nd row.

Shape armholes

Next row Sl st across first 5 sts, ch 1, 1sc into sl st at base of 1ch, pat to last 4 sts, turn. 73 [77:81] sts.

Next row Sl st across first 5 sts, ch 3, 1dc into sl st at base of 3ch, pat to last 4 sts, turn. 65 [69:73] sts.

Beg with a first row, work even in pat until work measures 21¼in. Fasten off.

Front

Using A, make 104 [108:112] ch.

Base row (RS) Using A, 1dc into 4th ch from hook, *skip next 3ch, 3dc into next ch, rep from * to end, ending last rep with 2dc into last ch. Do not turn, but return to beg of row.

Next row (RS) Join B with a sl st to top of first 3ch, * 3dc into center ch of next 3ch skipped on base row, rep from * to end, sl st into last dc of base row. Turn.

Beg pat

1st row Using A, ch 3, 1dc into first sl st, * 3dc into center dc of next 3dc worked on previous row in A, rep from * to last sl st, 2dc into last sl st. Do not turn, but return to beg of row.

2nd row Using B, sl st into top of first 3ch, * 3dc into center dc of next 3dc worked on previous row in B, rep from * to last dc, sl st into last dc.

First and 2nd rows form front pat. Cont in front pat until work measures 12¼in, ending with a 2nd row.

Shape armholes

Next row Sl st across first pat rep, pat to last pat rep, turn.

Rep last row twice more. 19 [20:21] pat reps.

Divide for neck

Next row Work 9 [10:10] pat reps, turn.

Shape left neck

Cont on these sts only, work even in pat for 3 rows.

Next row Pat to last pat rep, turn. Rep last 4 rows 3 more times. 5 [6:6] pat reps.

Work even in pat until work measures 21¼in. Fasten off.

1st and 3rd sizes only

Return to beg of neck shaping, skip center pat rep and keeping pat correct, rejoin yarn to next pat rep.

2nd size only

Return to beg of neck shaping and keeping pat correct, rejoin yarn to next pat rep.

All sizes

Next row Work to end. Turn. 9 [10:10] pat reps.

Shape right neck

Cont on these sts only, pat 3 rows without shaping.

Next row Work to last pat rep, turn. Rep last 4 rows 3 times more. 5 [6:6] pat reps.

Work even in pat until work matches left side of neck. Fasten off.

Back waistband

With RS facing, using knitting needles and A, pick up and K 104 [110:114] sts evenly along lower edge.

Work 2¾in in K1, P1 ribbing.

Bind off loosely in ribbing.

Front waistband

With RS facing, using knitting needles and A, pick up and K 102 [106:110] sts evenly along lower edge.

Work 2¾in in K1, P1 ribbing.

Bind off loosely in ribbing.

Front neckband

Fold corners of front decs to WS and sew in place using slipstitch.

With RS facing, using knitting needles and A, pick and K 68 sts down left front neck, one st from center V and 68 sts up right front neck.

Sizes

Men's sizes 38 [40:42]

Length from shoulder *24in*

Note: *Instructions for larger sizes are in brackets [ ]; where there is only one set of figures it applies to all sizes.*

Materials

11 [12:13] oz of knitting worsted-weight yarn in main color A
4 [6:6] oz in contrasting color B
Size F crochet hook
Pair of size 3 knitting needles

Gauge

4 pat reps and 12 rows to 4in over back pat worked on size F hook
5 pat reps and 14 rows to 4in over front pat worked on size F hook

To save time, take time to check gauge.

SPECIAL TECHNIQUE

One-row stripes

1 *When changing color at the end of each row in a two-color pattern, you can avoid breaking yarn (and having to darn in dozens of ends later) by turning only after every alternate row as in the pattern. Work the base row. Remove the hook from the loop and leave the first color at the side of the work. The loop can be held with a safety pin.*

2 *Do not turn, but return to the beginning of the row. Join the second color to the top of the first stitch with a slip stitch. Pattern to the loop left in step 1. Insert the hook first into the top of the last stitch and then into the loop. Remove the safety pin, wind the second color around the hook and draw through all loops on the hook. Turn.*

3 *Drop the second color and draw the first through the loop on the hook. Pull both ends of yarn firmly but not so tightly that the fabric puckers. Pattern to the end, leaving a loop as in step 1. Return to the beginning of the row, rejoin the first color as in step 2 and pattern to the end, working into the last stitch and loop as before.*

1st row (P1, K1) to within 2 sts of center st, K2 tog, P1, K2 tog, (K1, P1) to end.
2nd row K1, (P1, K1) to within 2 sts of center st, P2 tog, K1, P2 tog, (K1, P1) to end.
Rep last 2 rows twice more.
Bind off loosely in ribbing, at the same time dec one st at each side of center st as before.

Back neckband

Place a contrasting marker on last row of back 5 [6:6] pat reps from each armhole edge.
With RS facing, using knitting needles and A, pick up and K 45 sts between markers. Work 6 rows in K1, P1 ribbing. Bind off loosely in ribbing.

Armbands (alike)

Join shoulder seams.
With RS facing, using knitting needles and A, pick up and K 130 sts evenly along armhole edge.
Work 6 rows in K1, P1 ribbing.
Bind off loosely in ribbing.

To finish

Press or block as appropriate.
Join side and armband seams.
Press seams lightly.

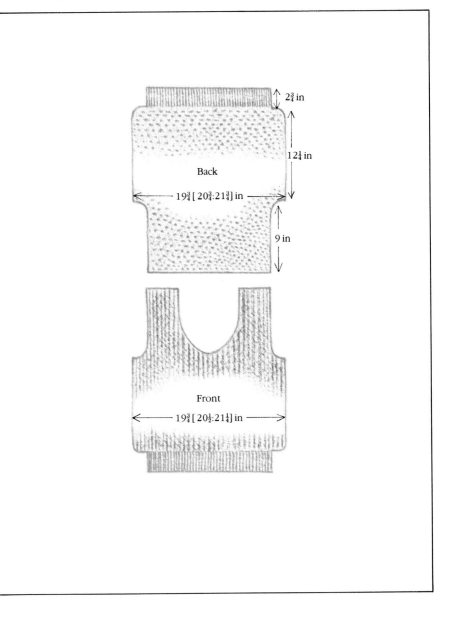

DIAGONAL-STITCH PULLOVER

This comfortable V-neck pullover has a diagonal stripe pattern worked in surface crochet.

Sizes

Men's sizes 36-38 [40-42]
Length from shoulder 27in
Sleeve seam 19 [19¼] in

Note *Instructions for larger size are in brackets [ ]; where there is only one set of figures it applies to both sizes.*

Materials

35 [37] oz of a knitting worsted-weight yarn
Size G crochet hook
Size H crochet hook
Pair of size 3 knitting needles

Gauge

16sc and 20 rows to 4in worked on size G hook

To save time, take time to check gauge.

Back

Using smaller hook, make 81 [89] ch.
Base row (RS) 1sc into 2nd ch from hook, 1sc into each ch to end. Turn. 80 [88] sc.
Next row Ch 1, skip first sc, 1sc into each st to end. Turn.
Work even in sc on these 80 [88] sts until work measures 24in, ending with a WS row.
Shape shoulders
Next row Ch 1, skip first sc, 1sc into each sc to last 7 [8] sts, turn. Rep last row 7 more times. 24 sts. Fasten off.

Front

Work as for back until work measures 15in, ending with a WS row.
Divide for neck
Next row Ch 1, skip first sc, 1sc into next 34 [38] sc, turn.
Working on first set of sts only, dec 1sc at neck edge on next and every following 3rd row 7 times in all. 28 [32] sc. Work even in sc until work measures 24in, ending with a RS row.
Shape shoulder
Next row Ch 1, skip first sc, 1sc into each sc to last 7 [8] sts, turn.
Next row Ch 1, skip first sc, 1sc into

each sc to end. Turn.
Rep last 2 rows twice more.
Fasten off.
Return to rem sts. With RS facing, skip next 10sc and rejoin yarn to next st, ch 1, skip first sc, 1sc into each of next 34 [38] sts. Turn. Complete to match first side, reversing shaping.
Fasten off.

Sleeves (alike)

Using size G hook, make 41ch and work base row as for back. 40sc.
Cont in sc as for back on these 40 sts, inc 1sc at each end of next and every following 4th row until there are 72sc.
Work even until work measures 15¾ [16] in.
Fasten off.

Surface diagonals

Back
With RS facing and using larger hook, follow chart to work surface slip stitch (see page 19) over first 78 rows of back and front to form diagonals, each 4 sts wide.

Front
Work as for back.

Waistbands (back and front alike)

Using knitting needles pick up and K 104 [114] sts evenly along lower edge.
Work in K1, P1 ribbing for 3in.
Bind off loosely in ribbing.

Cuffs

Using knitting needles pick up and K 56 sts evenly along lower edge.
Complete as for waistbands.

Neckband

Using knitting needles, cast on 140 sts and work in K1, P1 ribbing for 2in.
Bind off loosely in ribbing.

To finish

Press or block, as appropriate.
Join shoulder seams.
Set in sleeves, placing center of top of sleeve at shoulder seam.
Join side and sleeve seams, matching surface crochet diagonals on front and back.
Sew neckband in place, overlapping left over right at center front as shown.

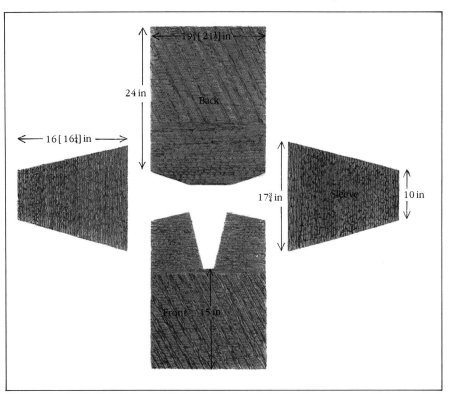

TRIANGLE PATCHWORK SWEATER

This rugged sweater, worked in a yarn with an interesting tweedy fleck, is great for the outdoor life.

Men's sizes 38-40
Length from shoulder *27 in*
Sleeve seam *19 in*

Materials
24oz of a knitting worsted-weight tweed yarn in main color A (dark brown)
13oz in contrasting color B (medium brown)
18oz in contrasting color C (beige)
Size H crochet hook
Pair of size 4 knitting needles

Gauge
14 sts and 10 rows to 4in over pat worked on size H hook

To save time, take time to check gauge.

Large triangles
Make 2 in C.
Make 97ch.
Base row 1dc into 4th ch from hook, 1dc into each ch to end. Turn. 95 sts.
1st row (RS) Ch 2, skip first 2 sts, inserting hook from right to left and from front to back work 1dc around stem of next dc – 1dc front worked –, * inserting hook from right to left and from back to front work 1dc around stem of next dc – 1dc back worked –, 1dc front, rep from * to last 2 sts, skip next st, 1dc into top of turning ch. Turn. 93 sts.
2nd row Ch 2, skip first 2 sts, 1dc front, * 1dc back, 1dc front , rep from * to last 2 sts, 1dc into next st, turn. 91 sts.
3rd row As 2nd row. 89 sts.
4th row Ch 2, skip first 2 sts, work next 2dc tog, 1dc front, * 1dc back, 1dc front, rep from * to last 4 sts, work next 2dc tog, 1dc into next st, turn. 85 sts.
5th row Ch 2, skip first 2 sts, 1dc back, * 1dc front, 1dc back, rep from * to last 2 sts, 1dc into next st, turn. 83 sts.
6th-8th rows As 5th row. 77 sts.
9th row Ch 2, skip first 2 sts, work next 2dc tog, 1dc back, * 1dc front, 1dc back, rep from * to last 4 sts, work next 2dc tog, 1dc into next st, turn. 73 sts.
10th-13th rows As 2nd row. 65 sts.
Rep 4th-13th rows once more, then rep 4th-12th rows once more. 19 sts.
33rd row As 4th row. 15 sts.
34th-36th rows As 5th row. 9 sts.
37th row Ch 2, skip first 2 sts, work next 2dc tog, 1dc back, work next 2dc tog, 1dc into next st, turn. 5 sts.
38th row Ch 2, skip first 2 sts, 1dc front leaving last loop on hook, 1dc into next st leaving last loop on hook, yo and draw through all 3 loops on hook. Fasten off.

Medium triangles
Make 4 in B.
Make 53ch. Work base row as for large triangle. 51 sts.
Work first-17th rows as for large triangle. 11 sts.
18th row As 9th row of large triangle. 7 sts.
19th row As first row of large triangle. 5 sts.
20th row As 38th row of large triangle. Fasten off.

Small triangles
Make 6 in A, 4 in B and 6 in C.
Make 39ch. Work base row as for large triangle. 37 sts.
Work first-12th rows as for large triangle. 9 sts.
13th row Ch 2, skip first 2 sts, work next 2dc tog, 1dc front, work next 2dc tog, 1dc into next st, turn. 5 sts.
14th row As 38th row of large triangle, work 1dc back instead of 1dc front. Fasten off.

Sleeves (alike)
Using A, make 47ch.
Base row 1dc into 4th ch from hook, 1dc into each ch to end. Turn. 45 sts.
Beg pat
1st row (RS) Ch 2, skip first st, 1dc front, * 1dc back, 1dc front, rep from * to last st, 1dc into top of turning ch. Turn.
2nd row Ch 2, skip first st, 1dc back, *1dc front, 1dc back, rep from * to last st, 1dc into top of turning ch. Turn.
First and 2nd rows form pat.
Shape sleeve
Keeping pat correct, inc one st at each end of next and every following 5th row until there are 59 sts.
Work even in pat until work measures 13½in, ending with a WS row.
Divide for top
Next row Pat first 29 sts, turn.
Next row Ch 2, skip first 2 sts, pat to end. 28 sts.
Next row Pat to last 2 sts, 1dc into next st, turn. 27 sts.
Rep last 2 rows 3 more times. 21 sts. Fasten off.
With RS facing, return to sts skipped at beg of top, skip next st and rejoin A to next st.
Next row Ch 2, skip st at base of joining, pat to end. 29 sts.
Complete to correspond with first side of sleeve top, reversing all shaping.

To finish
Block if necessary.
Cuffs (alike)
With RS facing, using knitting needles and A, pick up and K 44 sts along lower edge of sleeve.
Work 2½in of K2, P2 ribbing.
Fasten off.
Place a contrasting marker 8in from

each end of longest side of large triangles.

Join triangles as shown in diagram on page 159 to form back and front. Join long edges of large triangles between corners and markers, leaving edges between markers open for neck.

Back waistband

With RS facing, using knitting needles and A, pick up and K 92 sts along lower edge of back.

Work 2½in of K2, P2 ribbing.

Bind off in ribbing.

Front waistband

Work as for back waistband.

Set in sleeves.

Join side and sleeve seams.

Press seams very lightly.

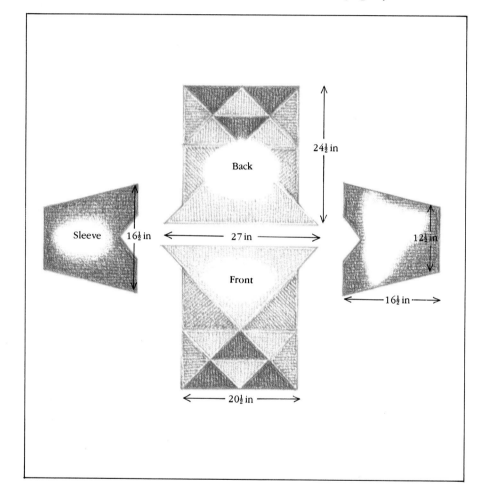

Join triangles as shown in diagram on page 159 to form back and front.

Right-side seaming

1 *Right-side seaming is an easy method of achieving an exact match on seams when joining a complex garment like the sweater shown here. Hold the edges of the two triangles together with wrong sides facing — clothespins are better than dressmaker's pins on thick crochet. Use a tapestry needle and two strands of spliced yarn matching one of the triangles.*

2 *Join the yarn to the wrong side of the corner of the triangle nearer to you. Insert the needle from back to front into the edge of the farther triangle, catching one strand only of the edge stitch. Then insert the needle from front to back slightly farther along the edge of the same triangle. Draw up the yarn tightly.*

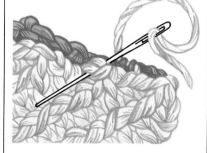

3 *Insert the needle from front to back into the edge of the nearer triangle. Insert the needle from back to front slightly farther along the same edge. Draw up the yarn tightly. Continue in the same way to the end. This method produces a flat, invisible seam which is very strong.*

SPECIAL TECHNIQUES
Tunisian crochet

Also known as Afghan stitch, Tunisian crochet is worked with a long hook of uniform thickness with a knob at the end to retain the stitches. The firm fabric produced by this technique has in the past been used mainly for articles that receive hard wear such as rugs, jackets and coats. At one time Tunisian crochet was called "shepherd's knitting" and was used to make peasant garments.

In the 19th century people used Tunisian crochet to make rugs and blankets with very long so-called "blanket hooks". These were made from three detachable pieces which could be screwed together to make a

hook approximately 30in long.

With modern yarns such as mohair and bouclé, however, it is now possible to use the same traditional techniques to create unusual and exciting fashion garments. Some of the close, firm stitches found in Tunisian crochet look very much like knitting, but they produce a much firmer fabric, which in some cases can even be cut up to make tailored coats and jackets using dressmaking patterns.

The fluffy texture of mohair and other similar yarns appears on the wrong side of the work, and often this can be so attractive that, with care, you can make a completely reversible gar-

ment – one which is fluffy on one side and much smoother on the other. Different stitches can be combined, as can different textures of yarn, although it is important that the yarns be of the same thickness. The end result can be a high fashion garment in an exciting mixture of colors and textures.

Hooks The special hooks used for Tunisian crochet are extra long to hold a large number of stitches and are available in sizes ranging from E to K.

Yarns and wools Any yarn or wool suitable for knitting and crochet can be used for Tunisian crochet. It is advisable, however, to begin with a small sample using smooth thread such as crochet cotton, worked with a size E hook, until the basic techniques have been mastered.

The basic technique

Tunisian crochet is quite easy to learn, especially if you have already learned normal crochet techniques. It is worked from one side only: one row is worked from right to left in a crochet stitch (for example, single or double crochet), but with one loop per stitch left on the hook; then the next row is always a return row worked from left to right. For this row, the yarn is wound around the hook and pulled through the first loop on the hook. The yarn is then wound around the hook a second time and pulled through two loops. Keep winding the yarn around the hook and pulling it through two loops on the hook until the row has been completed and one loop remains on the hook. The next row can then be started in crochet stitch. These two rows form the basic Tunisian crochet stitch repeat, (see basic Tunisian stitch opposite).

Binding off A firm edge can be produced by working a row of single crochet or slip stitches into the last return row.

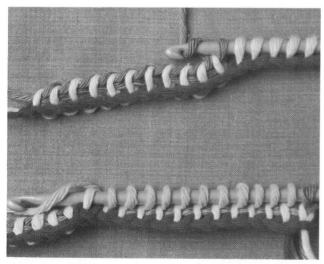

Basic Tunisian stitch (Tst)

This is also called knit stitch. It resembles a woven fabric and can be used as a background for cross stitch embroidery. Begin with a length of chain as for ordinary crochet (the pattern will specify the number, which will include 1 extra for turning).

1st row Work from right to left: skip 1 ch, * insert hook into next ch, yo and draw through a loop, leave loop on hook, rep from * to end.

2nd row (return row) Yo, draw through 1 loop, * yo, draw through 2 loops, rep from * to end of row. 1 loop on hook.

3rd row Ch 1, * insert hook from right to left under next vertical st, yo and draw through a loop, leave loop on hook, rep from * to end.

Rep 2nd and 3rd rows throughout.

Tunisian double stitch (Tdst)

Work any number of ch plus 1.

1st and 2nd rows As first and 2nd rows of basic Tunisian st.

3rd row Ch 1, skip first vertical thread, * insert hook from right to left under next vertical thread of previous row, yo and draw through 1 loop, yo and through 1 loop, leave loop on hook, rep from * to end of row.

4th row As row 2 of basic Tunisian st. Rep 3rd and 4th rows throughout.

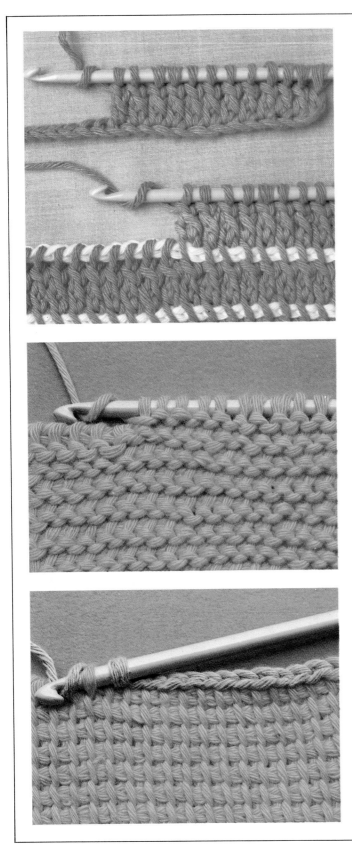

Tunisian triple (Ttr)

Work any number of ch plus 2.

1st row Yo, insert hook into 4th ch from hook, yo and draw through 1 loop, yo and draw through 2 loops, yo and draw through 1 loop. * Yo, insert hook into next ch, yo and draw through 1 loop, yo and draw through 2 loops, yo and draw through 1 loop, rep from * to end.

2nd row As 2nd row of basic Tunisian st.

3rd row Ch 1, * yo, insert hook into 2nd vertical loop, yo and draw through 1 loop, yo and draw through 2 loops, yo and draw through 1 loop, rep from * to end. Rep rows 2 and 3 throughout.

Tunisian purl stitch (Tp)

Work any number of ch plus 1.

1st and 2nd rows As first and 2nd rows of basic Tunisian st.

3rd row Ch 1, skip first vertical thread, * with yarn to front insert hook from right to left under next vertical thread, pass yarn under, then over hook and draw through loop, rep from * to end.

4th row As row 2 of basic Tunisian st. Rep 3rd and 4th rows throughout.

Binding off

The edge that is produced by the return row of Tunisian crochet can be left as it is and joined in a seam in the usual way; however, this is not always satisfactory, since holes tend to appear along the seam line. A neater and much firmer edge can be obtained by working a row of slip stitch, as shown here, or single crochet, using either an ordinary or an afghan hook.

The seam can then be joined by sewing or crochet as appropriate.

Bobble stitch (Tb)

The bobbles are worked on a background of Tunisian double st. Work a multiple of 6 ch plus 4.

1st and 2nd rows As first and 2nd rows of basic Tunisian st.

3rd row 1 Tdst, * yo, insert hook from front to back into next st, yo and draw through 1 loop, ** yo, insert hook into same st, yo and draw through 1 loop**, rep from ** to ** once, yo and draw through 6 loops, yo and draw through 1 loop (1 bobble made), 5 Tdst *; rep from * to *, working 1 bobble into next-to-last st, 1 Tdst.

4th-8th rows Work Tdst.

9th row 4 Tdst, * 1 bobble into next st, 5 Tdst *, rep from *, 1 Tdst into last st.

10th-14th rows Work Tdst. Rep rows 3-14 throughout.

Tunisian triple treble (Ttrtr)

This is a decorative stitch worked over a background of basic Tunisian stitch or Tunisian triple. Here it is worked over a background of basic Tunisian in color A, using a contrasting color, B, to produce a pattern called "brick stitch".

1st and 2nd rows Using A, as first and 2nd rows of basic Tunisian st.

3rd row Using B, as 3rd row of basic Tunisian st.

4th row Using B, return (2nd) row of Tst.

5th row Using A, as 3rd row of Tst.

6th row Using A, return row.

7th and 8th rows As 5th and 6th rows.

9th row Using B, ch 1, * 2 Tst, yo 3 times, insert hook into vertical loop 5 rows down, yo and draw through a loop, (yo and draw through 2 loops on hook) 3 times – called Tunisian triple triple or Ttrtr; rep from * to within last 4 sts, 4 Tst.

10th row Using B, return row.

Rows 5-10 form the pat.

Hairpin lace crochet

The origins of hairpin lace crochet are obscure. The special prong or loom which is used resembles a hairpin – hence the name. In the nineteenth century women often used their large bone hairpins for the work. Recently the adjustable hairpin loom has appeared on the scene, with the direct effect of eliminating the necessity of buying an assortment of looms in order to produce finished strips of different widths.

The technique consists of looping yarn around the loom and joining the loops in the center, using an ordinary crochet hook. The lace strips thus produced are then joined edge to edge, using one of several methods, to make the fabric. Individual strips can also be used as edgings or trimmings.

Any kind of yarn can be used for hairpin lace. Experiment with different yarns to see for yourself the variety of effects you can create.

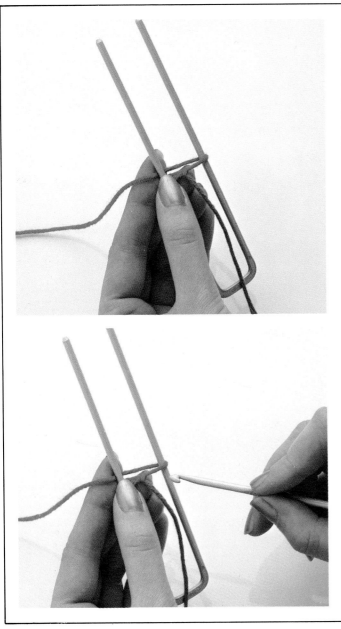

Preparing to crochet
Make a slip loop as for the start of a chain stitch and pull it out to half the width of the loom, then put it over the right-hand prong, with the knot in the center. Hold the yarn behind the left prong with the thumb and forefinger of the left hand, then turn the prong over from right to left so that the yarn is passed around what has now become the right prong. Hold the yarn behind the (left) prong as before.

The first stitch
Take the crochet hook and insert it through the left-hand loop. Put the yarn over the hook and draw it through the loop, then put the yarn over the hook again and draw it through the loop on the hook to complete the first crochet stitch at the center of the work. (There should now be a loop around each prong and one on the crochet hook.) Keeping the loop on the hook, take the other, free end of the hook over the right prong to lie behind it.

A single crochet
Turn the prong from right to left so that the yarn passes around the prong and insert the crochet hook from below through the front of the loop on the left prong. Take the yarn over the hook and draw a loop through so that there are two loops on the hook. Put the yarn over the hook and draw it through both loops, completing a single crochet into the loop. Lift the end of the crochet hook over the right prong and turn the prong from right to left.

Continuing
Continue turning the hook and working the single crochets as described to form a braid of loops with a center ridge of single crochet. When the loom is filled with loops, slip the work carefully off the loom and gently replace the last four or five pairs of loops worked back on their respective prongs, while leaving the rest of the braid to hang free.

Finishing a strip
When you have worked the number of loops required (check that you have an equal number on each side of the strip), simply cut off the yarn and draw the end through the loop on the hook. Do not pull a strip around too much while working, for the loops are easily unraveled at this stage and the work does not become firm until the loops of the separate strips have been joined (see next page).

Joining strips

The simplest method of joining is to pull the loops through each other. Place two strips side by side on a flat surface, making sure that each strip has the beginning knot at the bottom and the last loop end at the top. Working up from the bottom, insert the hook into the first loop of one strip. Insert it through the first loop of the other strip (two loops on hook) and then pull the second loop through the first.

Joining – continued

Insert the hook into the next loop on the second strip and draw it through the loop already on the hook. Proceed in this way, alternating sides and checking continually on the wrong side of the work to make sure that you have not missed any loops. Pass the ends of the yarn through the last loop to finish off. The appearance of the work may be varied by linking loops two, or even three, at a time.

Abbreviations used in this book

approx	approximately	rep	repeat
beg	begin(ning)	RH	right hand
ch	chain(s)	RS	right side
cont	continu(e)(ing)	sc	single crochet
dc	double crochet	sl st	slip stitch
dec	decreas(e)(ing)	sp(s)	space(s)
dtr	double triple crochet	st(s)	stitch(es)
gr(s)	group(s)	tog	together
hdc	half double crochet	tr	triple crochet
in	inch(es)	tr tr	triple triple crochet
inc	increas(e)(ing)	WS	wrong side
K	knit	yo	yarn over hook
LH	left hand		
oz	ounce(s)		
P	purl	Additional abbreviations are
pat	pattern	explained within the pattern in
rem	remain(ing)	which they are used.

INDEX